Sea of Collective Destiny
Bay of Bengal and BIMSTEC

Sea of Collective Destiny
Bay of Bengal and BIMSTEC

Vijay Sakhuja
Somen Banerjee

Vivekananda International Foundation
New Delhi

PENTAGON PRESS LLP

Sea of Collective Destiny: Bay of Bengal and BIMSTEC
By Vijay Sakhuja and Somen Banerjee

ISBN 978-81-942837-3-7

First Published in 2020

Copyright © Vivekananda International Foundation, New Delhi

All rights reserved. No part of this publication may be reproduced, stored in a retrieval system, or transmitted in any form or by any means, electronic, mechanical, photocopying, recording or otherwise, without the prior written permission of the Publisher.

Disclaimer: The views and opinions expressed in the book are the individual assertion of the Authors. The Publisher does not take any responsibility for the same in any manner whatsoever. The same shall solely be the responsibility of the Authors.

Published by
PENTAGON PRESS LLP
206, Peacock Lane, Shahpur Jat,
New Delhi-110049
Phones: 011-64706243, 26491568
Telefax: 011-26490600
email: rajan@pentagonpress.in
website: www.pentagonpress.in

Printed at Aegean Offset Printers, Greater Noida, U.P.

CONTENTS

	Foreword	*vii*
	Introduction	*ix*
1	Regionalism: A Political, Economic and Social Project	1
2	Sea of Collective Destiny	15
3	Transnational Organised Crimes: Trafficking of Drugs, Humans and Wildlife	26
4	Transnational Organised Crime: Terrorism and Piracy	34
5	Manmade Non-traditional Security Challenges: Global Warming and Bay of Bengal	44
6	Manmade Non-traditional Security Challenges: Marine Pollution	55
7	Human Induced Non-Traditional Threats and Challenges: Digital and Illegal Migration	62
8	Nature Induced Non-traditional Threats at Sea	68
9	Connectivity: Shipping, Ports, Tourism and Digital	78
10	Economic Regionalisation: Trends and Challenges	89
11	Economic Corridors, Regional Value Chain and Gender Sensitivity in Border Trade	109
12	Blue Economy: Regional Approach Takes Roots	118

13	Towards a Sustainable Bay of Bengal	131
14	Geopolitical Underpinnings in the Bay of Bengal Region	142
	Conclusion and Policy Recommendations	154
	Index	162

FOREWORD

It is often said that the 21st century belongs to Asia and the oceans and seas are shaping its destiny. In fact Asia is reliving its period of ancient glory that was marked by complex networks of politico-diplomatic, economic and strategic engagements as far as Persia, Eurasian landmass and the Mediterranean. During those times, the Bay of Bengal was central to three civilizations: India, China and Southeast Asia. It was also the entrepôt for traders from Rome, Egypt, Arabia, and Persia who frequented the region and their ships sailed through these waters. Besides, Hinduism, Buddhism and Islam originated/ arrived in Asia through the Bay of Bengal.

Today, the littoral states of Bay of Bengal—Bangladesh, India, Myanmar, Thailand, and Sri Lanka are at a crossroads; they are recalling the glorious past and are shaping their destiny by participating and partaking the globalized world of the 21st century. They are making seminal contribution and playing a significant part in the prosperity of Asia individually and collectively.

At the regional and sub-regional level, the Bay of Bengal littorals have invested in a variety of cooperation initiatives but have endorsed the Bay of Bengal Initiative for Multi-Sectoral Technical and Economic Cooperation (BIMSTEC) as a symbol of their 'regionalism' which is poised and ready for taking the region to new levels of consolidation and prosperity.

This book has been written from the vantage point of the first BIMSTEC Think Tank Dialogue on Regional Security organised by Vivekananda International Foundation (VIF) in November 2018 in New Delhi. This seminar was a meeting ground of officials and experts and a melting pot of innumerable ideas. This encouraged VIF to pursue this book project.

The authors, Dr Vijay Sakhuja and Commodore Somen Banerjee, who bring with them decades of naval experience, have analyzed the Bay of Bengal and the BIMSTEC in theory-policy-operational matrix and their efforts are significant and merit acknowledgement and appreciation.

The authors concluded that BIMSTEC is a positive experiment to foster regionalism in the Bay of Bengal area but a lot more needs to be done on a sustainable basis to generate a feeling of "we-ness" amongst the people of the region. BIMSTEC project cannot remain just a state-sponsored project. People must be involved in a big way. The authors feel that Bay of Bengal has potential to create an identity of its own. But it will need to generate a critical mark in terms of economy, diplomacy and military for that to happen.

This book deals with a variety of issues, which are of great concern to the inhabitant of the region, namely, transnational organised crime, terrorism, global warming, marine pollution, non-traditional threat at sea, connectivity, economic regionalisation, blue economy, etc. Authors make useful and specific policy recommendations to strengthen the existing BIMSTEC framework. The main message of the book is that the people of Bay of Bengal region had historically shared a collective destiny. This is the time to resurrect old ties, which got badly disrupted due to geopolitics. I am confident that the book will be a useful addition to the growing literature on the Bay of Bengal region.

New Delhi
Aug 2019

DR ARVIND GUPTA
Director,
Vivekananda International Foundation,
New Delhi

INTRODUCTION

For centuries the Bay of Bengal was crossed by troops, traders, slaves and workers. It was a maritime highway between India and China, navigable by mastery of its regularly reversing monsoon winds. The rise and decline of the Bay as a connected region is a story almost completely untold.

—**Sunil S Amrit**

The above quote from the book *Crossing the Bay of Bengal* sums up the past of the Bay that had once etched the eons of history.[1] Constants of geography, maritime contiguity, socio-cultural and religious connections and trading contacts had provided a sound foundation for transactions that blended the region into a distinctive flavour. Ironically, the modern divide between South Asia and Southeast Asia seems to belie Bay's symphony of the waters and shared legacy. As affluence returns to the region, states have started to gaze outwards beyond their immediate domestic concerns and yearn to rediscover the ancient links with neighbours around the Bay. This has rekindled the belief that the Bay has neither been an artificial concept, nor is it a figment of geographical imagination; instead it is reminiscent of shared identities and enduring ties of culture, religion, trade and migration.

Bay of Bengal is hemmed by developing nations, several having modest impact on the world economy as also on geopolitics. Yet, these nations seem to attract global consciousness, as each one of them has lately recorded impressive rates of growth. This attention has kindled a desire to collaborate for mutual development and reap the benefits of their combined strengths and regionalisation.

Bangladesh, Bhutan, India, Myanmar Nepal, Thailand, and Sri Lanka have mustered their hopes under the institutional framework of Bay of Bengal Multi-Sectoral Technical and Economic Cooperation (BIMSTEC) and aspire to emulate other successful regional forums like the Association of South East Asian Nations (ASEAN). These aspirations are rooted, as much in common future as it is in their shared history.

BIMSTEC is a natural link between South Asia and Southeast Asia that ties together nearly 1.5 billion people, which corresponds to 22 per cent of the world population and over US$ 3 trillion of GDP. There are significant human and economic incentives for these countries to converge and harness their mutual complementarities. Like any other regional grouping, BIMSTEC had a humble beginning in 1997 with fewer countries and a modest vision. Today it has more members and focuses on 14 sectors of cooperation spearheaded by the member states on a voluntary basis. However, the policies, praxis and performances of each country have differed due to disparate national institutional structures and processes. After two decades the 'we-ness' appears to elude barring a few exception. The member states interact more with the outside world than among themselves. This is one of the many reasons that led us to investigate the underlying reasons and understand the principles that undergird the process of regionalisation.

During the writing of this volume we came across significant challenges confronting the region and these have been captured in various chapters. However, we also admit that these may not be all inclusive. Nonetheless, this academic-policy study attributes the disjuncture in BIMSTEC to essentially two broad reasons. One is due to the propensity of operating mostly at the macro levels, which has invariably left the underlying issues to fester, remain unsolved and an inability of synergising policies for the region on various issues. The second reason can be attributed to centralisation by respective governments which preclude public participation.

This book, titled *Sea of Collective Destiny: Bay of Bengal and BIMSTEC*, visits the dialectic of regionalism and regionalisation, alongside the sweeping changes of a globalising world. The book has been arranged under three themes: security, economy and geopolitics and is broadly divided into 14 chapters, so as to enable busy readers to easily access information and analysis related to their respective interest without having to read the entire book. Moreover, each chapter is brief but sufficient, although the number of chapters are more. Furthermore, not all challenges can be discussed in the book; neither can this study claim to have studied any single problem to its finality.

The first chapter delves into theory of regionalisation and identifies some conceptual frameworks for analysis. The second chapter visits the shared culture and history of the region and discovers the common roots that bind its people. Chapter three to eight relate to security issues and address transnational organised crimes, human induced environmental issues, human induced digital crime and migration, and natural disasters. Chapter nine to thirteen discuss some of the trends and challenges of economic integration and connectivity in the region. Chapter fourteen draws attentions to the structural rumblings of geopolitics that impinge upon peace and stability of the region. In the concluding chapter, the policy recommendations have been coalesced.

The book has scanned a wide spectrum of topics that are under active consideration of policy makers, experts who follow the region closely and academics who study and teach regionalism and multilateral institutions. So it has something for all. Additionally, each chapter has been written in the format of an issue brief which delves sufficiently into each of the topics and suggest implementable policy vectors that have been set out in the last chapter.

We thank the Vivekananda International Foundation for facilitating this project. It is also our hope that the book will attract the attention of academics, analysts and policy makers who are interested in restoring and invigorating the identity of the Bay of Bengal as a region.

VIJAY SAKHUJA
SOMEN BANERJEE

1

Regionalism:
A Political, Economic and Social Project

Regional integration has been experienced in varied forms ever since humankind wanted to trade and had the urge to expand territory. The Mauryan Empire integrated large parts of Iran, China and India around 300 BC over several centuries. Likewise, between 27 BC and 476 AD, the Roman Empire integrated the Mediterranean Sea region into a monetary and political union. These empires were precursor to the modern forms of regionalism. The colonial era witnessed regionalisation of disparate nations under the suzerainty of imperial powers.[1]

Regions were also apolitical. For instance, during the pre-colonial era, the Bay of Bengal region was integrated with many other regions through exchange of culture, religion, people and trade. But its nature changed drastically with the advent of colonisation. The economy of the Bay of Bengal region was integrated by the British Raj for exploitation and rent-seeking. In the post-World War II period, its form took another twist, as colonialism faded into history. Since the 1960s there has been an upsurge of regional structures across the world.

Some of the existing groupings based on political frameworks include the African Union (AU), Organisation of American States (OAS) and Shanghai Cooperation Organisation (SCO). The European Union (EU), the Gulf Cooperation Council (GCC), Association of Southeast Asian Nations (ASEAN) and the South African Development Community (SADC) are characterised as politico-economic groupings.

Exclusive economic groupings too have mushroomed and can be seen in the Economic Community of West African States (ECOWAS), Asia Pacific Economic Cooperation (APEC), the Regional Comprehensive Economic Partnership (RCEP) and North American Free Trade Area (NAFTA). The international system has been also dominated by security groupings, such as the Organisation of Security and Cooperation in Europe (OSCE), the ASEAN Regional Forum (ARF) and the North Atlantic Treaty Organisation (NATO). These present unique hues of political diversity, levels of economic strengths and security agendas and as a mix of inchoate overlays. Also, the roles of individual regional forums continue to evolve and their motives tend to shift in response to the global and domestic environment.

To understand the underlying causes, praxis, and prospects of regionalism, this chapter answers two questions: (a) what does regionalism mean and how does it take shape?; and (b) what kind of regionalism will be functional and efficient for stemming the tides of modern challenges?

Stages of Regionalisation

In the past, regionalism was believed to be a State-led phenomenon. However, globalisation through economic integration, trade, human connectivity, modern communication and travel have made regions more complex. As a result, events and developments in one corner of the world can be felt far away in various ways and intensity. For instance, terror attacks carried out by a small group of radicalised people on an Easter Sunday in Sri Lanka in April 2019 had a profound impact on the future of Bay of Bengal region comprising 21 per cent of humanity. To make sense of this milieu it is necessary to study various forms of regionalism from the perspective of the Westphalian State system.

Whereas old regions were created from above, new ones are more voluntary in nature. Today, the constituent states and non-state actors experience an *urge to merge* for tackling global challenges. Whilst old regions were economically inward looking and protectionist, new are more open and compatible with the interdependent world. Whereas, the old regions were mainly concerned with relations between groups of neighbouring countries, new ones are formed as part of global structural transformations and globalization.[2]

Regions are always in a state of evolution and change. Hence, a region must be understood as a process and a social construction. Like a nation, a region is an imagined community and in general, has five levels of 'regionness' that make up the regionalisation process:[3]

(a) Regional Space is a geographic area, delimited more or less by natural barriers. In social terms, a territory is inhabited, at first by isolated communities, but later by more trans-local relationships. A regional space is never static but transforms with societal changes and migrations.

(b) Regional Complex implies interdependence for stability of a regional system. At its lowest level, Barry Buzan's regional security complex (RSC) can be anarchic and sustained by balance-of power equation. South Asian Association for Regional Cooperation (SAARC) is an example for this kind of security complex, which is paradoxically united by conflict and regional process is coercive. RSC could also be a security complex of amity and cooperation.

(c) Regional Society is organised by cultural, economic, political or military interests. Societies are more formal and States are normally the dominant actors. This pattern of relations is nevertheless regulated by rules like that in a 'housing-society'.

(d) Regional Community takes shape when an enduring organisational framework (formal or informal) promotes societal communication and convergence of values and actions, and is characterised by social trust. In security terms, this corresponds to Karl Deutsch's security community.

(e) Regional Institutionalised Polity has a more fixed structure of decision making and stronger actor capability for intervening and handling natural catastrophes, emergencies and conflicts in the region that operates as a loose federation. In security terms it would be an amalgamated security community.

The aforesaid regionalisations have evolutionary logic but are not necessarily prescriptive. These must be combined with endogenous and exogenous factors in order to understand how globalisation is changing State behaviour and creating different pathways for regionalisation. Even though the process of globalisation has been uneven and incomplete, it is sufficiently developed to impact upon any regionalisation project.[4]

Regionalism: Regionalisation vs Globalism - Globalisation

Contemporary world order is different from post-1945 period. Latter was characterized by the US-led Bretton Woods economic system, and was premised on exchange rate relations between national economies. However, this started to change with the dawn of globalisation in the 1970s and was accompanied by a concomitant crisis in US global hegemony. The ensuing vacuum in leadership was quickly filled by 'transnational managerial classes' or the 'international business civilisation' comprising the private banks and global corporations. States could no longer confine international relations to their traditional State-led engagements and inter-state organisations. They also took cognisance of international capital, the banks, foreign exchange markets and capitalist interests. In this changed scenario, States adopted both offensive and defensive strategies. Offensive strategies supported national industries to face market competition, while the defensive strategies protected industries from world competition. In effect, governments had to now ride two-tigers simultaneously, i.e. respond to the structural powers of international capital and open economy as also to the continuing pulls of national interests. Robert Cox averred that regionalist and globalist projects have to coexist in post-hegemonic world order; however he didn't amplify on the nature of such coexistence.[5]

Regionalism "is a State-led project designed to reorganise a particular regional space along defined economic and political lines." It can be distinguished from globalism, which is a State-led project at the global level. But, in both projects, the State is the key actor. The calculations a State does on cost-benefit and interests, are start-point for understanding State behaviour. State behaviour is also informed by past social interfaces and current social interactions. Together they provide both opportunities and constraints.[5]

Unlike regionalism and globalism, globalisation and regionalisation are not State projects; instead combine historical and emergent structures. They are complex articulation of established institutions, rules and new patterns of social relations between non-state actors. States typically seek to accelerate, modify or reverse the process of globalisation or regionalisation. But, one-sided strategic calculation by states will be narrow and inadequate.[6]

Core and Periphery of Regionalisation

Regionalisation refers to those processes that deepen the integration of particular regional economic spaces. Conventional ways of measuring it are: the flow of people, investments and trade. Regionalisation can develop before cultural or political unification or may occur in a territory that has already achieved political unification. In the process, some areas of the region will be integrated and some will be marginalised. Unless the core of the regionalist project addresses the issue of inequality, the process of integration leads to further polarisation.[7]

The world order now has three major economic regions – North America, the European Union and East Asia. Each of these regions has a core. The relations between the cores and their respective peripheries are complex and diverse.[8] The structural weight of each of the three cores has created asymmetric relations in their respective regions. The core acts as a powerful magnet and drags other states in its orbit. This model becomes even more pronounced with the collapse of alternative models of development.

For instance in East Asia, the core was represented earlier by Japan. The result was an economic structure where Japanese production were located in other parts of East Asia, but the technology and business strategies were under the firm control of Japan. The mantle of core State in East Asia is gradually shifting from Japan to China. Countries are eager to interact with the core for increasing their rate of growth and social development, however, unequal the relationship.

These structural inequalities between the core and periphery continue to grow, due to the lack of alternative institutional mechanism for redistribution of wealth. The position is stark in the EU as well, with Germany, France and Benelux countries forming the core. Because of the difficulties in achieving convergence between the economies, those on the periphery are reduced to the status of being satellites. The potential hegemonies in all the three areas do not endeavour to construct more permanent and inclusive frameworks.[9]

Regional Dimensions of World Order

Henry Kissinger in his book *World Order* avowed that no truly global order has ever existed. What passes for order in our time is the Westphalian system of sovereign states, refraining from interference in each other's affairs, and extensive network of international legal and organizational structures, designed to foster free trade and stable international financial system.[10] A regional order is based on similar principles, albeit under the influence of regional dynamics characterised by connectivity, trade, shared resources, communication, crime, territorial disputes and internecine conflicts. Regional dimensions of world order can be identified in mainly four patterns of interactions through the links between regionalism as:[11]

(a) Negative Globalism refers to unaccountable power and influence exerted by multi-national corporations, transnational banks, and financial institution with their ideology of consumerism and maximizing growth. It also includes crime and terror with global reach. Neo-liberal ideology on one hand respects freedom and rule of law, but on the other, it harbours

the destructive elements of greed, extreme individualism and materialism. Regionalism has the ability to counter the effects of negative globalism.
(b) Hegemony of superpowers is established through measures of non-territorial influences such as counter-terror operations, change of regime, coercive diplomacy, arms race and militarisation of space. Regional balance can keep the influence of the extra-regional powers under check.
(c) Pathological Anarchism breaks down the established regional order associated with political normalcy and governance. It could lead to sustained violence, genocidal outbreaks, crime against humanity, safe-haven for terrorists, and massive displacement of people from their natural habitats. Both states and the United Nations have failed to check pathological anarchism. Regional communities can build institutions, capabilities and norms to address them at the regional scale.
(d) Positive Globalism promotes sustainability, human rights, development accountability, rule of law, demilitarisation, etc. However, there are concerns about homogenization of identity and excessive centralism. Regional order can reconcile the quest for governance *vis-à-vis* the need to protect the sensitivities of heterogeneous cultures within.

Economic Regionalism

In the post-World War period, regional economic initiatives were characterized by increase in intra-regional trade and capital flows; reducing tariffs and non-trade barriers; and removal of impediments to investment flows. It can be empirically established that tariff reduction does not enhance intra-regional cross-border trade significantly; instead it is the non-tariff and administrative barriers that hinder integration and discourage regionalism. Some examples of non-tariff barriers are—monetary and payment barriers, production barriers, and barriers to investments. Other barriers hindering regional integration are structural adjustments, slow convergence, differences in ethnicity, policy instability, and competing or overlapping regional institutions.[12]

Regionalisation of Security

In the past, especially during the pre-Cold War period, political and military sectors were the principle sectors of security relations. Politico-military security was normally associated with proximity, as threats were more easily understood over short distances. Indigenous regional security dynamics like the India-Pakistan tensions in South Asia surfaced post- decolonisation and were influenced by superpower rivalry. Security is not always state-cenric:

(a) *Security transcending States:* Post-Cold War landscape of regional security has altered significantly due to diffusion of power and relative introversion of superpowers. Also, sources of power within nation-states are not concentrated solely with the government anymore. This is because security agenda have grown beyond territoriality to domains such as economy, environment and identity. Some of these extra-territorial issues cannot be dealt with through business-as-usual approach by States. They have emerged as existential threats and require exceptional measures to overcome. Hence, they legitimise the departure from normal politics characterized by use of force, additional executive powers and secrecy.[13]

(b) *Referent object:* State is no more the only referent object, as sources of threat have diversified. Referent objects can be either larger than a State, or a peer institution or it could be a sub-state actor. Those that are above state system include enforcement of liberal international economic order, transnational crimes, climate change, weapons of mass destruction, chemical weapons conventions, and missile technology control regime. Alongside the states are referent objects like identity and religion. Sub-state referent objects are issues of human rights and individuals. Some of these referent objects are better addressed under regional frameworks as they have inter-state linkages and some of them resonate with transnational bonds of culture, identity and values across multiple states.

(c) *Regional values:* Each region has its distinct character. Whilst Europe is institutionalised on social democratic values, North America is organised on liberal values, Middle-East banking system is organised on Islamic norms and Asians reflect national developmental values.[14] So, on more occasions than one, regional solutions are more effective, even if the concern is global. However, in the case of some global sectors like environment, regions have weaker influence.[15]

Approaches to Understanding Regionalism in International Relations

Regionalism can be understood through multiple approaches of traditional international relations. But no single approach can explain all the nuances of conflict, competition or cooperation. Regional interactions will always conflate aspects of realism, liberalism constructivism, functionalism, hegemony and globalisation. So, it becomes essential to understand each of these perspectives to be able to appreciate the influence of the whole.

Realism has been efficacious in explaining many trends in regionalism. It has been able to justify the underling geopolitical perspectives of regional alliances. Systemic trends of the international system normally press states to engender common responses despite their internal differences. NATO is one such geographically oriented regional framework. In addition, mercantile economic competitions can garner regional cooperation between states to stem competing market forces. Neo-realists believe that the outside-in pressures of mercantilist rivalry greatly influenced the European integration. It came into being in the 1960s as a counter (*le defi americain*) to the exorbitant economic American privileges. Its re-launch in the 1980s was another response against the rising Japanese domination and loss of competitiveness in strategic technology market. Similarly, NAFTA served a bargaining ploy for the US against the Japanese and the Europeans and APEC against Europe. Smaller and vulnerable states too have engaged in regional collaboration to stem the challenges from powerful nations. The erosion of Non-Aligned Movement (NAM) post-Cold War pushed developing countries in Africa, Latin America and Asia to form new regional forums.[16] Neo-realism is equally applicable to the Bay of Bengal region in the light of an emerging world order that is increasingly being shaped by China. The likely contours of a Chinese order had been summarised by Michael Pillsbury in his book *The Hundred Year Marathon*. According to him, Chinese suzerainty will be characterized by a world with Chinese values, where personal rights will not matter and internet will be censored. Democratically elected governments will be undermined and the UN and the WTO would be made irrelevant.[17] In this backdrop, cooperation between democracies of the Bay of Bengal can emerge as a bulwark against Chinese irredentism, geo-economic onslaught and military influence.

China's Belt and Road Initiative (BRI) has already made its inroads into Sri Lanka, Myanmar, Nepal, Bangladesh and Thailand. It would be difficult for individual nations to deny the Chinese largesse due to the legitimacy it provides to an incumbent government. China has substantial leverage and influence in the New Development Bank (NDB) and the Asian Infrastructure Investment Bank (AIIB). Approvals for electrical projects worth $20-million and $165-million in Myanmar and Bangladesh in 2016 vindicate the point.[18] Similarly, mercantilism by China has undercut large sectors of domestic farmers and industries in the region and each country maintains trade deficit with China. These ominous signs need to be averted by becoming more competitive through synergetic policies on issues such as border management, infrastructure, tariffs, security and regional value chains (RVC). India's growing power also provides BIMSTEC the political muscle to resist sovereign capitulation. China's loss of face during the Doklam standoff and India's refusal to join the BRI has dented China and Xi's legitimacy significantly. The ongoing US's trade war with China has further exposed Chinese vulnerabilities. Bay of Bengal as a region need not direct its actions against any specific country, but it can take advantage of the size of its intrinsic market comprising over 22 per cent of the world's population. Together, the region has the potential to deter, balance or contain coercive political and economic challenges, and command greater voice in the international fora.

As far as Hegemony is concerned, literature on the relationship between regionalism and hegemony is quite sparse. According to Andrew Hurrell, the existence of a powerful country in a region can impair the formation of an inclusive regional organisation. But, theoretically hegemony can also stimulate the creation of regional institutions in four ways:[19] First, a regional grouping can be an effective means for balancing an external hegemony.[20] ASEAN against China and GCC against Iran are two such regional organisations. Similarly, BIMSTEC has the potential to deter China, without a formal military alliance. Second, regionalism can be leveraged to constrain a hegemonic power within a region. While Soviet Union was the external stimulus for European integration, constraining Germany provided the internal stimulus. Similarly, BIMSTEC can be a useful forum to allay the fears of its member states against the growing might of India through confidence-building measures, non-aggression agreements and non-coercion treaties, which will ensure greater stability to an already tranquil region. However, regional disarmament will be impractical due to the structural constraints of the current geopolitical scenario. Third, weaker states could seek accommodation with the local hegemony for strategic and economic advantage. This kind of behaviour is most likely when the power differentials are exceptionally great.[21] However, such an accommodation or band-wagoning with India may not be practical for other countries in the Bay of Bengal rim due to the lack of domestic consensus within the constituent states. Fourth, a hegemonic state could take the initiative to generate international support and legitimacy for itself. According to Antonio Gramsci, successful hegemony requires consensus to predominate coercion.[22] India's hegemony in the region could be counterproductive due to its predominant power, and runs the risk of making the regional institutions irrelevant. Hence, downplaying India's hegemony will be the essential for creating regional institutions in the Bay of Bengal region. India has a major role to play in building the legitimacy and relevance of the organisation. Interestingly, India's foreign policy has undergone drastic changes in the recent past. India had played an active role in democratisation of its neighbourhood by weaning them away from monarchy and military regimes.²³ India's foreign policy is now founded on five parameters – *Samman, Samvad, Samridhi, Suraksha, Sabyata and Sanskriti*, which means dignity and self-respect, dialogue and negotiations, development and prosperity, security and defence and culture and civilisation. Government of India has taken proactive steps to undo the alienation of its neighbours, streamlined its delivery mechanisms and is engaging all stakeholders.²⁴ Denouncing hegemony, sharing greater regional burden during contingencies, investing in regional infrastructure projects, supporting neighbours with technical infrastructure like satellite communication facilities are some of the measures initiated by India to deepen mutual trust. India's Act East and neighbourhood-first policies too are in consonance with peaceful growth and development of the region.

Although globalisation cannot be anchored in any IR theory, it has become a powerful theme for increased interconnection and interdependence between businesses, investments, industries, governments, non-government organisations (NGOs), education and plenty of other social activities. State autonomy has been transgressed in many disciplines by the constant exchange of people, information and goods across the borders. Thus the relationship between globalisation and regionalism has evolved in complex ways. The economic rise of the 'South' has started to decouple global growth from advanced countries, leading to considerable enthusiasm about global governance. India had been one of the top 10 developing countries in terms of FDI inflows and outflows in 2017.²⁵ The difference between gross export and value added export of Thailand was 35 per cent in 2013 and that of India was 22 per cent.²⁶ In Bangladesh, garment manufacturing has become a major driver of its industrial development and global connect. Myanmar has witnessed the fastest growth of FDI at 45.2 per cent in 2017 and Nepal has been able to capture some of the niche low volume, high value markets like tea and coffee.²⁷ Such global incentives and enhanced levels of universal interactions are obvious challenges for regionalism. Radical theorists argue that state's authority on market is losing ground to transnational governance. Nevertheless, globalisation can also provide stimulus for regionalism. Common culture, history, homogeneity, political and security interests of a region facilitate common standards, regulations and implementation. The diminishing control of domestic governments has had a positive impact on people-to-people contact by creating conditions for more balanced distribution of wealth and power across a region.²⁸ In other words, globalisation can reify spontaneity amongst people in the region and garner regional consciousness—the *we-ness* for doing business.

In so far as Liberalism is concerned, Goldstein and Keohane in their book *Ideas, Beliefs, Institutions and Foreign Policy* aver that both realism and liberal institutionalism adopt rationalist approach in which self-interested actors try to maximise their utility;[29] but, the start point is an idea. Ideas influence policies in three ways: providing causal roadmaps, affecting strategies and getting embedded in political institutions.[30] Once ideas are transformed into rules and norms, in other words they are institutionalised, they constrain public policy.[31] Role of institutions is not to replace the mechanisms of decentralization but to support cooperation in situations where states or organisations alone would fail. Normally institutions are not intended to enforce rules or norms but are designed to help a community to reduce uncertainty and moderate expectations.[32] BIMSTEC has been organised into 14 sectors of cooperation in order to reduce transaction cost between states and enhance mutual understanding. Hence, institutions are pre-requisite for regional cooperation, but are not adequate.

Nicholus Onuf in his book *International Relations in a Constructed World*, states that constructivism is the proposition that humans are social beings and social relations make or *construct* (emphasised) people. But it is a two-way process where, people also construct a society. However, people and societies are held together by a third element called *rules* (emphasised).[33] A family of rules and related practices is called regime.[34] Constructivists emphasise on regional identity based on shared sense of belonging or cognitive regionalism. There are two main variants of regionalism. One, spawns from a sense of community or 'we-ness', mutual sympathy, loyalty or shared identity, which is based on shared principles, collectively held norms and common understanding. Second, is a *process* (emphasised) by which a community emerges based on social values (capitalism or democracy) or based on a process of social communication or transactions.[35] From a constructivist perspective, the Bay of Bengal region has all the ingredients of common history and compatible modern values for maturing into a robust regional organisation. However, a few centuries of oblivion had weakened these bonds. Hence, these bonds need to be recreated by expanding the scope of transactions. Security too is an essential element in region-building process. Andrew Hurrell points out that security regime such as ASEAN Regional Forum (ARF) should not be seen as balance-of-power or alliance formation against any particular state, but it should be conceived as opportunity for enhancing communication, information, transparency and for reducing mutual threat perception.[36]

Ernest B Hass remarked in his book *The Uniting of Europe* that there are other ways to peace than either power (realism) or law (idealism). Instead of struggling for power, states can pursue neo-functionalism by advocating democratic pluralism in policy making. Governments are normally inclined towards institutional approach based on rational choices. Experts find rational choice to be a constraint in the evolution of regionalism because of its path-dependencies. Path-dependency seeks to establish stability in institutional functioning and thereafter locks-in to achieve long-term permanency. This kind of institutional approach is not dynamic and cannot evolve real-time values and interests of multiple actors in a globalised world. In contrast, theory of neo-functionalism (NF) advocates that regional integration occurs when societal actors, rely on supranational institutions rather than their own governments. These institutions, in turn enjoy increasing authority and legitimacy. In short, neo-functionalism is about disaggregating the state into its actor-components, as they become source of policies meeting the demands of the social actors.[37] According to Hass, there are no fixed national interests and policies, as governments should be responsive to shifting domestic needs. NF uses the logic of unintended consequences and entertains different hierarchy of values and interests for different private actors. For BIMSTEC to evolve its regional consciousness, it has to reduce influence of governments in shaping policies and provide adequate leeway to private players to interact and devise their norms for horizontal interaction. Governments would have to be adept to endorse and facilitate such norms.

Conclusion

This chapter outlines multiple conceptual frameworks that can guide the analysis on regionalisation of the Bay of Bengal region. Theories of international relations inform the complexities of the structure of international environment and offer a peek into the motivations of individual behaviours of states. It is also essential to understand the distinction between regionalism and regionalisation to comprehend the intra-regional, inter-regional and trans-regional interactions. The stages to regionalisation discussed aforesaid, provide a proximate yardstick for measuring the level of regionness achieved between the littorals of Bay of Bengal thus far. A glimpse into barriers of economic integrations will require further amplification in the book. Post-Cold War elements beyond territoriality, such as economy, environment and identity, have shifted the security agenda from pure politico-military domain. So a state is no more the only referent object and sources of threat are diverse. This book demonstrates how some of these referent objects are better addressed under regional frameworks, not only because of their transnational character, but also the compatibility of culture, identity and values of the Bay of Bengal region. Lastly, the geopolitical relevance of regionalisation has been explained through the dialectics on 'core-periphery' and 'regional dimensions of world order'.

Littoral states of the Bay of Bay already have the natural advantage of shared socio-cultural, religious, language and trading links. The next chapter explores the historical bonds and perspectives that are gradually welding the seams of a nascent regional identity.

NOTES

1. Percy S Mistry, "New Regionalism and Economic Development", (ed) *Theories of Regionalism* Fredrik oderbaum and Timothy M Shaw (New York: Palgrave, 2003), p.120.
2. Bjorn Hettne "The New Regionalism Revisited, in Theories of Regionalism", (ed) Fredrik Soderbaum and Timothy M Shaw (New York: Palgrave, 2003), pp. 23–24.
3. Ibid., pp. 28-29.
4. Andrew Gamble and Anthony Payne, " The World Order Approach, in Theories of Regionalism", (ed) Fredrik Soderbaum and Timothy M Shaw (New York : Palgrave, 2003), pp. 48–49.
5. Ibid., pp. 50.
6. Ibid.
7. Ibid., pp. 57.
8. Ibid., pp. 51.
9. Ibid., 57–58.
10. Henry Kissinger, *World Order*, (UK: Penguin Random House, 2014), pp. 2–7.
11. Richard Falk, "Regionalism and the World Order", (ed) Fredrik Soderbaum and Timothy M Shaw *Theories of Regionalism* (New York: Palgrave, 2003), pp. 69–79.
12. Percy S Mistry, "New Regionalism and Economic Development", (ed) *Theories of Regionalism* Fredrik Soderbaum and Timothy M Shaw (New York: Palgrave, 2003), pp. 126–31.
13. Barry Buzan, "Regional Security Complex Theory", (ed) Fredrik Soderbaum and Timothy M Shaw, *Theories of Regionalism* (New York : Palgrave, 2003), pp. 141–50.
14. Ibid., pp. 150–6.
15. Ibid, pp. 155–6.
16. Andrew Hurrell, "Explaining the resurgence of regionalism in world politics", *Review of international studies*, Volume 21, Issue 04, October 1995, pp. 331–58.
17. Michael Pillsbury, *The Hundred Year Marathon* (New York: St Martin's Griffin, 2014), p.178.
18. UNCTAD, "Forging a path beyond borders; the global south", Geneva, 2018, https://unctad.org/en/PublicationsLibrary/osg2018d1_en.pdf (accessed 31 December 2018).
19. Andrew Hurrell, "Explaining the resurgence of regionalism in world politics", *Review of international studies*, Volume 21, Issue 04, October 1995, pp. 331–58.
20. Ibid.
21. Ibid.
22. Valeriano Ramos Jr, "The concepts of ideology, hegemony and organic intellectuals in Gramsci's Marxism", *Theoretical Review*, No 27, 1982.

23 SD Muni, *Neighbourhood initiatives of the Modi Government*, (ed) Nalini Jha and Sreelekha (New Delhi: Pentagon Press, 2018), p. 9.
24 Ibid., p. 14.
25 UNCTAD, "Forging a path beyond borders; the global south", Geneva, 2018, https://unctad.org/en/PublicationsLibrary/osg2018d1_en.pdf (accessed 31 December 2018)
26 Rashmi Banga, "Regional value chain, Measuring value of GVC", UNCTAD, 2013, https://unctad.org/en/PublicationsLibrary/ecidc2013misc1_bp8.pdf (accessed 31 December 2018)
27 UNCTAD, LDC Report 2018, "The local entrepreneurship dimensions of global production system" https://unctad.org/en/PublicationChapters/ldcr2018_ch3_en.pdf (accessed 31 December 2018)
28 Andrew Hurrell, "Explaining the resurgence of regionalism in world politics", *Review of international studies*, Volume 21, Issue 04, October 1995, pp. 331–58.
29 Ibid, p. 4.
30 Judith Goldstein, Robert Owen Keohane, *Ideas, Beliefs, Institutions and Foreign Policy* (1993: Cornell University Press, 1995), p. 8.
31 Ibid, p. 12.
32 Ibid, p. 184.
33 Nicholas Onuf (et al), *International Relations in a Constructed World* (London: ME Sharpe, 1998), p. 59.
34 Ibid, p. 70.
35 Andrew Hurrell, "Explaining the resurgence of regionalism in world politics", *Review of International Studies*, Volume 21, Issue 04, October 1995, pp. 331–58.
36 Ibid.
37 EB Hass, *The Uniting of Europe: Political, Social and Economic Forces - 1950-1957* (Indiana: University of Notre Dame Press, 2004), p. xiv.

2

Sea of Collective Destiny

Geography, history, social practices, cultural connections and religious beliefs are among the many cardinals and determinants to understand a region. Further, it is an established axiom that interrelationship among the indices of geography and the people create *joie de vivre* in the region. States draw upon their shared histories, cultural and religious connections and practices, linguistic transmissions and mutations, and trading links towards common futures. The Bay of Bengal is a space of 'collective destiny' marked by deep-rooted cultural connections, religious affinities and vibrant trading connections. In the 21st century, the Bay of Bengal is reliving the ancient glory and exhibits new-found vibrancies that are shaping its future.

In the above context, this chapter attempts to highlight the idea of 'collective destiny' of Bay of Bengal based on geography, cultural connections, trading links and collective understanding of contemporary challenges that confront the region. These are also the critical determinants that help regional and sub-regional organisations and institutions to thrive and support the purpose for which these were conceptualized. Further, the chapter provides the contemporary outlook of the Bay of Bengal marked by cooperative agendas that promote collective fortunes to be shared by the littoral countries.

Geography of the Bay

The Bay of Bengal is a semi-enclosed sea and shaped like a horseshoe.[1] Its western edge is largely India and the northern waters wash the shores of Bangladesh; in the east, the Bay of Bengal is bound by Myanmar, Thailand and west coast of peninsular Malaysia. The Bay is boxed in the south by two countries—Sumatra, Indonesia and eastern Sri Lanka. It opens to the Indian Ocean in the south and can be described as the 'extended arm' of the Indian Ocean.

In terms of exact cartographic representation, the Bay of Bengal is the largest Bay and is spread over 2.2 million square kilometres (868,000 square miles).[2] It lies between longitudes 80 degree east and 100 degree east and latitudes 0 degree (Equator) and 22 degrees north. It stretches over a large body of water and is spread over nearly 2.2 million square kilometres. The average depth in the Bay of Bengal is 2,600 metres with a maximum depth of 5,258 metres.[3]

Several perennial rivers drain into the Bay of Bengal. Amongst these, a few originate in the Himalayan glaciers: Gangotri and Yamunotri in Uttarakhand, India; Nubra, Biafo and Baltoro in the Karakoram region; Zemu in Sikkim; and Khumbu glaciers in the Mount Everest region.[4] The Yarlung Tsangpo River of Tibet runs into India to become the Brahmaputra; it moves eastwards and then south and through the plains of Assam into the Bay of Bengal. Likewise, Ganga originates in the Himalaya and is joined by several smaller rivers—Ramaganga, Gomati, Ghagra, Gandak and Kosi that also have their origins in the Himalayas in Nepal.[5] The Surma-Meghna river system flows through Bangladesh.

The confluence of the three rivers is also referred to as Ganga-Brahmaputra-Meghna (GBM) basin and drains an area of 10,86,000 square kilometres.[6] Between Ganga and Brahmaputra rivers, they carry nearly 1,000,000,000 metric tons of sediment into the northern Bay of Bengal. Further, the GBM combine form the largest depositional system in the world. It is a high depositional activity and the delta front advances at 15 metres annually.[7] In the east, the 2170 kilometres long Irrawaddy River in Myanmar also has its source in Tibet in the Himalayas and drains into the Andaman Sea. These river systems affect the sediment deposits and shape the underwater topography of the Bay of Bengal. Furthermore, they affect the hydrographic and oceanographic characteristics of the Bay of Bengal.

Right in the middle of the Bay of Bengal are the Andaman & Nicobar Islands. These 572 islands, small and big, lie in the north-south axis and spread over about 825,000 hectares. They have a coastline of 1,962 kilometres (25% of India's coastline) which generates 6 Lakhs square kilometres of Exclusive Economic Zone (EEZ) or 30 per cent of India's EEZ.[8] These are under the sovereign control of India.

Cultural Connections and Trading Links

The difficult and challenging overland geography represented by the Himalayas and the tropical forests of Indo-China had imposed major constraints on the movement of people across Asia. The seas were the most promising medium to undertake voyages and engage in trade. Bay of Bengal was central to three civilizations—India, China and Southeast Asia. I-Tsing, the famous Chinese traveller, visited India in AD 673 and had disembarked at the port of Tamralipti (Tamluk on the mouth of the Ganges in Bengal).[9] He visited Palembang en route to India and has also recorded the itineraries of 60 Chinese pilgrims to India clearly showcasing the constant traffic in the Bay of Bengal. Similarly, Fa-hien returned to China by the sea route via Ceylon.

The Roman, Arab, Persian traders also frequented the Bay region and their ships sailed through these waters. The southern Bay of Bengal was the major trading route and served as the primary passageway for traders from Arabia, Persia, India, Malaya and China. Their ships sailed between 7 and 9-degree latitudes making easterly and westerly voyages. Ships sailing from south India followed the coastal routes till the eastern shores of Ceylon before setting course across the Bay of Bengal and thence along south Sumatra coast through Sunda Strait to Palembang and finally making land fall on the western shores of the Malay Peninsula at Kedah.[10]

The intra-Asian trade was essentially 'high value low volume' in nature and comprised Chinese silk and porcelain, Southeast Asian spices, cotton from India, incense from Persia, etc. As recorded elsewhere, "Funan ships that sailed to Bengal in India were large and could carry up to 100 oarsmen and Indian built ships also engaged in India–China trade illustrating the fact that the two states were engaged with each other through maritime trade since ancient times... The Chinese overseas trade at that time comprised a variety of goods and of the 1141 items of trade, 339 items were imported from Southeast Asia, India and Middle East.[11] Arab vessels from the Emporia in Arabia and the Persian Gulf shipped goods to Srivijaya ports in Southeast Asia from where these were transshipped to China."[12]

The Asian mariners had acquired good knowledge of the prevailing winds and currents in the Bay of Bengal. The period between December-March (the north-easterlies begin to turn NNE beginning December till March) was preferred for voyages. Similarly, the seafarers had acquired sophisticated astronavigation knowledge which ensured safe west-east sailing.[13]

In the Bay of Bengal, the Kalinga kingdom had established trading links with

China through the sea route. For instance, archaeological evidences "throw light on Kalinga-China relationship. The Chinese celadon wares, the Chinese porcelain with blue floral design on white background and Chinese copper coins, one complete and the other fragmented belonging to 14th century CE which are discovered from Khalkatapatna provided substantial evidences to testify Odisha's relation with ancient China. Similarly, the excavations at Manikpatna (Cheli-ta-lo of Hiuen Tsang) yielded two types of evidences for maritime connections of Kalinga with China, i.e. celadonware and Chinese copper coins."[14] Besides, cultural contacts with several kingdoms in Southeast Asia are symbolized and recalled in Odisha, India, in folklore and festivals such as the Bali Yatra which accurately means 'The Journey to Bali'.[15]

Likewise, traders, mariners and people from India, China, Southeast Asia, Persia, Arabia and even the Roman Empire had facilitated a large maritime trading ecosystem in the Bay of Bengal. This is best understood by the Tamil merchant guilds at Nakorn Si Thammarat (Thailand) and Barus (Sumatra, Indonesia).[16]

Tansen Sen's study needs to be highlighted here, "Indian records also confirm the trips of Indian merchants to the markets in Southeast Asia and China. The eighth-century work Kuvalayamiilii, for example, recounts the discussions of Indian merchants who dealt in horses, elephants, pearls, ivory, and silk about their travels to Southeast Asia and China. Another eighth-century text, Samariiiccakahii, reports one prince's plans for a commercial trip to China. This work also notes of a sailor called Suvadana who had returned to India from China via Southeast Asia."[17] Further, "From the eighth century onward, the maritime route between India and China, that either transverse through the Andaman and Nicobar Islands or skirted around the ports of the Bay of Bengal to Sumatra and into the South China Sea, became more popular than the overland routes mentioned above."[18] Sen also states that "While internal land routes connected Nagapatinam to the ports in the Malabar coast, ports of the Bay of Bengal, including those in coastal Bengal and Myanmar, were linked through maritime channels. Srivijayan, Muslim, Jewish, and later the Chinese, sea-faring traders are known to have established their diasporas at Nagapatinam. In fact, the port seems to have continued to be an important emporium in East West trade in the sixteenth century, when Portuguese and Chinese ships harboured at the Coromandel coast".[19]

Bay of Bengal Geopolitics

In the civilisational history of India, the role of the Chola kings in building maritime power was an unparalleled achievement. The Chola kings had engaged in sea-based commerce thus opening the Chola heartland to the overseas trading systems. These overseas commercial ventures flourished thereby ensuring the rise of the economic power of the Chola monarchs who pursued aggressive trading policies that established trading networks and political relations in the Mediterranean, Persia and Malaya, Sumatra and China through trade missions.

The Chola Empire was perhaps the most respected Hindu State that possessed, though only for a brief period, influence over the Malay Peninsula and Sumatra. The maritime ascendancy of Cholas in the waters of Bay of Bengal was acknowledged among the littorals and was demonstrated by the merchant guilds or 'ainnuruvar' at several places in Southeast Asia and Ceylon. The Bay of Bengal became a Chola trading lake with a flourishing maritime enterprise.

Although the trading relations were well established and flourished in the Bay of Bengal, the region had its fair share of competition marked by geopolitics. For instance, relations between the Chola Kings and the Srivijaya ruler had deteriorated presumably due to unfavourable trade practices favouring China. The commercial rivalry may have angered the Chola king Rajaraja I (A.D. 1012–A.D. 1044) who launched a naval expedition against the Srivijaya Empire.[20]

The naval expedition ordered by the Chola king Rajendra Choladeva I to Southeast Asia is mentioned in the inscription dated 1030-31 of the big temple of Tanjavur reads:[21]

> (who) having dispatched many ships in the midst of the rolling sea and having caught Sangrama – Vijayottunga Varman, the king of Kadaram, together with the elephants in his glorious army, (took) the large heap of treasures, which (that king) had rightfully accumulated; (captured) with noise, the (arch) called Vidyadhara torana at the 'war gate' of his extensive city, Sri Vijaya with the ' jeweled wicket gate' adorned with great splendour and the 'gate of large jewels'; Pannai with water in its bathing ghats; the ancient Malaiyur with the strong mountain for its rampart; Mayirudingam surrounded by the deep sea (as) by a moat; Ilangasoka, undaunted (in) fierce battles; Mappappalam having abundant (deep) water as a defence; Mevilimbangam having fine wall as defence ; Valaippanduru having Vilapandur ; Talaittakkolam praised by great men (versed in the sciences); Madamalingam, firm in fierce and great battles; Ilamuridesam whose fierce strength rose in war; Manakkavaram, in whose extensive flower gardens honey was collecting and Kadaram, of fierce strength, which was protected by the deep sea.

The inscription lists place names that were attacked by the invading Chola forces and these have been subjected to historical geography; six can be found on the Malay Peninsula, four in Sumatra, Manakkavaram has been identified as

Nicobar Islands and two, i.e. *Valaippanduru* and *Mevilimbangam* are unknown. However, the sequence in which these places were attacked has also been a subject of debate and discussion.

It is worth mentioning that the Chola Kings had no plans to expand their empire into Southeast Asia and exercise political control, instead for them primacy was trade and this was also flavoured with cultural diplomacy. Nilakanta Sastri notes that 'neither the merchants nor the state in South India had any idea of possibilities of economic imperialism'.[22] For the Indians, the trade was an end in itself and Indian traders were willing to trade as long as it was profitable and 'it never occurred to them that foreign lands may be compelled to buy and sell at the point of the bayonet'.[23]

During 1328–98, under the first Ming dynasty ruler Zhu Yuanzang, several maritime trade restrictions were introduced that forbid private trade with countries in Southeast Asia. This was essentially to bring maritime trade under state monopoly and discourage competition, but this had led to smuggling of goods leading to loss of revenue.

Under Emperor Chengzu (1403), China had achieved phenomenal maritime capability with a large navy and is best represented by the Zheng He's seven expeditions between 1405 and 1433. He called at ports in Southeast Asia, India Persian Gulf and East Africa and conducted trade, engaged in diplomacy as also projecting China's glory.[24] These expeditions showcased China's maritime prowess of the times that was built around a fleet of more than three hundred vessels of various types manned by a large crew.[25]

Contemporary Geoeconomic Outlook

Bay of Bengal region is geostrategically important to international commerce. It connects the vital sea route between Indian Ocean and the Pacific Ocean also referred to as the Indo-Pacific in contemporary strategic discourse. The Straits of Malacca experiences heavy maritime traffic and on an average 200 ships transit every day through this strategic choke point. The sea lane, before entering or after exiting the Straits of Malacca, transits through the Bay of Bengal and this mercantile reality endows the Andaman and Nicobar Islands enormous strategic advantage to the maritime world particularly for India.

Bay of Bengal littorals—Bangladesh, Myanmar, Thailand, Malaysia, Singapore, Indonesia, Sri Lanka and India—are in throes of maritime rejuvenation showcased by the burgeoning maritime enterprise, which displays strong elements of continuity from the historical past. In fact, the Bay of Bengal is a mirror image of the sophisticated maritime trading system that emerged in ancient Asia that contributed not only to their growth, but had linkages with other trading systems of the Indian Ocean and as far as the Mediterranean.

The Bay of Bengal littorals are also good examples of globalized states marked by interconnectedness with a strong belief that their destiny is shaped by the sea given that a bulk of which is carried out via the seas. At another level, these countries have shed their colonial past which came to their shores from the seas and are building sufficient capability to preclude the dominance of their littorals by an external power as protect trade over the sea-lanes, and to ensure safety of marine resources in the Exclusive Economic Zones. They are confident to harness the potential of the seas for a full realisation of their power potential and place in the international system.

In the context of the latter, many of the Bay of Bengal littorals have chosen to seek external support to harness the seas in terms of infrastructure development, development of Blue Economy, naval capability to preclude external intervention, policing capacity to safeguard their sea areas such as the EEZ which have enormous value to enhance their economic growth. China's 21st century Maritime Silk Road under the Belt Road Initiative has resonated among several countries of the Bay of the Bengal and some of its key components are marine economy, maritime connectivity, marine environment protection and scientific research, maritime search and rescue and fishery.[26] Although such support is generally accepted as benign in nature, it has been a subject of intense debate and is marked by deep-rooted suspicion among a few and these have unfolded into 'debt traps'.

The Bay of Bengal maritime connectivity projects and initiatives are also the bridgehead for land-locked countries and hinterland areas. These are far from the ports and unable to participate in seaborne commerce and contribute to national growth. These maritime nodes in the Bay of Bengal not only help the landlocked states and regions to overcome the tyranny of geography, but help them to participate in global commerce, bulk of which moves over the seas.

There are currently forty-eight countries designated by the United Nations as "least developed countries" (LDCs) including Bangladesh, Bhutan, Myanmar, and Nepal. Two among these are landlocked and are dependent on their neighbours for international seaborne trade.[27] Although India is not a LDC, its northeast region is landlocked and connectivity is a major issue. Besides, the two neighbours, Bhutan and Nepal, benefit from access to Indian ports of Kolkata/Haldia for sea-based commercial activity. The 1971 Transit Treaty between India and Nepal allows the latter to engage in international seaborne commerce through the port of Kolkata/Haldia. This issue is discussed in greater detail in a succeeding chapter.

Several Asian powers are attempting to recall their ancient maritime glory. China's Maritime Silk Road (MSR);[28] India's Project 'Mausam';[29] and Indonesia Global Maritime Fulcrum.[30] These countries are harnessing the seas for a full realization of their position in the 21st century international system and demonstrate to the international community that during ancient times, they were highly interconnected and globalized and the seas had shaped their destiny in significant ways, and continue to do so.

Regional Maritime Boundary Issues

Bay of Bengal littorals are signatory to the 1982 UNCLOS and have ratified the Convention. India, Bangladesh and Myanmar resolved their boundary disputes. The case between Bangladesh and Myanmar, i.e. "Dispute concerning delimitation of the maritime boundary between Bangladesh and Myanmar in the Bay of Bengal (Bangladesh/Myanmar)" was adjudicated by the International Tribunal for the Law of the Sea (ITLOS) through their judgement on 14 March 2012[31] and the Permanent Court of Attribution (PCA) passed orders in the dispute between Bangladesh and India. In the case of the latter, an area of 19,467 square kilometres, four-fifth of the total area of 25,602 square kilometres disputed maritime boundary in the Bay of Bengal with India was awarded to Bangladesh.[32]

There are no major boundary disputes among the littorals barring a few such as the ones between Myanmar and Thailand. Myanmar has maritime boundaries with India, Bangladesh, and Thailand. The boundary dispute with India and Bangladesh has since been resolved, but 'a dispute with Thailand over the 'ownership of three small islets (Ginga Island/Ko Lam, Ko Khan Island and Ko Ki Nu), has on occasion sparked the occasional naval confrontation.'[33]

Regional Groupings Take Shape

Bay of Bengal littorals have invested in regional and sub-regional cooperation initiatives—South Asian Association for Regional Cooperation (SAARC); Bangladesh-China-India-Myanmar Forum for Regional Cooperation (BCIM); Bay of Bengal Initiative for Multi-Sectoral Technical and Economic Cooperation (BIMSTEC); Mekong Ganga Cooperation (MGC); Ayeyawady-Chaophraya-Mekong Economic Cooperation Strategy (ACMECS); and Bangladesh, Bhutan, India, Nepal (BBIN) Initiative. Likewise, several Bay of Bengal littorals are members of the Association of Southeast Asian Nations (ASEAN), ASEAN Regional Forum (ARF), East Asia Summit (EAS), ASEAN-led security initiatives such as ASEAN Defence Minister's Meeting (ADMM), Expanded ASEAN Maritime Forum (EAMF), etc.

These structures and arrangements have over the years matured and are performing well at the functional and operational levels. At the policy level, many of the above groupings have endorsed and promoted multilateral maritime cooperation that spans several thematic issues such as maritime safety, security and delivery of 'public goods at sea' through Search and Rescue (SAR) and Humanitarian Assistance and Disaster Relief (HADR).

At another level, cooperative agendas have percolated into security and strategic issues in the Bay of Bengal and are represented by multi-nation meetings such as the MILAN, joint and coordinated naval patrols and mechanisms for sharing of information and intelligence.

Conclusion

The contemporary relations among the Bay of Bengal littorals are reminiscent of the ancient and represent strong civilisational underpinnings. This is best reflected in the current politico-diplomatic engagements which exude confidence in the partnership, bilateral trade which is expected to grow in the future, and cooperative security and strategic agendas.

Given the above vision and the policy mechanism, BIMSTEC as a multilateral institution is consolidating the existing and building new agendas. It is also time to explore "new vistas" for maritime cooperation in the coming decades keeping in mind the dynamic nature of the maritime environment, abundance of maritime issues which merit attention, and the changing nature of the security threats and challenges.

The study now moves on to explore the challenges of Transnational Organised Crimes that transcend borders and hence need coordinated approach for efficacious response.

NOTES

1. The horseshoe is believed to possess powers to protect against evil. Apparently, HMS Victory, Admiral Nelson's flagship had carried horseshoe nailed to the mast to bring good luck during battle.
2. "Water Facts", https://www.windows2universe.org/?page=/earth/Water/fact.html (accessed 20 October 2018).

3   H M Rahman, *Legal regime of marine environment in the Bay of Bengal* (New Delhi: Atlantic Publishers & Distributors, 2007), pp.35–36.
4   Sanjay Chaturvedi and Vijay Sakhuja, *Climate Change and the Bay of Bengal* (Singapore: ISEAS, 2015), p.31; Also see Arshad Mehmood Abbasi, Mir Ajab Khan, Mushtaq Ahmad, Muhammad Zafar, *Medicinal Plant Biodiversity of Lesser Himalayas-Pakistan* (New York: Springer, 2012), p.5.
5   Sanjay Chatiuvedi and Vijay Sakhuja, *Climate Change and the Bay of Bengal* (Singapore: ISEAS, 2015), p.31.
6   'Ganga Basin', 'Ganga Flood Control Commission (GFCC), Ministry of Water Resources, Government of India,' http://gfcc.bih.nic.in/ (accessed 30 November 2018). Also see Sanjay Chaturvedi and Vijay Sakhuja *Climate Change and the Bay of Bengal* (Singapore: ISEAS, 2015).
7   For more details see http://www.banglapire.org/Research/rivers-sediments (accessed 20 February 2019).
8   "Skill Development in Andaman & Nicobar Islands", http://planningcommission.nic.in/reports/genrep/reginal_conf2/A%20&%20N%20I/an_govt.pdf (accessed 20 February 2019).
9   Benudhar Patra, "Kalinga and China: A Study in Ancient Relations", http://magazines.odisha.gov.in/Orissareview/2014/July/engpdf/47-51.pdf (accessed 20 February 2019).
10 For a detailed treatment of this issue see Vijay Sakhuja and Sangeeta Sakhuja ' Rajendra Chola I's Naval Expedition to Southeast Asia", in Hermann Kulke, K. Kesavapany, Vijay Sakhuja (eds.), *Nagapattinam to Suvarnadwipa: Reflections on the Chola naval expeditions to Southeast Asia* (Singapore : ISEAS, 2009), pp.76-90.
11 Vijay Sakhuja, *Asian Maritime Power in the 21st Century*: Strategic Transactions China, India and Southeast Asia (Singapore: ISEAS, 2011), p.255.
12 Ibid.
13 For more details see B. Arunachalam, *Chola Navigation Package* (Mumbai: Maritime History Society, 2004).
14 Benudhar Patra, "Kalinga and China: A Study in Ancient Relations", http://magazines.odisha.gov.in/Orissareview/2014/July/engpdf/47-51.pdf (accessed 20 February 2019).
15 Asad Latif, *India in the Making of Singapore* (Singapore: ISEAS, 2008), p.75.
16 Leong Sau Heng, "Collecting Centres, Feeder Points and Entrepots in the Malaya Peninsula. 1000 B.C. – A.D. 1400", J. Kathirithamby-Wells and John Villiers (eds.), *The Southeast Asian Port and Polity: Rise and Demis* (Singapore : Singapore University Press, 1990), pp.28-29.
17 Tansen Sen, *Buddhism, Diplomacy, and Trade the Realignment of Sino-Indian Relations, 600-1400* (US: University of Hawaii Press, 2003), p.162.
18 Ibid., p.176.
19 Ibid., p.179.
20 Vijay Sakhuja and Sangeeta Sakhuja ' Rajendra Chola I's Naval expedition to Southeast Asia", in Hermann Kulke; K. Kesavapany; Vijay Sakhuja (eds.), *Nagapattinam to Suvarnadwipa: Reflections on the Chola Naval Expeditions to Southeast Asia* (Singapore : ISEAS, 2009), pp.76-90.
21 K. Nilakanta Sastri, *Cola* (Madras: University of Madras, 2000), pp.211–13.
22 Ibid., p.598.
23 Ibid.

24 Tan Sen, "Did Zheng He Set Out To Colonize Southeast Asia", Leo Suryadinata (ed.), *Admiral Zhang He & Southeast Asia*, (Singapore : Institute of Southeast Asian Studies, 2005), p.43.
25 Vijay Sakhuja, *Asian Maritime Power in the 21st Century*: Strategic Transactions China, India and Southeast Asia (Singapore : ISEAS, 2011), p.256.
26 Foreign Ministry Spokesperson Hua Chunying's Regular Press Conference on 10 October 2013 http://kw.chineseembassy.org/eng/fyrth/t1086912.htm (accessed 10 December 2018).
27 "The Least Developed Countries Report 2016: The Path to Graduation and Beyond – Making the Most of the Process", https://unctad.org/en/PublicationsLibrary/ldc2016_en.pdf (accessed 10 December 2018).
28 "Work Together to Build the Silk Road Economic Belt and The 21st Century Maritime Silk Road", Speech by H.E. Xi Jinping President of the People's Republic of China at the Opening Ceremony of The Belt and Road Forum for International Cooperation, 14 May 2017 http://www.xinhuanet.com/english/2017-05/14/c_136282982.htm (accessed 10 December 2018).
29 "Project Mausam", Press Information Bureau, Ministry of Culture, Government of India, http://pib.nic.in/newsite/PrintRelease.aspx?relid=168923 (accessed 10 December 2018).
30 "Indonesia Sebagai Poros Maritim Dunia", http://www.presidenri.go.id/berita-aktual/indonesia-sebagai-poros-maritim-dunia.html (accessed 10 December 2018).
31 International Tribunal for The Law of the Sea Reports of Judgments, Advisory Opinions and Orders Dispute Concerning Delimitation of the Maritime Boundary Between Bangladesh and Myanmar in the Bay of Bengal (Bangladesh/Myanmar) Judgment of 14 March 2012, https://www.itlos.org/fileadmin/itlos/documents/cases/case_no_16/published/C16-J-14_mar_12.pdf (accessed 15 December 2018).
32 "In the Matter of the Bengal Maritime Boundary Arbitration – Between The People's Republic of Bangladesh and The Republic of India", https://pcacases.com/web/sendAttach/383 (accessed 15 December 2018).
33 Jürgen Haacke, "Myanmar and Maritime Security", http://www.theasanforum.org/myanmar-and-maritime-security/ (accessed 23 March 2019).

3

Transnational Organised Crimes:
Trafficking of Drugs, Humans and Wildlife

During the preceding centuries, the gravest security threat faced by nation-states was invariably the military of another state. This has undergone a radical shift in the 21st century. Having been outlawed by the United Nations, military offensive is considered legitimate only in self-defense and collective security under a UN mandate.[1] Yet peace remains an illusion due to the emergence of non-state actors. Terrorism and trafficking are transnational organised crimes (TOCs) that have proliferated significantly and claim considerable resources of the governments. Portfolios of TOCs have widened with the emergence of cybercrime and environmental crimes. To thrive and expand, criminals exploit the legitimate economic and social activities for criminal purposes. Off-late they have become exceedingly creative, multifaceted and global.

In the past few decades, the Bay of Bengal region comprising five littorals and two land locked states has experienced rapid economic and social development. Ironically, growth with its attendant challenges of crime and inequality, can exacerbate the regulating authorities of any state. Sandwiched between the 'Golden Crescent' and the 'Golden Triangle', the Bay of Bengal region is no exception. It remains vulnerable from within as a source of supply, a destination from beyond, as also a conduit for transit.

What are Transnational Organised Crimes (TOCs)?
There are at least two competing definitions for TOCs: while one focuses on

criminals, the other focuses on the types of crime. Both definitions have some validity, but neither is all-fulfilling. Understanding the way organised crimes are arranged is important, for adopting appropriate strategies against them. When referring to a 'mafia', the focus is primarily on the person or groups committing the crime. Law enforcement agencies like to emphasise on criminal groups and not the nature of the crime because criminal justice systems are designed to arrest and prosecute specific individuals for specific offences.[2] The United Nations Convention against Transnational Organized Crime (UNCTOC) defines 'organised crime' as any serious offence committed by a group of three or more people with the aim of making money.[3] Criminal groups are normally consistent territorially, and adapt to different criminal activities based on changing situations; today it could be extortion, and tomorrow the same group may indulge in drugs trafficking or perhaps fraud another day. TOCs also need to be viewed from the prism of its incentives, because the organising principle of such activities is the market. In this backdrop, neutralising a particular criminal group does not solve the problem until the incentives (market) remain in place.

This chapter examines the collusion and extent of transnational crimes that impact the security of the Bay of Bengal region, involving the enterprises of trafficking that manifest in the forms of drugs, human and wildlife trafficking.

Drug Trafficking

There are fewer groups today exclusively involved in drug trafficking. Investment in multiple TOCs makes economic sense by distributing risks. However, drug trafficking is the most lucrative, and is estimated to have contributed between fifth and third of revenue earned in the year 2014. It is no longer the preserve of big criminal gangs as advanced communication technologies have circumvented the need for groups to make personal contact with their clients. Besides, 'darknet' enables users to buy drugs with crypto currency. In the short-term drug money seems lucrative and tends to boost a region's economy. But, its long-term effects are negative, impacting property prices, distribution of wealth, increase in corruption, and weakening of law enforcement.

Corruption pervades all along the drug supply chain and they mutually reinforce each other. The Bay of Bengal region is especially susceptible to narco-economics due to poor socio-economic conditions, internal fault-lines and ineffective judicial systems. Drug trade especially benefits the terrorist and insurgent groups by providing them the financial means for sustenance. Taliban's involvement in production, manufacturing and trafficking of drugs in Afghanistan has been well documented by the United Nations Security Council.[4]

In recent years, traditional drug markets have diversified into new psychoactive substances (NPS), which are derivatives of prescribed medicines that are difficult to regulate. Unprescribed opioids (pharmaceutical derivative of opium) are also being used to produce counterfeit medicines disguised as pharmaceutical products.[5] As many as 106 countries had reported the emergence of 739 different types of NPS between 2009 and 2016. Some countries detected sales of NPS under the name of controlled drugs such as 'LSDs' and 'Ecstasy'.[6] Drug trafficking has increased during the past years, particularly cocaine and synthetic drugs appear to thrive. Drug flows alter course based on tactics adopted by enforcement agencies, changes in modus-operandi and concealment techniques.[7] According to a UNODC survey, Myanmar and Afghanistan together account for over 90 percent of the world's opium production. Apart from opiates, cannabis and amphetamine are the most widely consumed drugs in the Bay of Bengal region. Increase in consumption of synthetic and prescription drugs have also been reported in some countries.[8]

Bay of Bengal countries straddle the transit routes for opiates and heroine between Afghanistan, Myanmar and Laos. Although cocaine market is still small, large seizures in Djibouti (en-route) and Sri Lanka in 2016 and 2017 show that their market in the Bay of Bengal region is on the rise.[9]

Prospects of Mitigation

During the 5th meeting of BIMSTEC Sub-Group on Prevention of Illicit Trafficking in Narcotic Drugs, Psychotropic Substances (NDPS) and Precursor Chemicals in Nepal in May 2018, UNODC had urged BIMSTEC and South Asia Regional Intelligence and Coordination Centre (SARICC) to collaborate their efforts.[10]

Since SARICC is planned to be a full-fledged organisation with a dedicated headquarters likely in Colombo,[11] it would be prudent for BIMSTEC to piggyback on SARICC. SARICC was conceived during the Network of Networks meeting held at New Delhi in November 2015 for combating TOCs. SARICC comprises seven nations of South Asia (Maldives, Sri Lanka, India, Nepal, Bhutan, Bangladesh and Myanmar) with the mandate of facilitating collation and analysis of criminal intelligence, coordination of operational activities of the law enforcement agencies and provide information sharing platform on security for the region.[12] Thailand and Myanmar's intelligence will also have to be plugged into SARICC for effective coordination within BIMSTEC. For pan-Asia coordination, SARICC would eventually have to connect with the existing Central Asian Regional Information and Coordination Centre (CARICC) and Asia-Pacific Information & Coordination Center for Combating Drug Crimes (APICC).

Human Trafficking

The most widely accepted definition of human trafficking is mentioned in the Protocol to the United Nations Convention against TOCs, adopted in 2000. It specifies that crime of trafficking constitutes three elements – act, means, and purpose (exploitation).[13] No country is immune from human trafficking. However, the profile of trafficking victims continues to change. In the past 10 years, even men have started to make a large share (21 percent in 2014) of the victims. In comparison, children were 28 percent and women accounted for 51 percent of the victims.

People are trafficked for several exploitative purposes such as forced begging, forced labour, child soldier, sexual exploitation, forced marriages, or organ removal. Often, traffickers and their victims belong to same community, ethnicity and language. So, trafficking can be significantly reduced by increasing awareness within the vulnerable communities.

Information regarding the citizenship of victims in South Asia is scarce; however, UNODC report of 2016 notes that these flows are primarily local (within the region). Almost 96 percent of the detected victims of South Asia were trafficked domestically. In Southeast Asia the intra-regional trafficking is close to 93 percent.

Large proportions of intra-regional human trafficking can be attributed to countries with large populations, high levels of socio-economic inequalities, and intense internal migratory flows. Men's trafficking is the highest in Myanmar. Trafficked men form Myanmar and India have been rescued by Thailand authorities employed for forced labour on fishing boats off Thailand.[14]

Prospects of Mitigation

Given the complexity of human trafficking, the strategy for mitigation would have to be customised and embedded into respective policy areas. The solution lies in implementation of UN General Assembly Resolution 55/25 of November 2000 and its relevant Protocols.[15] For harmonizing a regional efforts BIMSTEC sub-group on human trafficking and migration needs to facilitate coordination in following areas (based on Protocol to the Convention Annex II):[16]

(a) Adoption of legislative and other measures and harmonizing regional procedures to establish criminal offence (Article 5).
(b) Region wide policy on protection of privacy and identity of victims of trafficking (Article 6).
(c) Permit victims of trafficking to remain in the territory, temporarily or permanently, as the case may be (Article 7) and resolution of safe extradition.
(d) Information exchange and training (Article 10).
(e) Strengthen, border control to prevent and detect trafficking (Article 11).
(f) Security and Control of travel documents (Article 12).

Wildlife Trafficking

Animals caught from the wild each year and sold as food, ornamental plants, pets, medicines, tourist curios and leather. Large proportions of this are legal, but it is the illegal trade that threatens the survival of many endangered species.[17] Wildlife crime is estimated to be worth $7 to 23 billion out of the total environmental crime between $91 and 258 billion. This is expected to grow two to three times the speed of the global economy.[18] Poaching of elephant ivory, rhino horn and tiger skin are well known, but many other species such as pangolins, marine turtles and rose wood are being exploited for illegal trade. Border areas world over, like the Golden Triangle at the intersection of China, Myanmar, Laos, Thailand and Vietnam are places where wildlife trade thrive and is hardest to regulate.[19]

Prospects of Mitigation

International trade of over 30,000 species of plants and animals is regulated by the Convention on International Trade in Endangered Species of Wild Fauna and Flora (CITES), 1973 through system of 'certificates and permits'.[20]

The magnitude of this crime in Bay of Bengal region is quite serious and merits commissioning a new Sub-Group on wildlife trafficking for effective implementation of the CITES guidelines. Its mandate could be:

(a) Assist countries to comply with the Convention.
(b) Facilitate countries to create national and local laws. Assistance to professional NGOs like the TRAFFIC and WWF could be sought for this purpose.
(c) Run regional training and exchange workshops for customs officers, border police, conservation officers and traders.

(d) Provide assistance and funding to countries for enforcement efforts.
(e) Regional information sharing and coordination across the borders.
(f) Coordinate scientific and technical advice between states.

Conclusion

Drug trafficking is one of the most lucrative TOCs and a revenue spinner. BIMSTEC and SARICC can coordinate a variety of TOCs including drugs trafficking. Myanmar and Thailand will have to plug-in to SARICC for effective coordination with the BIMSTEC. Concomitantly, to facilitate pan-Asia coordination, SARICC would have to connect with the existing Central Asian Regional Information and Coordination Centre (CARICC) and Asia-Pacific Information & Coordination Center for Combating Drug Crimes (APICC). For countering human trafficking, implementing UN General Assembly Resolution 55/25 of November 2000 and its relevant Protocols would be critical. As also, trafficking can be significantly reduced by increasing awareness within the vulnerable communities. For mitigating wildlife trafficking, the Convention on International Trade in Endangered Species (CITES) of Wild Fauna and Flora, CITES 1973 needs early implementation. The magnitude of the latter in Bay of Bengal region is high and commissioning a new Sub-Group on wildlife trafficking will be essential for earnest implementation of the CITES guidelines with the aforesaid mandate.

A number of institutional mechanisms exist for tackling TOCs. During the sixtieth session of UN General Assembly in March 2017, the Commission on Narcotic Drugs adopted resolution 60/1 prescribed 100 recommendations. Sustainable Development Goals (SDGs) 5.2 and 16.2, call for effective measures to end forced labour, modern slavery, and human trafficking, as well as child labour in all its forms.

TOCs have regional roots with global and regional linkages. A multitude of institutions are at work at the global, regional and national levels to neutralise these criminals. But, mitigation of the crimes will also need addressing the underlying causes that are unique to each region. Bay of Bengal region has its own unique geography, cultural background, fault-lines and socio-economic conditions. Hence, customised security frameworks have to be devised for the region, while conforming to international conventions and protocols.

Having examined the dynamics of trafficking and their mitigation mechanisms, in the next chapter, the study will explore the linkages of terrorism and piracy with TOCs and the necessity for securitizing BIMSTEC.

NOTES

1. Divya Srikanth, *Non-Traditional Threat in the 21st Century*, International Journal of Development and Conflict, Volume 4, Issue 1, p 60-68, http://www.ijdc.org.in/uploads/1/7/5/7/17570463/2014junearticle4.pdf (accessed 06 December 2018)
2. UNODC, *The Globalisation of Crime, A Transnational Organised Crime Threat Assessment*, 2010, p.19.http://www.unodc.org/res/cld/bibliography/the-globalization-of-crime-a-transnational-organized-crime-threat-assessment_html/TOCTA_Report_2010_low_res.pdf (accessed 06 December 2018)
3. Ibid., p.20.
4. Ibid., p.23.
5. UNODC, *Executive Summary Conclusions and Policy Implications*, World Drug Report 2017, p.13, https://www.unodc.org/documents/scientific/Booklet_1_Executive_ Summary_conclusions_ and_policy_implications.pdf, (accessed 07 December 2018)
6. Ibid., p.14.
7. Ibid., p.18.
8. UNODC, *Regional Program for South Asia 2013-2015 – Promoting the Rule of Law and Countering Drugs and Crimes*, p.13, https://www.unodc.org/documents/southasia//webstories/RP_South_Asia_FINAL.pdf (accessed 08 December 2018)
9. UNODC, *Executive Summary Conclusions and Policy Implications*, World Drug Report 2017, p.19, https://www.unodc.org/documents/scientific/Booklet_1_Executive_ Summary_conclusions_ and_policy_implications.pdf, (accessed 09 December 2018)
10. BIMSTEC website, https://bimstec.org/?event=fifth-meeting-of-the-bimstec-sub-group-on-prevention-of-illicit-trafficking-in-narcotic-drugs-psychotropic-substances-and-precursor-chemicals (accessed 09 December 2018)
11. UNODC, https://www.unodc.org/southasia//frontpage/2018/April/india_-south-asian-officials-and-experts-extend-support-to-unodcs-regional-intelligence-sharing-initiative.html, (accessed 09 December 2018)
12. Press Information Bureau, Ministry of Finance, Government of India, November 06, 2015, http://pib.nic.in/newsite/PrintRelease.aspx?relid=130290, (accessed 09 December 2018)
13. ILO and Walk Free Foundation, *Global Estimate of Modern Slavery*, Geneva 2017, p5, https://www.ilo.org/ wcmsp5/groups/public/—dgreports/—dcomm/documents/publication/wcms_575479.pdf (accessed 08 December 2018)
14. UNODC, *Global report on Trafficking in Person Report 2016*, https://www.unodc.org/documents/data-and-analysis/glotip/2016_Global_Report_on_Trafficking_ in_Persons.pdf (accessed 08 December 2018)
15. UNODC, UN Conventions on TOCs, 2004, https://www.unodc.org/documents/middleeastandnorthafrica/organised-crime/UNITED_NATIONS_CONVENTION_AGAINST_TRANSNATIONAL_ORGANIZED_CRIME_AND_THE_PROTOCOLS_THERETO.pdf (accessed 10 December 2018)
16. Other articles of Annex II are relevant for national implementation in addition to the above. For more details see https://www.un.org/en/development/desa/population/migration/generalassembly /docs/globalcompact/A_RES_55_25.pdf (accessed 09 December 2018)
17. WWF, http://wwf.panda.org/our_work/wildlife/problems/illegal_trade/ (accessed 09 December 2018)

18 Mary Utermohlen and Patrik Bain, *Flying under the Radar,* USAID, Traffic, WWF et al, Report 2017, https://www.traffic.org/site/assets/files/2100/flying_under_the_radar_final-web.pdf (accessed 09 December 2018)
19 For country wise database dashboard on import and export of wildlife see http://cites-dashboards.unep-wcmc.org / (accessed 09 December 2018)
20 WWF, *Fact Sheet on illegal and sustainable wildlife trade.* http://d2ouvy59p0dg6k.cloudfront.net/downloads/wildlife_trade_factsheet2006.pdf (accessed 19 December 2018)

4

Transnational Organised Crime:
Terrorism and Piracy

Criminals play on globalisation of communication, financial transactions and international travel and flourish, diversify and extend their activities. Today, victims, suspects and criminal groups of a single crime can be located in multiple countries. Hence, transnational organised crime (TOC) is now a universal occurrence and calls for concerted global and regional response.[1]

Terrorism and TOC

Terrorism is not a new phenomenon and has been part of political movements all through human history. In the 20th century, terrorism took roots as nationalist movement, against colonial imperialists to garner sympathy and support beyond the immediate theatres of action. In the post-World War II time, terrorism assumed an international character, as aggrieved and victims discovered that it could be effectively used to bring together international condemnation.[2] However, it took the terrorist attacks on 11 September 2001 to change the American and Western perceptions, which led to their commencement for 'war on terror'.

Many of the Bay of Bengal littorals have been victims of terror attacks for decades. Fatal and non-fatal injuries from terror attacks in these countries during the last 45 years (1972-2017)[3] are illustrated in Figures 4.1 and 4.2.[4] Bangladesh ranks 21st, Myanmar 37th, Thailand 16th and India 8th in the 2017 Global Terrorism Index (GTI) promulgated by the Institute of Economics and Peace (IEP). India is

Figure 4.1: Fatal Injuries from Terror Attacks

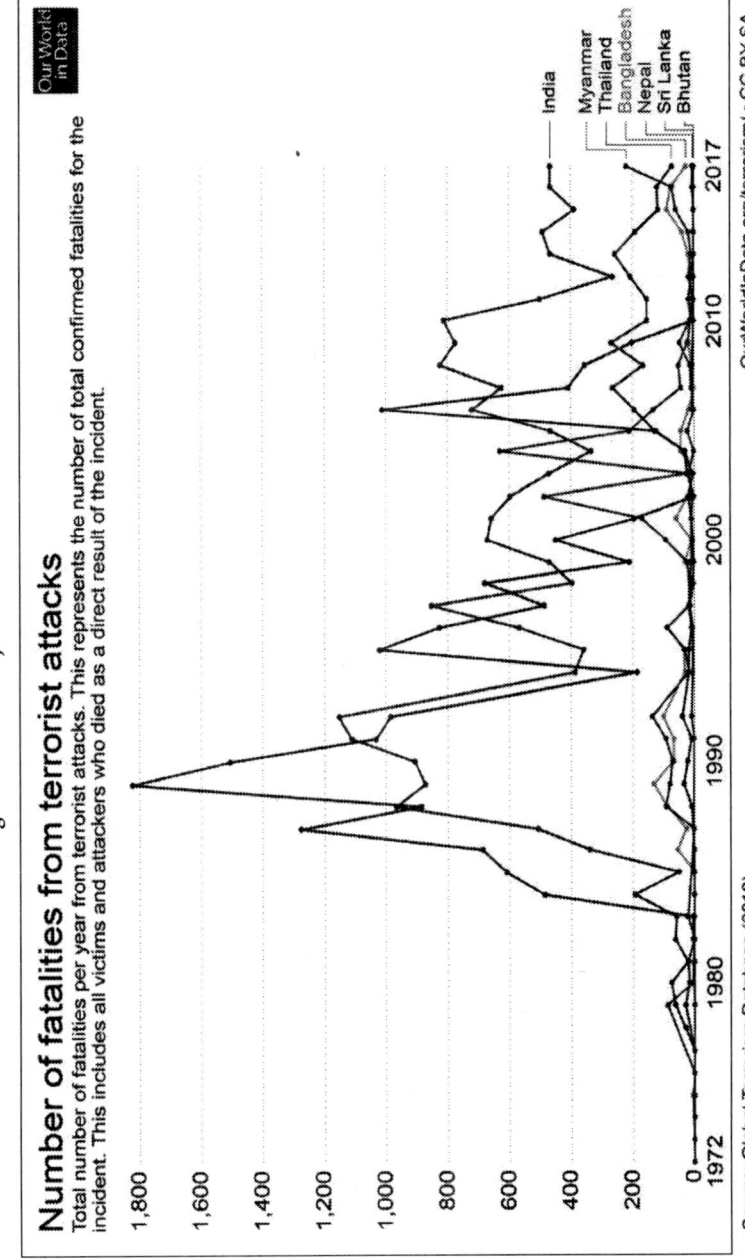

Figure 4.2: Non-fatal Injuries from Terror Attacks

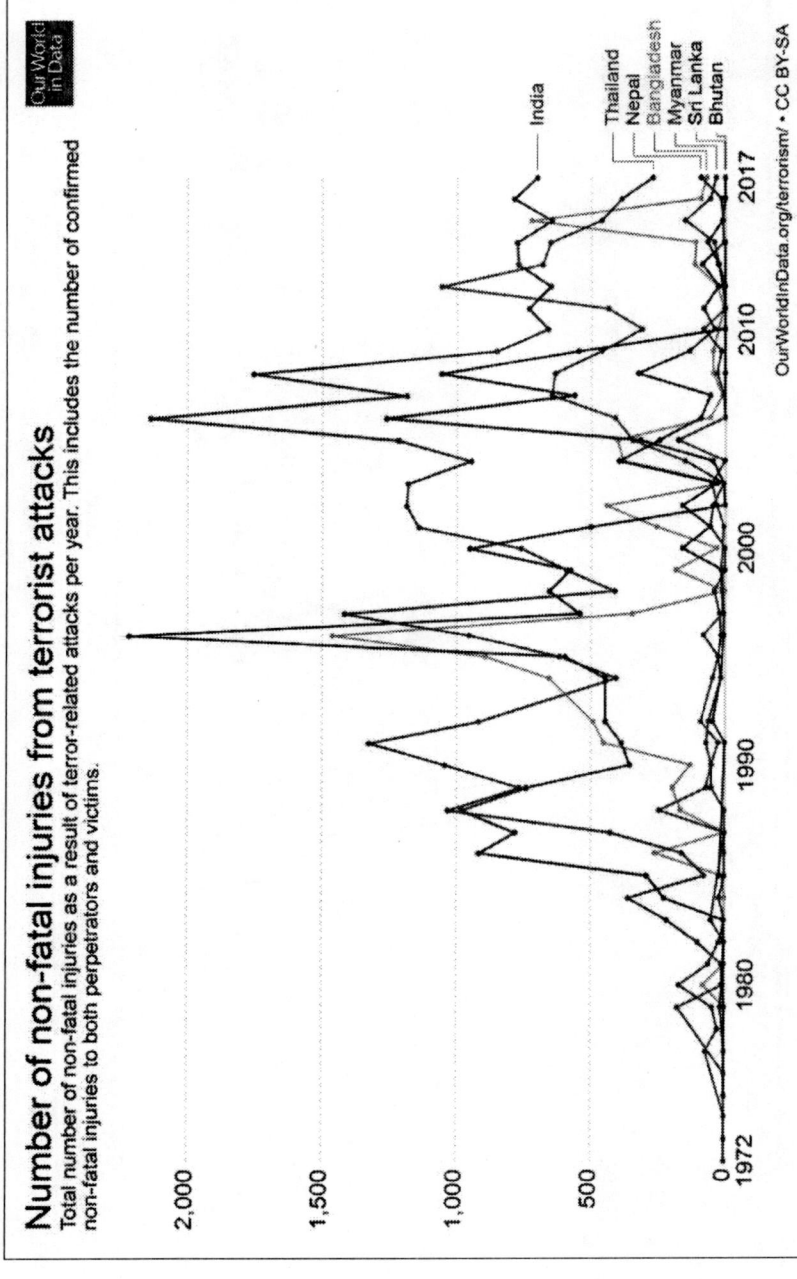

Sources: Author; based on OurWorldData.org

the worst effected by terrorism among the Bay of Bengal littoral followed by Sri Lanka 68th, Nepal 44th, and Bhutan at 129th has experienced the lowest terrorism in the region.[5]

Further, the graphs indicate that India and Bangladesh have suffered maximum casualties from terror attacks. India witnessed 18 percent increase in 2016 from the preceding year, which declined marginally in 2017 and 2018.[6] Despite a large number of terror groups operating in India, the rate of death per attack (0.4) is low, primarily because they are not aimed at killing people, but seeking political recognition. Maoists groups operate in the eastern, central and the southern areas of India known as the Red Corridor. Pakistan remains the main source of Islamic terrorism in the state of Jammu and Kashmir. Two deadliest Islamist terrorist groups Lashkar-e-Taiba (LeT) and Hizbul Mujahideen, have also been involved in terror activities in Pakistan, Afghanistan, Iran and Bangladesh. The National Democratic Front of Bodo land (NDFB) and United Liberation Front of Assam (ULFA) are perhaps the most notorious terror groups operating in India's north-eastern region.[7]

Bangladesh had seen a sharp rise in terrorism in 2016, which progressively reduced in 2017 and 2018. In Bangladesh, the Jamaat-ul-Mujahideen Bangladesh and Ansarul Islam are the leading jihadi group.[8]

In Rakhine province, west Myanmar, there has been a surge in violence since October 2016. Security forces were attacked twice by insurgents of the ethnic Rohingya Muslim minority. This snowballed in violence resulting in the mass migration of Rohingya refugees to neighbouring countries particularly Bangladesh. Apparently, attack on security forces is believed to be the handiwork of the Arakan Rohingya Salvation Army (ARSA).[9]

In Thailand, the military junta had taken over power in May 2014 and two years later the country voted for amendments to the constitution giving more power to the ruling military junta. This caused a series of bombings by suspected Malay–Muslim rebels in the southern provinces that continued in 2017 as well. Subsequently, negotiations were facilitated by Malaysian government between the Junta and Mara Patani, an organization representing the insurgents. It is also believed that Thailand could be a transit point for terrorist groups such as the Al-Qaeda, Jemaah Islamiyah (JI), and Hezbollah.[10]

During the Fourth BIMSTEC Summit meeting in Nepal in August 2018, the Heads of States acknowledged that targeting terrorists, terror organizations and networks would not be adequate. The States and non-State entities encouraging, supporting, financing, and providing sanctuaries to terrorists would also have to be held responsible. Inclusion of 'States sponsoring terrorism' in the joint-statement of the BIMSTEC was indeed a unique achievement, one that SAARC could not achieve all this while. A strong commitment was also reiterated by all member countries to prevent cross-border movement of terrorists, curb radicalization, foil misuse of internet, and dismantle terrorist safe havens.[11] It merits highlighting that Internet is the primary medium for terrorists to communicate, organise, recruit, evade surveillance, coordinate attacks and undertake propaganda campaigns.

Surprisingly, some member States are yet to ratify the BIMSTEC Convention on Cooperation in Combating International Terrorism. The Fourth Summit meeting in Nepal in August 2018 was followed by an inaugural edition of BIMSTEC Nations Military Field Training Exercise – MILEX 2018, in Pune (India) in September 2018. Tactical drills included hostage rescue, helicopters-based insertion of troops, room intervention and house clearing drill, search operations, neutralization of improvised explosive devices (IEDs) and raid on a terrorist hideouts.[12] Two meetings of National Security Chiefs have reviewed the progress on terrorism coordination in March 2017 and 2018. However, BIMSTEC does not have a nodal agency for coordination of activities on counter-terrorism.

Two terror attacks in 2019 have reaffirmed the requirement of close regional coordination between intelligence and enforcement agencies.[13] It also highlights the requirement of addressing the underlying social causes and ideological intolerances in the region. More importantly, it emphasises the necessity of countries to harmonising national constitutions with the principles of liberal natural law and equality. Whilst, in India some minorities enjoy more rights than the rest, in some countries of the region, minorities are constitutionally discriminated as second-rate citizens. Nature of both these inequalities is recipe for incessant conflict.

The magnitude of terrorism in the Bay of Bengal region cannot be sustained without sustained funding. Terrorist need money for training, travel expenses, accommodation and operations. Sources of these funding can be traced to TOCs discussed in the chapter. To counter terrorism, not only the financial flows would have to be disrupted, but their sources have to be tackled. Future terror attacks can be prevented by isolating their material support and footprints of purchases. Counter-terror finance tracking needs to be steered at the regional level as the supporting TOCs are invariably situated across the border. Often it is the lack of coordination between security agencies as also between States is effectively exploited by the criminals.

There is concern and awareness to fight terrorism among the BIMSTEC member States. A sub-Group group on Counter Terrorism of the BIMSTEC is mandated to coordinate efforts but the absence of a coordination centre for fusion and analysis of data has precluded its effectiveness which is exploited by terror groups and their financiers.

South Asia Regional Intelligence Sharing and Coordination Centre (SARICC) can potentially be the nodal agency for coordination and information sharing. But for that, Thailand will have to be integrated into the SARICC to conflate an effective regional picture on terrorism. The Convention on CTTC is still awaiting ratification and instrument on Mutual Legal Assistance in Criminal Matters (MCLACM) which can provide for measures to locate, freeze and forfeit or confiscate any funds or finances meant for the financing of all crimes in other's territory is awaiting signature by member states.

Sea Piracy

Piracy and armed robbery is a criminal act and threatens maritime security. The concomitant affects include disruption of navigation, unsettling of commerce, rise of insurance premiums and investments in security. The UN Security Council renewed the authorisation for use of naval forces against Somali pirates under resolution 2383 (2017), Chapter VII.[14] This initiative underscores the potential of such crimes in exacerbating stability of a country, fueling corruption, promoting terrorism and disrupting maritime order. The Bay of Bengal is witness to armed robbery at sea and not necessarily piracy, which means that these crimes are primarily restricted to the territorial waters (12 nautical miles) of the states and are purely under a state's jurisdiction.

Despite regional coordination and national efforts, piracy and armed robbery at sea continue to linger signifying that the underlying conditions fuelling piracy remain unchanged. These include weak coastal enforcement against poaching by foreign fishing vessels; strong network between criminals, pirates and financiers; weak legal framework to capture, prosecute and convict; lack of alternative jobs for coastal communities; and poor border control. However, national and regional focus is always biased towards prosecuting the criminals, with scant attention towards the underlying causes.

Article 105 of the 1982 UN Convention on the Law of the Sea (UNCLOS) gives every state jurisdiction upon the high seas to seize a pirate ship or aircraft irrespective of its nationality, arrest the persons and seize their property onboard.

The courts of a state which carried out the seizure are empowered to decide upon the penalties. But when such act is carried out within the national jurisdiction (within 12 nautical miles) of a state, as is mostly the case, universal jurisdiction over piracy does not apply, which would imply that there is no need for regional cooperation in the Bay of Bengal for piracy.

However, when viewed from the prism of causes, regional cooperation becomes mandatory by the way of training; information sharing; coordinating intelligence; coalescing capacities; targeting financing networks; and neutralising transnational organised groups that sponsor such piracy and armed robbery at sea. Table 4.1 that follow shows incidents of armed robbery in the Bay of Bengal region in 2018.[15,16]

Table 4.1: Incidents of Armed Robbery in the Bay of Bengal Region

Location	2014	2015	2016	2017	2018
Bangladesh	15	11	3	7	11
India	10	7	14	2	3
Total	25	18	17	9	14

Piracy and armed robbery at sea are best addressed both from the perspective of convicting criminals, as also by mitigating the underlying causes by strengthening the national legal framework. Further, by bolstering intra and inter-region information exchange of information and intelligence can help track network between criminals, pirates and financers.

Institutional Frameworks to Combat TOCs

The United Nations Convention General Assembly resolution 55/25 of November 15, 2000 is the overarching international instrument against TOC. **The treaty came into force on September 29, 2003 and has been ratified by 147 states as on December 2018.** This Convention has been supplemented by three protocols, on specific issues: trafficking women and children, migrants, and firearms.[17] During the 16th session of UN General Assembly in March 2017, the Commission on Narcotic Drugs adopted resolution 60/1 reinforcing commitment to implementing the outcome document of 2016 which contains 100 recommendations. Sustainable Development Goals (SDGs), in particular to Target 5.2 and 16.2, call for effective measures to end forced labour, modern slavery, and human trafficking, as well as child labour in all its forms. In addition, SDG target 16.4 relates to reductions of illicit financial and arms flow, strengthen recovery and return of stolen assets, and combating all forms of organized crime. An integrated approach towards SDG 16 and 5 within Bay of Bengal littorals would provide a viable platform for regional cooperation for curtailment of TOCs.

The Regional Cooperation Agreement on Combating Piracy and Armed Robbery against Ships in Asia (ReCAAP) is a regional organisation comprising 14 Asian nations and six extra-regional nations (Norway, the Netherlands, Denmark, and the United Kingdom, Australia, and the United States) to promote cooperation and armed robbery against ships in Eastern Indian Ocean and Western Pacific. All Bay of Bengal littoral nations are members of ReCAAP. The ReCAAP Information Sharing Centre (ReCAAP ISC) operates from Singapore. Except Nepal and Bhutan all Asian countries have ReCAAP Focal Points for coordination and reporting against piracy.[18]

Indian Ocean Rim Association (IORA) is a regional organisation of 22 nations and 9 dialogue partners to primarily facilitate and promote economic cooperation. Maritime safety and security is one of the eight focus areas of IORA with the aim of coordinating piracy, armed robberies at sea, irregular movement of persons, drugs trafficking, terrorism, human trafficking, trafficking of weapons, illegal unregulated and unreported fishing, illicit trafficking in wildlife, degradation of ocean health, climate change and unlawful exploitation of marine resources. An IORA Working Group on Maritime Security and Safety (WGMSS) was commissioned in September 2018 under rotating chairmanship of Sri Lanka for two years.[19] BIMSTEC needs to earmark a Sub-group on maritime security to tackle the underlying causes of financing and collusion and interact with IORA and ReCAAP for update on events at sea.

Indian Ocean Naval Symposium (IONS) comprising 32 nations is a voluntary initiative, to improve coordination amongst navies of the Indian Ocean region, including Pakistan. The interaction is carried out through workshops, seminars and academic interactions. Participation by Bay of Bengal littorals enhance interaction between their maritime agencies.

At the sub-regional level, the Counter-terrorism and transnational crime (CTTC) is one of the 14 sectors of BIMSTEC instituted through a convention signed by member states in 2009. Led by India, the Joint Working on CTTC has six Sub-groups:

(a) Sub-Group on Narcotic Drugs, Psychotropic Substances and Precursor Chemicals (SGNDPSPC); (Lead Shepherd: Myanmar)
(b) Sub-Group on Intelligence Sharing (SGIS); (Lead Shepherd: Sri Lanka)

(c) Sub-Group on Legal and Law Enforcement Issues (SGLLEI); (Lead Shepherd: India)
(d) Sub-Group on Anti- Money Laundering and Combating the Financing of Terrorism (SGAML-CFT); (Lead Shepherd: Thailand)
(e) Sub-Group on Human Trafficking and Illegal Migration; (Lead Shepherd: Bangladesh) Sub-Group on the Cooperation on Countering Radicalization and Terrorism. (Lead Shepherd: India)

Although the Convention on CTTC is yet to be ratified, an instrument on Mutual Legal Assistance in Criminal Matters (MCLACM) provides for measures to locate, freeze and forfeit or confiscate any funds or finances meant for the financing of all crimes in other's territory. This instrument is awaiting signature by member states.

This Chapter has attempted to explore the linkages of TOCs with terrorism and sea piracy and infers that mitigation of these is even more complex. The study now examines impending environmental catastrophes induced by human interventions.

NOTES

1. 'UNODC', https://www.unodc.org/unodc/en/organized-crime/intro.html (accessed 06 December 2018)
2. Max Roser and et al, "Terrorism, Our World in Data", https://ourworldindata.org/terrorism (accessed 10 December 2018).
3. 'Our World in Data', https://ourworldindata.org/terrorism (accessed 10 December 2018).
4. 'South Asia Terrorism Portal (SATP)' http://www.satp.org/App_Themes/User/images/South%20Asia%20map_2015.jpg (accessed 11 December 2018).
5. 'Global Terrorism Index 2017', p.21. http://visionofhumanity.org/app/uploads/2017/11/Global-Terrorism-Index-2017.pdf(accessed 11 December 2018)
6. South Asia Terrorism Portal (SATP), Datasheet India, http://www.satp.org/datasheet-terrorist-attack/india (accessed 11 December 2018)
7. 'Global Terrorism Index 2017', p.29. http://visionofhumanity.org/app/uploads/2017/11/Global-Terrorism-Index-2017.pdf (accessed 11 December 2018)
8. International Crisis Group, https://www.crisisgroup.org/asia/south-asia/bangladesh/295-countering-jihadist-militancy-bangladesh (accessed 11 December 2018)
9. Counter Terrorism Project, Myanmar, https://www.counterextremism.com/countries/myanmar (accessed 11 December 2018)
10. Counter Extremism Project, Thailand, https://www.counterextremism.com/countries/thailand (accessed 11 December 2018)
11. Press Information Bureau, Prime Minister's Office PMO), August 31, 2018, http://pib.nic.in/newsite/PrintRelease.aspx?relid=183185 (accessed 11 December 2018)
12. Press Information Bureau, Ministry of Defence, September 16, 2018, http://pib.nic.in/newsite/PrintRelease.aspx?relid=183495 (accessed 11 December 2018)

13 Suicide attacks killing 40 Indian security forces in Pulwama on February 14, 2019 and approximately 200 Sri Lankan minorities on April 21, 2019.
14 UNSC Meeting Coverage, SC/13058 of 07 November 2017, https://www.un.org/press/en/2017/sc13058.doc.htm (accessed 12 December2018)
15 ICC, IMB Piracy and Armed Robbery Map 2018, https://www.icc-ccs.org/piracy-reporting-centre/live-piracy-map (accessed 12 December 2018)
16 ICC-IMB, Piracy and Armed Robbery at Sea, Report 01 January-September 2018, London, October 2018, p.5.
17 United Nations Treaty Collection, https://treaties.un.org/pages/ViewDetails.aspx?src=TREATY&mtdsg_no=XVIII-12&chapter=18&clang=_en (accessed 16 December 2018)
18 ReCAAP, Regional Guide on combating Piracy and Armed Robbery in Asia, http://www.recaap.org/resources/ck/files/guide/Regional%20Guide%20to%20 Counter%20 Piracy%20and%20Armed%20Robbery%20Against%20Ships%20in%20Asia%20(high-res).pdf (accessed 12 December 2018)
19 IORA, http://www.iora.int/en/priorities-focus-areas/maritime-safety-and-security (Accessed December 12, 2018)

5

Manmade Non-traditional Security Challenges:
Global Warming and Bay of Bengal

> *The number and magnitude of manmade disasters worldwide have risen since the 1970s and continue to grow in both frequency and impact on human wellbeing and economies, particularly in low and middle-income countries.*
>
> – **Mami Mizutori (2015)**
> Special representative of the UN Secretary General for disaster risk reduction

According to an estimate of the United Nations International Strategy for Disaster Reduction (UNISDR), the economic impact of all disasters worldwide was US$ 175 billion in 2016, of which US$ 9 billion stemmed from manmade disasters. These numbers continue to grow each year, as a result of climate change, rapid urbanisation and industrialisation. The Fukushima radiological disaster displaced 165,000 people and cost US$ 235 billion. Similarly, pipeline accidents, train derailment, aircraft crash, and oil spills can cause catastrophic damage around the globe and attract considerable attention of governments and media. Usually, such manmade disasters are caused by unexpected accidents due to negligence or material failure and pertain purely to the realms of safety. UNISDR, regional and national agencies are constantly streamlining their strategies to deal with such challenges. But there are a number of manmade disasters that are deliberate manifestations of man, which would be the focus of this chapter.

Some manmade disasters impact at the global scale, yet they are often given short shrift due to their slow onset or lack of cognizance. These are beyond the domain of mere safety but lie in the realms of security as they impact the very survivability and well-being of mankind. Sendai Framework 2015 is not adequate to mitigate them. Climate change, ocean acidification and air and water pollution affect all alike, rich, poor and middle income countries. Though these changes have been spurred by human interventions, they are the least palpable in the short-term, but have considerable impact in the long-term. As a result, major ecosystems of the earth have started to unravel and cause irreparable damage to many a vulnerable species on land and at sea. If they continue unabated, mankind would be enveloped in its wake, for the want of decisive action. This chapter delves into the impact of 3 such man-made non-traditional challenges, namely, global warming, ocean acidification and oxygen depletion on the Bay of Bengal region. As a regional organisation, BIMSTEC may not be able to reverse the global trends by itself, but 22 percent of the globe's population residing here can certainly make significant contributions towards sustainable use of natural resources endowed upon them. A question arises here: What is the relevance of regional initiative in mitigating manmade disasters like global climate changes?

The logic of environmental issues does not point strongly towards regionalisation. Regional logic builds on greater intensity of interaction among neighbouring units and environmental issues often do not work that way. It produces diverse set of causes and effects. Some global causes (CFCs in atmosphere) have local effect (ozone hole at the poles) and some have global effect (warming and sea level rise). Some local causes have local effects (many forms of pollution) and some may have wider effects (nuclear accidents). Regionalising logic comes into play in environmental sector if either (i) regional actors create common problem in their own environment, like the water systems involving sea, rivers, lakes, aquifers or fisheries management, etc. or (ii) an environmental impact elsewhere encompasses the region, like the ozone hole. As elaborated in Chapter 1, environmental sectors have weak regional logic.[1] This chapter highlights issues related to climate change, sea level rise, ocean acidification, oxygen depletion and plastic pollution, as all of them have reached serious irreversible levels and need urgent attention to avert major calamities with implication on security. Sea level rise can cause large-scale migration and ocean pollution can deplete animal protein sources drastically affecting food security.

Climate Change

The earth is habitable because its surface temperature is 35°C warmer than the surrounding black body. This is primarily due to the protective layer of greenhouse gases (GHGs) comprising carbondioxide (CO_2), methane (CH_4), ozone (O_3) and nitrous oxide (N_2O) amongst others. However, the atmosphere has become warmer than required due to human activities. Global warming has reached between 0.8°C and 1.2°C above the pre-industrial (1750) levels. If it persists at the current rate, it is expected to reach 1.5°C between 2030 and 2052. Anthropogenic (manmade) emissions caused by greenhouse gases, aerosols and their precursors are increasing global warming at the rate of 0.2°C per decade.[2] Synthetic GHGs emitted by industrial activities such as refrigerants and air conditioners also contribute to global warming and include chlorofluorocarbons (CFCs), hydrofluorocarbons (HFCs), perfluorocarbons (PFCs), and sulfur hexafluoride (SF_6).[3] The non-CO_2 GHGs are important to track as they have added 1.17 watts per square meter or close to 44.5 percent of total climate temperature from the year 1750 to 2000.[4]

In comparison to CO_2 emissions, non-CO_2 GHGs are easier to limit. The composition of the latter has been listed in the Kyoto and Montreal protocols. The Montreal Protocol has managed to reduce the concentration of CFCs and chlorinated solvents by almost 8 percent between 1993 and 2005.[5] The cumulative emissions of CO_2 and non-CO_2 will determine the extent of global warming in future.

If CO_2 emission are capped by 2040 (graph b) then limiting the rise in temperature to 1.5°C seems feasible. However, if the non-CO_2 emissions are not reduced by 2030, the chances of meeting the 1.5°C target become bleak. Graph (a) encapsulates the entire spectrum of all future eventualities.

Consequences of climate change due to global warming would be widespread on humans and ecosystems involving corals, coastal mangroves, low-latitude fisheries, glaciers, terrestrial ecosystems, coastal flooding, fluvial flooding, crop yields, tourism and heat-related mortality.

Impact of climate change on Bay of Bengal countries: The question arises: Will arresting global rise in temperature to 1.5°C stop the rise of ocean levels and prevent extreme weather?

Sea levels Rise (SLR): According to an IPCC report of 2018, extreme hot days on land in mid-latitudes (30-60°N) will be warmer by 3°C over the global mean surface temperature (GMST); number of hot days will increase in the tropics; and SLR is likely to be between 0.26 and 0.77 meters by 2100, at global warming of 1.5°C. SLR will continue beyond 2100 even if GHGs stabilises and global warming is limited to 1.5°C. These conditions will become much more severe, if the temperature were to rise by 2°C. Thus, global warming will eventually inundate the low-lying coastal areas, islands and deltas of the Bay of Bengal region and cause saltwater intrusions, damage to infrastructure, displacement and risks to multiple ecological systems.

Table 5.1: Population displacement due to sea level rise by 2100

Country	Displaced personnel
Bangladesh	334,762
Bhutan	Nil
India	5,892,150
Myanmar	247,191
Nepal	Nil
Sri Lanka	250,825
Thailand	595,000
Total	7,319,928

Assuming that water levels are going to rise by 30 inches (0.77 meters) in 2100, the estimated human displacements within Bay of Bengal rim countries (*globalfloodmap*)[6] is tabulated. India would be the worst effected followed by Thailand.

Response to SLR:[7] There are varying estimates of economic impact due to SLR. According to an ADB report (2017), the loss to GDP from SLR mitigation could range between 0.3 per cent to 9.3 per cent. Adaptive strategies against SLR include retreat, accommodation and protection. Retreat strategy involves planned relocation or migration and needs to cater for loss of property, resettlement cost and rebuilding infrastructure. According to one estimate cost of migration alone is likely to cost 2.7 to 3.5 percent of GDP by 2050 and 4.6 to 10.9 percent by 2100.[8] Accommodation strategies include optimal usage of vulnerable areas by converting agricultural lands to fish farming, growing salt tolerant crops; limiting damages by building piles; improving drainage systems; and positioning alarm and evacuation systems. Protection strategy would entail erection barriers and sea walls. A reference cost for building wall per meter vertical was US$ 6.02 million per kilometre in 2010.[9] Most governments are yet to cater to these scenarios in their national plan.

Crop yield: One is intrigued to know if crop yield would be affected by climate change, as it directly impacts subsistence of humans on earth. Researchers have found that crop yields are expected to increase due to rising CO_2 in the atmosphere and should have minor impact on global food production due to climate change. But the effect will not be uniform worldwide.[10] Another narrative predicts that food production in Bay of Bengal region will be the worst affected due to the compounded effects of disappearing glaciers, increased desertification, droughts and floods. This is likely to unsettle the stability of food security in the region. Based on the findings of International Food Policy Research (IFPRI) US, impact on food production, consumption and hunger in 2010, 2030 and 2050 due to climate change is tabulated for the Bay of Bengal region.[11]

Table 5.2: Impact of Climate Change on food production, consumption and hunger

	Food in Kcal			Hunger in million		
	2010	2030	2050	2010	2030	2050
Bangladesh	2426	2653	2781	26	14.8	8.7
India	2354	2651	2883	189.7	90.5	44.9
Myanmar	2169	2420	2487	10.5	7.2	6
Nepal	2425	2625	3028	2.7	2.4	1.5
Thailand	2742	2975	3103	6.2	3.5	2.3

Source: Author, based on IFPRI report

Despite global warming, it can be found from the IFPRI models that per capita food consumption of the region will improve and millions will be lifted out of poverty and hunger. India will still have to tackle millions with stunted growth due to hunger. FPI of the Bay of Bengal region are estimated to improve, despite the global warming. India stands out with a robust increase in FPI. This can be attributed to the investments made in research and technology and considerable improvements in land productivity. Agricultural efficiency is measured by the ratio of agricultural output to input resources and is called total factor productivity (TFP). India, China and Brazil are the drivers of TFP in the developing world. India's production capacities and TFP is a positive indicator for the entire region and the world.

Ocean Acidification

A quarter of CO_2 released into the atmosphere is absorbed by the oceans, which helps in reducing GHGs in the atmosphere. But the downside to this is that CO_2 absorbed by seawater increases its acidity and reduces the calcium-carbonate concentrations. This phenomenon is called ocean acidification (OA). CO_2 emissions have increased substantially in the atmosphere post-industrialisation. As a result, ocean chemistry is undergoing fundamental change throughout the world. The National Oceanography and Atmospheric Association (NOAA), USA, had lowered a buoy in the Bay of Bengal in position 15°N and 90°E in November 2013, from an Indian Research Ship Sagar Nidhi. Since then NOAA has been monitoring OA of the Bay of Bengal.

It can be observed that atmospheric CO_2 concentrations have increased marginally over the years and so has the CO_2 absorption.[12] Concomitantly, the pH levels of the Bay of Bengal has been reducing (graph not shown, available on NOAA website), which means that acidity has been increasing steadily. Interestingly, OA rises sharply during summers, and falls substantially with the advent of the monsoons through the winters. It can thus be inferred that due to higher ambient temperatures in the tropics, the Bay of Bengal is more vulnerable to OA in comparison to mid-latitude and higher-latitude seas.

The silver lining is that the total CO_2 emissions of Bay of Bengal countries in 2017 were 2944.2 $MtCO_2$ as compared to world emissions of 36153 $MtCO_2$.[13] In other words, 22 percent of the world population in the Bay of Bengal rim produces just 8 percent of carbon emissions.

Impact of OA on Bay of Bengal: Marine fish is an important constituent of animal protein for littoral countries of the Bay of Bengal. OA affects the marine food chain, and consequently the fishing industry and food security. It also affects marine shell and skeletal species like corals, oysters, clams, mussels, and snails. Coral reefs server as habitat for fish, natural barriers for the coastline and attraction for tourism. Almost 19 per cent of the world's coral reefs are estimated to have already been damaged by OA. 26 out of 66 coral species of the Saint Martin's Island, Bangladesh, are believed to have disappeared between 1997 and 2008.[14] Increased acidity is also depleting calcium carbonate concentration in clams, sea snails, lamp shells and sea urchins.

Mangroves play an essential role in maintaining the balance of coastal ecosystems by providing habitat for aquatic species and protecting the coastline. Mangroves of Ganga basin act as nursery for fin-fishes, shrimps, crabs, and cockles. However, increasing OA is believed to be damaging the roots of mangroves. Mangroves in Thailand are believed to be dying due to acidification from the root upwards.[15]

Oxygen Depletion

The Intergovernmental Oceanographic Commission of the United Nations Educational, Scientific and Cultural Organization (UNESCO) has warned of an impending ecological crisis due to declining levels of oxygen in the oceans and that the situation is worsening rapidly.[16] Decline in oxygen is due to incessant discharge of shore-based pollutants sewage, and industrial waste into the sea. The impact of this indiscriminate activity has led to the loss of dissolved oxygen in the seas and oceans, particularly in tropical waters where the rate of loss has gone up to nearly 20 per cent. Further, "the oxygen minimum zones (OMZs) are expanding rapidly impacting on the survival of marine organisms that rely on dissolved oxygen for survival and affecting the biogeochemical cycling of carbon and nitrogen, potentially aggravating global warming."[17] According to Professor Andreas Oschlies, from GEOMAR Helmholtz Centre for Ocean Research Kiel, "Data shows that in the past half-century, the area in the open ocean, in which all oxygen is lacking, has grown more than fourfold. We also expect oxygen levels to continue to fall outside these areas as the Earth continues to warm."[18]

OMZs have been discovered generally at depths of 200 and 800-meters depth and the biggest OMZ patch is in the Indian Ocean, i.e. in Arabian Sea (spread over approximately 70,000 square mile the Gulf of Oman) and the Bay of Bengal (60,000 square kilometres).[19] A study by scientists from India, Denmark and Germany warned that "should a similar global trend apply to the Bay of Bengal, its OMZ will trip to anaerobic mode, like in the Arabian Sea."[20]

The current state of OMZ in the Bay of Bengal is attributed to pollutants from rivers. For instance, the Buriganga River in Bangladesh is highly polluted and Dhaka, the country's capital, dumps nearly 4,500 tons of solid waste into the river daily and about 80 per cent of it is untreated.[21] Likewise, rivers from Myanmar and India carry untreated water which is discharged into the sea. It has been noted that the "physical processes and the temperature-salinity structure in the Bay of Bengal directly influence the OMZ and the depth of the oxycline and nutricline, thereby affecting the phytoplankton and marine mammal communities."[22]

It has been warned that the "dead zone of the Bay of Bengal is now at a point where a further reduction in its oxygen content could have the effect of stripping the water of nitrogen, a key nutrient. This transition could be triggered either by accretions of pollution or by changes in the monsoons, a predicted effect of global warming."[23]

Oxygen is as critical to marine species as it is to life on land. Oxygen also helps regulate the cycle of carbon and nitrogen in the oceans. Depletion of oxygen concentration can result in biochemical imbalance, habitat loss and can eventually alter the food web. This could lead to horizontal and vertical migration, loss of biodiversity and extinction. Since oxygen levels are much lower in the seawater than in the atmosphere, a minor fluctuation can cause oxygen related stresses for the marine life. Increase in temperature reduces the capacity of the oceans to hold oxygen. De-oxygenation results mainly from increasing GHGs in the atmosphere and chemicals discharged into the rivers and seas. Chemicals comprising nitrogen and phosphorus from agricultural nutrients, sewage and industrial pollution are especially responsible for de-oxygenation. Millennium ecosystem assessment released by the UN in 2005 had reported that supply of nitrogen compounds in the oceans has increased by a whopping 80 percent between 1860 and 1990.[24]

Hypoxia is a condition when body is deprived of oxygen. The threshold concentration for hypoxia for sub-lethal biological effect is considered to be 2 mg/Liter or 63 µmol/Liter. Oxygen minimum zones (OMZs) are areas below 20 µmol/Liter indicated in blue. Being an enclosed bay and located geographically in the tropical latitudes, Bay of Bengal is affected both by higher ambient temperature and pollutant discharge from its littoral states. It can be seen that Bay of Bengal has large areas of OMZs, with serious oxygen deficiencies.

Response to oxygen depletion:[25] The strategy to restore oxygen will require measures including:

- Reduction in GHGs.
- Reduction of nutrient infusion into the seas from the coast.
- Adoption of marine spatial planning.
- Unifying research, database collation and policies in BIMSTEC.

Prospects of Mitigating climate change: From the aforesaid it emerges that GHGs are the primary catalyst for sea level rise, ocean oxygen depletion and ocean acidification. However, a policy response to climate change needs to be global, which can then permeate to implementation strategies at the regional and national levels. Negotiations on climate change conference had begun under the UN's framework on climate change (UNFCCC) in the mid-1990s to negotiate the Kyoto protocol (adopted in December 1997) for establishing binding commitments on GHGs. Since 2005, these annual conferences have been rechristened as conference of parties or COP. COP 24 was concluded in December 2018 at Katowice, a Polish coal city, with mixed results, as the chasm between scientists, activists and politicians appears unbridgeable. In the end, COP 24 reached a face saving consensus on a truncated rulebook for implementing the Paris Agreement (COP 21 in December 2015) from 2020. Major setbacks of COP 24 include deferment of nation determined contributions (NDCs) till 2024 and market mechanisms like the clean development mechanisms (CDMs) to COP 25. There were differences on adaptation tax as well. The three strategies on adaptation have been explained earlier in the chapter. Interestingly, greatest opposition to COP24 came from the US, Saudi Arabia and Russia, who disagree to the very rationale of scientific warnings on temperatures beyond 1.5°C rise.

These differences are unlikely to be overcome soon. Even so, Bay of Bengal countries would be impacted severely by climate change to the tune of 9.3 percent of GDP and 7.3 million migrations. Hence, Bay of Bengal nations needs to evolve national and regional strategies on GHG reduction, adaptation plan and adaptation taxes. Bangladesh's climate change strategy and action plan (BCCSAP) and national adaptation plan (NAP) could be used as a benchmark for these purposes for the Bay of Bengal region by BIMSTEC. India's leadership towards clean energy, especially in solar power can be leveraged by the policy makers. Nepal and Bhutan can play a lead role by expanding and exporting clean energy to the region. Bay of Bengal region also needs to generate awareness and evolve clean energy strategies and CDM standards.

Conclusion

Manmade disasters caused by unexpected accidents due to negligence or material failure delve purely in the realms of safety. These are being addressed by UNDRR under the Sendai Framework 2015. However, disasters like climate change, ocean acidification, and air and water pollution are slow in onset and have far-reaching implications on the ecology. Climate change caused by global warming would have widespread impact on humans and multiple ecosystems involving corals, coastal mangroves, low-latitude fisheries, glaciers, terrestrial ecosystems, coastal flooding, fluvial flooding, crop yields, tourism and heat-related mortality. Bay of Bengal countries would be impacted severely by climate change to the tune of 9.3 percent of GDP and 7.3 million migrations. CO_2 emissions are also altering ocean chemistry through acidification. OA affects marine food chain, and consequently the fishing industry and human food security. De-oxygenation is another phenomenon that is mainly the result of increased GHGs in the atmosphere and chemical discharge into the rivers and seas by agricultural nutrients, sewage and industrial pollution.

Response to sea level rise (SLR) - Adaptive strategies against SLR include retreat, accommodation and protection. Retreat strategy involves planned relocation or migration and needs to cater to loss of property, resettlement cost and rebuilding infrastructure. Accommodation strategy includes optimal usage of vulnerable areas by converting agricultural lands to fish farming, growing salt tolerant crops; and limiting damages by building piles, improving drainage systems, alarms and evacuation systems. Protection strategy would require to erect barriers and sea walls. Adaptation tax would be an important political decision in this regard.

Response to oxygen depletion – The strategy to restore oxygen will require measures include reduction of GHGs; prohibition of nutrient infusion into the seas from the coast; adoption of marine spatial planning; and unifying research, database collation and policies of BIMSTEC. Bangladesh's climate change strategy and action plan (BCCSAP) and national adaptation plan (NAP) could be used as a benchmark for evolving national policies by BIMSTEC. India's leadership in clean energy, especially in solar power can be leveraged by BIMSTEC. Nepal and Bhutan play lead roles in expanding and exporting clean energy to the region. BIMSTEC also needs to generate awareness and evolve clean energy strategies and clean development mechanisms (CDM) standards.

The study will now move on to human induced environmental degradation as a consequence of marine pollution.

NOTES

1. Barry Buzan, *Regional Security Complex Theory*, in Theories of New Regionalism, edited by Fredrik Soderbaum and Timothu M Shaw, Palgrave Macmillan Ltd, NY, 2003, pp. 155-156.
2. IPCC, Summary for policy makers, Global warming of 1,5°C, 2018, p7 https://report.ipcc.ch/sr15/pdf/sr15_spm_final.pdf (Accessed on December 23, 2018)
3. NOAA, GHGs, https://www.ncdc.noaa.gov/monitoring-references/faq/greenhouse-gases.php (Accessed on December 23, 2018)
4. NOAA, Radiative forcings of non-CO_2 atmospheric gases, https://www.esrl.noaa.gov/research/themes/forcing/ (Accessed on December 23, 2018)
5. Ibid.
6. http://globalfloodmap.org/Bangladesh (Accessed on December 24, 2018)
7. Ruben Carlo and Minsoo Lee, Impacts of sea level rise on developing Asia, ADB no 507, 2017, https://www.adb.org/sites/default/files/publication/222066/ewp-507.pdf (Accessed on December 24, 2018)
8. Ibid, p.6.
9. Ibid, p.8.
10. Petr Havlik et al, Climate change, impacts and mitigation, assessment of agriculture and forestry. WB, 2015, https://openknowledge.worldbank.org/bitstream/handle/10986/23441/Climate0change0and0forestry0sectors.pdf?sequence=1&isAllowed=y (Accessed on December 24, 2018)
10. Amitav Ghosh and Aaron Savio Lobo, "Bay of Bengal: depleted fish stocks and huge dead zone signal tipping point", https://www.theguardian.com/environment/2017/jan/31/bay-bengal-depleted-fish-stocks-pollution-climate-change-migration (accessed 23 March 2019). Millennium Ecosystem Assessment Board, *Ecosystems and human wellbeing: Wetland and Water*, World Research Institute, Washington DC, 2005, p. 6 (Accessed on April 21, 2019) https://www.millenniumassessment.org/documents/document.358.aspx.pdf
    UNESCO, IOC, GO2NE, The Ocean is losing breath, https://unesdoc.unesco.org/ark:/48223/pf0000265196 /PDF/265196eng.pdf.multi (Accessed on December 25, 2018)
11. IFPRI, Food policy indicators, http://ebrary.ifpri.org/utils/getfile/collection/p15738coll2 /id/

12. NOAA, BOBOA, https://www.pmel.noaa.gov/co2/story/BOBOA (Accessed on December 24, 2018)
13. Global Ocean Atlas, http://www.globalcarbonatlas.org/en/CO2-emissions (Accessed on December 24, 2018)
14. M Shahadat Hussain et al, Vulnerability of BoB to ocean acidification, IUCN, Bangladesh, 2015, p. 13, https://portals.iucn.org/library/sites/library/files/documents/2015-049.pdf (Accessed on December 24, 2018)
15. Ibid, p.22.
16. "Intergovernmental Oceanographic Commission", http://www.unesco.org/new/en/natural-sciences/ioc-oceans/sections-and-programmes/ocean-sciences/global-ocean-oxygen-network/ (accessed 22 January 2019).
17. Nature, "Will ocean zones with low oxygen levels expand or shrink?", https://www.nature.com/articles/d41586-018-05034-y (accessed 22 January 2019)
18. Geomar "Oxygen depletion in the ocean is increasing", January 04, 2018. https://www.geomar.de/index.php?id=4&no_cache=1&tx_ttnews%5btt_news%5d=5630&tx_ttnews%5bbackPid%5d=185 (accessed 22 January 2019)
19. Vijay Sakhuja, "The Problem Of OMZs: Indian Ocean Is Fast Loosing Oxygen!", https//www.sspconline.org/index.php/opinion/Indian-ocean-fast-loosing-oxygen (accessed 22 January 2019).
20. Jayaraman, Dead zone' found in Bay of Bengal, https://www.natureasia.com/en/nindia/article/10.1038/nindia.2016.163(accessed 22 January 2019).
21. Soapboxie, "What Are the 10 Most Polluted Rivers in the World?" https://soapboxie.com/social-issues/What-Are-the-10-Most-Polluted-Rivers-in-the-World (accessed 22 January 2019)
22. V.V.S.S. Sarma, G.D. Rao, R. Viswanadham, C.K. Sherin, Joseph Salisbury, Melissa M. Omand, Amala Mahadevan, V.S.N. Murty, Emily L. Shroyer, Mark Baumgartner, Kathleen M. Stafford, "Effects of Freshwater Stratification on Nutrients, Dissolved Oxygen, and Phytoplankton in the Bay of Bengal", https://tos.org/oceanography/article/effects-of-freshwater-stratification-on-nutrients-dissolved-oxygen-and-phyt (accessed 23 March 2019)
23. Amitav Ghosh and Aaron Savio Lobo, "Bay of Bengal: depleted fish stocks and huge dead zone signal tipping point", https://www.theguardian.com/environment/2017/jan/31/bay-bengal-depleted-fish-stocks-pollution-climate-change-migration (accessed 23 March 2019).
24. Millennium Ecosystem Assessment Board, *Ecosystems and human wellbeing: Wetland and Water*, World Research Institute, Washington DC, 2005. Pp. 6, (Accessed on April 21, 2019) https://www.millenniumassessment.org/documents/document.358.aspx.pdf
25. UNESCO, IOC, GO2NE, The Ocean is losing breath, https://unesdoc.unesco.org/ark:/48223/pf0000265196 /PDF/265196eng.pdf.multi (Accessed on December 25, 2018)

6

Manmade Non-traditional Security Challenges:
Marine Pollution

A clean marine eco-system provides ambient conditions for a healthy aquatic life; however, marine litter and pollution can have undesirable impact on the very existence of living creatures including marine vegetation. This chapter highlights the environmental challenges being encountered by the Bay of Bengal by marine litter such as plastics and pollution from agriculture, industry, sewage and waste that run into the seas through river systems and other drainage and discharge processes.

Plastic Pollution in the Ocean

Plastics have become an integral part of today's economy and lifestyle. It is used for packaging, construction, healthcare, transportation, and electronics. Plastics now make up roughly 15 percent of a car by weight and about 50 percent of the Boeing dream liner. Since 1964 plastic production has increased from 15 million tons to 311 million tons and is expected to double by 2050. Packaging market occupies 25 percent of plastics industry by volume and is growing at 5 percent per annum.[1]

Nearly 95 percent of the packaging material by value, between US $ 80 and 120 billion is lost due to lack of effective recycling; close to 75 percent packaging is never recovered; 40 percent of which ends up in landfills and 32 percent leaks out of the collection system.[2] Almost 8 million tons of plastics leaks into the ocean.[3]

Plastic can be found almost in every corner of the ocean today. Instances have come to the fore wherein plastic have been found in mammals and there are fears that over 50 percent of sea turtles may have consumed plastic. It is found entangled around marine animals and birds, and is also being ingested by them.

According to one estimate 268,940 tons of plastic bottles, bags and microbeads amounting to 5250 billion pieces are floating in the oceans today. Indian Ocean shares 22 percent of the total plastic in the oceans corresponding to 59,130 tons by weight and 1300 billion pieces.[4] Distribution of plastic in the ocean is influenced by oceanic currents and surface winds. As a result they accumulate in five ocean gyres, two each in Atlantic and Pacific and one in Indian Ocean.[5] Even though Bay of Bengal is outside the Indian Ocean gyre, it accumulates high concentration of plastic due to its enclosed geography.

Asia, Europe and the US together produce 85 percent of the plastic, of which Asia produces 45 percent. But Asia alone contributes to 82 percent of the leakages.[6] Nearly 60 percent of the world's plastic waste originates in Southeast and East Asia, primarily from five countries, namely China, Indonesia, Philippines, Vietnam, and Thailand.[7]

Of the top 10 river sources polluting the oceans, two drain into the Bay of Bengal. Ganga (India and Bangladesh) ranks second after Yangtze (China), and Irrawaddy (Myanmar) ranks ninth.[8] In Indonesia, Brantas and Solo are described as highly polluting. Apparently, Indonesia is the second-largest contributor to marine plastic pollution after China, and is estimated to emit around 200,000 tons of plastic from rivers and streams, mainly from Java and Sumatra.[9] The fishermen from the Lhokseumawe area in the Aceh Province which lies in the south of Bay of Bengal complain about plastic and household waste found afloat and caught in the nets along with fish.[10] According to an estimate by Central Pollution Control Board (CPCB), India, close to 15,343 tons/day of plastic waste is being generated from 60 major Indian cities. 60 percent (9205 tons/day) of this gets recycled, while the remaining 40 percent gets mismanaged.[11]

Response Against Marine Litter

Like any large water body, the Bay of Bengal has its share of plastic litter and patches of debris have been discovered at sea as also along the coastlines of the littoral states. Ironically, the Bay of Bengal and the South China Sea are the new plastic hotspots in Asia, and the former is more polluted than the Indian Ocean gyre.[12] The Helmholtz Centre for Polar and Marine Research of the Alfred Wegener

Institute has compiled scientific data and published a map on marine litter which includes the Bay of Bengal as one of the most effected waters.[13]

An Indian National Institute of Ocean Technology (NIOT) study on Coastal Ocean Monitoring and Prediction System, undertaken as early as 2003, concluded that marine debris along the Great Nicobar and Nancowry Islands in the Nicobar Group was unusually high when compared to the population of the islands (1800 islanders and 1000 tribal based on 1992 census).[14] Further, the debris was not of local origin and it was observed that it may have originated in the neighbouring countries (Singapore, Malaysia, Indonesia, Sumatra, and other Southeast Asian countries), and had drifted towards the Nicobar Group of islands due to currents and wind.

The Bay of Bengal countries have made earnest efforts to address this problem. For instance, Myanmar, Bangladesh, India, Indonesia, Malaysia, Maldives, Sri Lanka and Thailand are part of the Bay of Bengal Large Marine Ecosystem (BOBLME) project and are engaged in efforts to better the lives of the coastal populations through improved regional management of the Bay of Bengal environment and fisheries. Under this project, Sri Lanka has noted that "Marine and beach litter in Sri Lanka are found along the beaches and shores, on the water surface, in the water column and on the seabed, along the shores of lagoons and estuaries. They can be found near the source of input but also can be transported over a long distance with sea currents and winds. The shore-lands where river or canals discharge are locations where marine litter is seen in significant quantities. This phenomenon is quite evident around Kelani Ganga river mouth, and Wellawatte and Dehiwala canal outlets in Colombo."[15] Marine litter observed along the coastline on beaches, fishery harbours and the port environment in Sri Lanka include vast category of items such as plastic polystyrene, rubber, medical and sanitary equipment.

In Bangladesh, since 2013, under 'Project Aware' and its 'Fighting Marine debris' programme, divers and volunteers engage in survey and removal of marine debris off the Saint Martin's Island.[16] In February 2016, the divers removed 1048 objects and of these, 90.31 percent were of plastic. Programmes like Swachh Bharat Abhiyan, Clean Ganga and Smart Cities have been initiated by the Government of India to control litter and build a sustainable environment. To spread awareness, 16 September each year is observed as coastal cleaning day.

Several global efforts like the Global Partnership on Marine Litter (GPML), the Honolulu Strategy (UNEP, 2011) and the G7 countries (G7, 2015) have been coordinating actions to reduce marine litter. Three goals set by the Honolulu strategy are:[17]

(a) Goal A: Land-based litter and solid waste introduced into the marine environment.

(b) Goal B: Sea-based sources of marine debris including solid waste, lost cargo, abandoned vessel, abandoned lost or discarded fishing gears (ALDFG).

(c) Goal C: Accumulated marine debris on shorelines, in benthic habitats, and in pelagic waters.

Countries are also steering actions against marine litter under the sustainable developmental goals (SDGs) targets 6.3, 11.6, 12.3, 12.4, 14.1, 14.2 and 14c. India too is putting together a comprehensive a National Marine Litter policy.

Underwater Noise

Marine pollution is also caused by underwater noise and can be attributed to shipping, fishing trawlers, offshore exploration, placing oil and gas pipelines and fibre optic cables on the seabed. Besides, warships use Sonar, a device to detect enemy submarines, which results in casualties among marine mammals. According to a study on the impact of underwater noise on marine life, it has been noted that "120dB can cause discomfort to these [marine] species, more than 170dB can cause serious internal injuries, bleeding and even haemorrhages, and noise beyond 200dB can cause instant death."[18] As one of us have argued elsewhere, powerful Sonar transmissions from the warships can potentially lead to internal bleeding in mammals causing damage to ear and brain tissues, resulting in disorientation or death of mammals. There is also a belief that whales may even misunderstand Sonar waves as an attacker, and cause panic driving them towards shores.[19]

In the Bay of Bengal, there have been incidents of sharks and whales washing ashore. In 1973, 147 whales were found on the beach off the Tuticorin coast; thereafter in 2016, 80 short-finned pilot whales were found stranded on the sand along the east coast. In 2017, a 3.5 tons 18-foot whale shark was sighted on the Pamban beach in Tamil Nadu.[20] In the latter case, necropsy revealed a plastic spoon in the whale shark's digestive system. The state wildlife authorities cautioned that plastic waste was harming the marine ecosystem and that marine species are unable to differentiate between floating plastic and prey.[21]

Pollution from Agriculture, Industry, Sewage and Waste

Some parts of the coasts have been significantly affected due to industrial and municipal effluents as indiscriminate development of brackish water culturing systems. The damage can be attributed to lack of awareness, poor planning, tardy enforcement, and ineffective coordination between concerned agencies. Sewage, industrial and pesticides are of particular concern as they are discharged without treatment. Industries like fertilizer, textile, cement, pulp, paper, food processing, pharmaceuticals, metal, petroleum, lubricants, etc., discharge heavy metals in the coastal waters.

The coast of Bay of Bengal is also deteriorating due to siltation, pollution and uncontrolled coastal development. As noted earlier, polluted rivers from Bangladesh, India and Myanmar drain into the Bay of Bengal carrying large volumes of pollutants. For example, the Bidyadhari river in West Bengal, draining into North Sundarbans, carry different heavy metals in the hierarchy of Fe>Mn>Zn>Cu>Pb>Cd, which are slightly different from the average hierarchy in the Bay of Bengal of Fe>Zn>Ni>Cr>Pb>Cd. Even though Cadmium is least among the six metals, it is the most harmful to human health.

Sediment quality analysis (SQA) show that average concentration of Nickel was higher than Effect Range Low (ERL) and Effect Range Medium (ERM). ERL signifies a concentration when toxic levels are rarely observed and ERM indicates a condition when toxic levels are always observed. High concentration of Nickel adversely affects biological species. Besides, toxic effect of Zinc and Lead are a great threat to shells and oysters. These species are engineers of the marine ecosystem and their endangerment make the next trophic level small mesopelagics and squids vulnerable. Eventually, the top trophic level of Tuna and mammals also get affected by ocean pollution.[22]

Conclusion

Mitigation will require effective industrial planning and the safe disposal of ship oil, industrial and urban waste. Reducing high levels of pollutants need urgent attention if the coastal ecosystem has to be preserved and marine resource of the Bay have to be saved. Programmes like Swachh Bharat Abhiyan, Clean Ganga and Smart Cities have been initiated by the Government of India to control litter and build a sustainable environment. Single use plastic has been banned across India from 02 October 2019 and its implementation is already visible. Mega awareness program have also been started by BIMSTEC governments.

Several global efforts like the Global Partnership on Marine Litter (GPML), the Honolulu Strategy (UNEP, 2011) and the G7 countries (G7, 2015) have been coordinating strategies to reduce marine litter. Countries are also steering actions against maritime litter under the sustainable developmental goals (SDGs) targets 6.3, 11.6, 12.3, 12.4, 14.1, 14.2 and 14c. Most countries in the region do not have national marine litter policy. It would be prudent to adopt such a policy by BIMSTEC nations to prevent maritime litter from spilling into the Bay of Bengal.

This chapter has attempted to highlight the magnitude of an approaching environmental catastrophe and has suggested some prospects for mitigation that need immediate attention. A regional approach to such mitigations has become equally essential as have been the national and global initiatives.

The study will now move on to human induced digital and cyber challenges in the maritime domain and discuss the security concerns of human migration.

NOTES

1. World Economic Forum, The new plastic economy, rethinking the future, 2016, p.10, http://www3.weforum.org/docs/WEF_The_New_Plastics_Economy.pdf (accessed 25 December 2018)
2. Ibid., p.12.
3. Ibid., p.14.
4. For more details see "Sailing Seas of Plastic", https://app.dumpark.com/seas-of-plastic-2/#oceans (accessed 25 December 2018)
5. Hannah Ritchie and Max Roser, "Plastic Pollution, Our world in Data", https://ourworldindata.org/plastic-pollution (accessed 25 December 2018)
6. World Economic Forum, The new plastic economy, rethinking the future, 2016, p.22., http://www3.weforum.org/docs/WEF_The_New_Plastics_Economy.pdf (accessed 25 December 2018).
7. Somen Banerjee, "Prospects of India China Maritime Cooperation", https://www.vifindia.org/2018/ september/05/prospects-for-india-china-maritime-cooperation (Accessed on December 25, 2018)
8. Hannah Ritchie and Max Roser, "Plastic Pollution, Our world in Data", https://ourworldindata.org/plastic-pollution (accessed 25 December 2018)
9. "Indonesian Contribution to the Sea of Plastic", http://www.youthpressagency.org/destinazionenews-clima?art=165 (accessed 24 January 2019).
10. "Fishermen in Aceh Complain of Plastic Waste at Sea", (accessed 24 January 2019).
11. UNEP, Government of India and SASEP, "Marine Litter in South Asian Sea Region", 2018, http://www.icmam.gov.in/mlitterJune2018.pdf (accessed 25 December 2018)
12. Vijay Sakhuja, "Fisheries and the Plastic Threat in Bay of Bengal", http://www.maritimeindia.org/View%20Profile/636074271086249914.pdf (accessed 24 January 2019).
13. Vijay Sakhuja, "Marine Debris Worry Indian and Indonesian Leaders" https://www.vifindia.org/print/5165?slide=%24slideshow%24 (accessed 24 January 2019).

14. "Marine Debris in Nicobar", https://www.niot.res.in/venkat/publications/Marine%20debris%20in%20Great%20Nicobar,%20Current%20science.pdf (accessed 17 July 2018).
15. S.A.M. Azmy, "Sri Lanka Report on Coastal Pollution Loading and Water Quality Criteria", http://www.boblme.org/documentRepository/BOBLME-2011-Ecology-14.pdf (accessed 12 October 2017).
16. "Bangladesh Underwater Cleanup 2016", https://www.projectaware.org/action/bangladesh-underwater-cleanup-2016(accessed 24 January 2019).
17. Ibid., p.12.
18. Badri Chaterjee, "Death by Noise: Sound of Ships Kills Marine Mammals in Mumbai", *Hindustan Times*, 3 September 2017.
19. Vijay Sakhuja, "Marine Mammal Stranding: Myth, Mystery and Facts", http://www.ipcs.org/comm_select.php?articleNo=5355 (accessed 22 January 2019).
20. Vijay Sakhuja, "Marine Mammal Stranding: Myth, Mystery and Facts", http://www.ipcs.org/comm_select.php?articleNo=5355 (accessed 22 January 2019).
21. Ibid.
22. T Rashid, et al, "Pollution in the Bay of Bengal: Impact of Marine Ecosystem", Open Journal of Marine Science, 2015, pp. 55-63.

7

Human Induced Non-Traditional Threats and Challenges:
Digital and Illegal Migration

This chapter analyses dissimilar set of threats and challenges that have major human footprint. In particular, these are human induced or human created. The chapter also discusses as cyber-digital threats in the maritime domain and human migration.

Digital Shipping and Cyber Threats

It is well established that maritime connectivity sustains economic development and deepens economic integration. It is also acknowledged that digital connectivity enhances productivity, augments trade, reduces logistical costs and bolsters economic development. In the process, an enormous amount of digital data is generated, processed and exchanged among stakeholders including regulatory bodies in the conduct of commercial transactions. For instance, it is possible to obtain real time data to track cargo onboard ships and other multimodal transport, receive automatic notifications on the status of shipment clearances, control and monitor transactions, synchronizing data among varied stakeholders and partners, thus reducing manual operations on account of paperwork for invoices and increases business efficiency and productivity. Likewise, mobile applications, i.e. "apps" facilitate exchange of information and financial transactions on the go by using wearable mobile devices such as smartphones and tablets.

However, there are several risks to use and transmit digital data; it is prone to cyber-attacks through viruses and Trojans, and the hackers are continuously prowling the digital space for gaps and weaknesses to access data, steal information, or interfere in operations thus causing disruption of critical infrastructure.[1]

The cyberspace and the associated digital ecosystem are important enablers for enhancing commercial maritime operations. Yet these present an entirely different dynamic for the maritime domain and its users and stakeholders. Maritime cyber-attack is a serious non-traditional security threat and has caught the attention of the United Nations, governments and the maritime industry. Any disruption of the maritime supply chains due to cyber-attack can severely affect the global trading system and disruption of the global supply and production chains particularly in the context of 'just in time' cargo.

Maritime cyber-attacks are of concern to marine enforcement agencies too. There are several documented cyber-attacks and the criminals were successful in breeching into computing systems. For instance, smugglers hacked into the port cargo handing data and were able to locate the containers with drugs which were pilfered without detection. Interestingly, the smugglers even managed to tamper the cargo manifest and deleted the data of the shipment.[2]

The International Maritime Organisation (IMO) has acknowledged that ships are vulnerable to cyber-attack. It has instructed all ship owners to incorporate cyber risk management into ship safety mechanism by 01 January 2021 failing which the vessels may be detained.[3] Also, 'cyber security requirements will be formalised in Chapter IX of the International Convention for the Safety of Life at Sea, SOLAS, Regulations 1-6, Management for Safe Operation of Ships'.[4] These are significant initiatives and would have to keep pace with future developments in maritime infrastructure that would be characterized by cutting-edge disruptive technologies such as Big Data, Marine Cyber Physical Systems (MCPS), Artificial Intelligence (AI), Autonomous Systems, etc., which would necessitate upending investments in digital maritime infrastructure.

Spoofing, AIS and LRIT

Spoofing is defined as an act of "disguising a communication from an unknown source as being from a known, trusted source" and can be applied to a variety of devices and systems used for "emails, phone calls, and websites".[5] It can infect networks and even generate false signals to gain control of the computer system which is a major concern for safety and security of shipping.

In the 1990s, Automatic Identification System (AIS) was introduced onboard ships to transmit a vessel's position, speed, and direction through information alerts. This has unquestionably helped shipping companies with regular information about the ships, prevented 'marine accidents, collisions and related incidents'.[6] According to an industry report titled 'AIS Data on the High Seas: An Analysis of the Magnitude and Implications of Growing Data Manipulation at Sea' data is increasingly manipulated by ships that seek to conceal their identity, location or destination for economic gain or to sail under the security radar" and the top five AIS manipulation practices are: (a) Identity Fraud; (b) Obscuring Destinations; (c) Going Dark; (d) GPS Manipulation; (e) AIS Spoofing.[7] Further, the report notes that 41 per cent of the vessels do not report their next port of call, 10 per cent vessels turn off their AIS transmissions, and there was 59 per cent increase in the use of GPS manipulation. Also, AIS can be 'spoofed' and inserted into the data stream, allowing people to create 'ghost ships' where none exist. It is the latter which presents complex challenges for the maritime enforcement agencies.

It is important to mention that the Somali pirates could choose ships to attack through online tracking the movement of the ship by breaking into the AIS and the Electronic Chart Display & Information System (ECDIS), a computer-based navigation information system which can be used as an alternative to traditional paper charts.[7] It has been noted that "Increasingly, the maritime domain and energy sector has turned to technology to improve production, cost and reduce delivery schedules.... These technological changes have opened the door to emerging threats and vulnerabilities as equipment has become accessible to outside entities."[8]

Another challenge posed by the AIS is its use by fishermen with their fishing nets. Large vessels "change course for the nets, thinking they were vessels" and the fishermen are bold to "contact the ships on the VHF radio and tell the bridge watch team what course they should steer in order to avoid the fishing nets."[9] Captain Mike Jessner, a ship master for the American President Lines, is seeking international support to prevent the use of AIS on fishing nets by fishing vessels and according to Jessner "equipment identifies these [AIS on fishing nets] as vessels and it is only able to track a couple of hundred at a time. When there are hundreds in use on fishing nets, the ECDIS cannot distinguish which are vessels and which are nets, so they all appear as vessels."

The offshore energy infrastructure is not immune to spoofing and in 2014, "hackers shut down a floating rig by inducing a list. Another offshore rig's computer system was so compromised by malware that it took 19 days to make it seaworthy again."[10] According the British government, attacks on energy infrastructure have already cost "UK oil and gas companies approximately US $672 million annually and cyber-attacks on energy infrastructure could cost nearly US $1.9 billion to the energy companies by 2018."[11] At another level, fishing vessels with suspicious AIS could be creatively used by terrorists to launch attack.

Illegal Human Migration

Migration, legal or illegal, has been a feature of civilizations since ancient times. The former is a construct of movement of people as part of socio-cultural exchanges while the latter is generally debated within the security framework. In the Bay of Bengal, illegal migration is quite common and is made possible due to good land and sea connectivity. Bangladeshi migrants to India travel by the land and sea routes and in the case of the latter, they arrive on board small boats particularly from areas in Bangladesh where there is severe impact of climate change and sea level rise.

A study notes that "Sea-level rise is also projected to aggravate storm surge, flooding, erosion and other coastal hazards, resulting in significant losses of coastal ecosystems. The coastal regions of Maldives, and Sri Lanka and India (Andaman, Nicobar and Lakshadweep Islands) are likely 18 to be worst affected by the phenomena."[12] The climate-displaced migration spills into neighbouring countries.[13]

While these migrants are victims of climate change, Tamil community in Sri Lanka fled the conflict in the country. In 2010, MV Sun Sea with over 200 Tamil migrants on board was intercepted, destined for Canada; earlier, in 2009, MV Ocean Lady was intercepted off Canada's British Columbia coast with 76 Tamil asylum seekers from Sri Lanka.[14] In 2008, large number of illegal immigrants from Bangladesh and Myanmar reached the A&N coast after they had been set adrift in the sea by the Thai military.[15] Several years later, in 2015, Rohingya, a minority Muslim community in Myanmar, were taking the sea route to escape ethnic cleansing in Myanmar due to tensions between the Buddhist and Muslim communities in the state of Rakhine. According to the UNHCR estimates, since 2012, nearly 170,000 people have made the crossing, and maritime movements across the Bay of Bengal have occurred on a consistent basis for at least a decade before that.[16]

The Bay of Bengal continues to witness Rohingya migration; in 2016, Thai security forces intercepted 73 Rohingya migrants overcrowded on a boat including women.[17] Another boat with 200 Rohingya migrants was caught off Phuket province in the Andaman Sea. Likewise, the Indonesian authorities reported that their fishermen had found adrift 121 Rohingya, including women and children, 25 kilometers from Cot Trueng in Aceh province. In February 2019, Myanmar navy vessel patrolling off Sittway capture a vessel bound for Malaysia with 14 illegal migrants including seven women and two agents; apparently, the migrants had paid US$ 2,000 each for the voyage.[18]

Conclusion

The foregoing discussions illustrate that the cyber-digital domain offers enormous opportunities in all facets of human activity; yet it engenders neo-security threats that are non-lethal yet more lethal.

Finally, illegal migration is a serious issue for the international community and a number of causal factors such as poverty, loss of economic opportunities, livelihood problems, religious persecutions, wars and social unrest and climate induced changes. However, these vary from region to region with peculiarities.

In the following chapter, the study will investigate natural disasters that know no boundaries. Expeditious response to natural emergencies can reduce the effects of such disasters.

NOTES

1. For a good discussion on 'infrastructure' see Munish Sharma, "Securing Critical Information Infrastructure : Global Perspectives and Practices", https://idsa.in/system/files/monograph/monograph60.pdf (accessed 20 February 2019). According to the author, "An infrastructure, as a system, is built up of numerous facilities and enables a specific set of activity for the society. Just as water, oil or gas pipelines enable flow and supply of water or oil from the source to the consumption end and roads, bridges, railway networks and aviation enable movement of people, goods and freight, telecommunication networks built over optical fiber, switches and microwave antennas enable voice and data communication. Interconnected banking operations, network of automated teller machines and other financial or banking services over Internet enable delivery of these services round the clock in every corner of the world. In general, these infrastructures are dependent on other infrastructure to dispense their core functions: for instance, banking system uses telecommunication network to deliver mobile banking or security functions such as one-time password. Similarly, payment systems of railways or civil aviation are dependent on the bank gateways for payments processing. The day-to-day societal functions and requisites, such as water and electricity, banking and financial services, transportation, fuel and food supplies and communications and Internet services, are completely dependent on these multi-layered physical or virtual infrastructures."

2. Vijay Sakhuja, "Maritime Cyber Attacks are a Reality", http://maritimeindia.org/View%20Profile/635718254600412804.pdf (accessed 28 December 2018).
3. "IMO Imposes Cyber Security on Ship ISM", https://www.marinemec.com/news/view,imo-imposes-cyber-security-on-ship-ism_48159.htm (accessed 13 December 2018).
4. "The Future of Maritime Cyber Security", https://securestatecyber.com/cyberbloggen-en/the-future-of-maritime-cybersecurity/ (accessed 30 June 2019).
5. "What is Spoofing?", https://www.forcepoint.com/cyber-edu/spoofing (accessed 13 December 2018).
6. "Hacking AIS", https://www.forcepoint.com/cyber-edu/spoofing (accessed 13 December 2018).
7. Vijay Sakhuja, "Maritime Cyber Attacks are a Reality", (accessed 28 December 2018). http://maritimeindia.org/View%20Profile/635718254600412804.pdf
8. Jeremy Wagstaff, "Hackers Target Global Tanker, Container Shipping Fleet" https://www.insurancejournal.com/news/international/2014/04/24/327195.htm (accessed 28 December 2018).
9. "AIS Problems Revealed in East China Sea", https://gcaptain.com/ais-problems-revealed-in-east-china-sea/ (accessed 31 December 2018).
10. "Cyber-attacks offshore", https://www.workboat.com/archived-workboat-magazine/cyber-attacks-offshore/ (accessed 18 November 2018).
11. Ibid.
12. Aparna Roy, "BIMSTEC and Climate Change: Setting a Common Agenda", https://www.orfonline.org/wp-content/uploads/2017/10/IB-203.pdf (accessed 23 March 2019).
13. Mohammad Zaman, "Confronting climate refugee issues in Bangladesh", https://www.thedailystar.net/opinion/environment/news/confronting-climate-refugee-issues-bangladesh-1677019 (accessed 23 March 2019).
14. "Captain of Tamil migrant ship MV Sun Sea loses first court battle to stop his deportation", https://nationalpost.com/news/politics/captain-of-tamil-migrant-ship-mv-sun-sea-loses-first-court-battle-to-stop-his-deportation (accessed 23 March 2019).
15. "Beckoning of Fortune Traps Rohingyas", *The Daily Star* [Bangladesh], 25 January 2009.
16. "The Rohingya Survey – 2016", http://xchange.org/map/RohingyaSurvey.html (accessed 16 October 2018).
17. Vijay Sakhuja, "How Asia' Boat People Exposed Maritime Weaknesses", https://asia.nikkei.com/Politics/How-Asia-s-boat-people-exposed-maritime-weaknesses (accessed 13 February 2019).
18. "14 Illegal Immigrants Bound for Malaysia Nabbed in Myanmar", https://www.nst.com.my/world/2019/02/459159/14-illegal-immigrants-bound-malaysia-nabbed-myanmar (accessed 13 February 2019).

8

Nature Induced Non-traditional Threats at Sea

Seismic, meteorological and hydrological fluctuations and vagaries on land cause natural hazards which unfold in the form of earthquakes, drought or floods. These catastrophic events result in loss of life, destruction of crops, and devastation of property and materials with long-term effects on the socio-economic development of the society. Similarly, natural events at sea occur in the form of Tsunamis that are results of underwater earthquakes, volcanic eruptions and landslides. These generate high and powerful waves that travel far into the sea; and those which crossover on land result in destruction of coastal infrastructure and damage to coastal communities. Likewise, cyclones and hurricanes are natural phenomenon caused by low atmospheric pressure at sea resulting in high speed winds that move landwards. On hitting the land, these leave behind a trail of devastation deep into the hinterland.

At another level, emergencies could take place at sea onboard ships and fishing vessels. These could be due to accidents, collisions, medical casualty, weather, cyclones, etc. Many of these would involve search and rescue wherein ships and aircraft are pressed into action by maritime agencies to rescue fishermen and evacuate sailors and passengers' onboard ships and cruise liners. Likewise, there are instances of rescue operations involving air crashes at sea, and rarely, a submarine crew may require rescue.

This chapter provides insights into the nature of catastrophes that take place in the Bay of Bengal. It begins by expounding on the concept of 'Public Goods at Sea' and argues that accidents caused due to natural events or accidents due to human errors or otherwise necessitate response from rescue agencies for which states do not levy charges given that these services are rendered or provided for humanitarian purposes. In this context, the paper addresses two major issues, i.e. Humanitarian Aid and Disaster Relief (HADR), and Search and Rescue (SAR) operations in the Bay of Bengal. An attempt is also made to theorize the delivery of HADR and SAR as an activity under the ambit of Disaster Diplomacy. Finally, the chapter argues that the regional response to accidents and natural events in the Bay of Bengal is weak, barring India which possesses enormous capacity to assist regional countries.

Concept of Public Goods at Sea

It is generally agreed that public goods have two characteristics; first, these are non-exclusionary and all users of these 'goods and services' can enjoy without paying. The second characteristic is the concept of 'non-rivalry' under which the potential users are not competing, and the goods are enjoyed by larger number of stakeholders without reducing the availability to others.[1] A commonly cited example of public goods is street lighting under which a common man is a beneficiary of services which are offered free by the State.[2] However, residents living in gated apartments are often charged for lighting in common space.

The concept of Public Goods has also found reference in international relations, global governance, and national security. The United Nations role in addressing global challenges through its institution, such as climate change, preventing violent conflict and collective response to terrorism and promote the seventeen Sustainable Development Goals (SDGs) can be labelled as public goods. These are pursued and promoted to bring benefits to the society.

In the maritime domain, meteorological services such as humanitarian assistance and disaster relief (HADR), Search and Rescue (SAR), etc., can be considered as public goods. These are offered for free to the maritime community. However, it was the lighthouse services which first found reference in economic analysis. It was noted "the lighthouse has often been cited as the classic example of a public good (whereby those who do not pay cannot be excluded from consuming it, and one's consumption does not reduce the consumption of others), leading to the prescription of a public production financed out of general taxation."[3] The example of lighthouses has been a subject of extensive study and debate among the economists who have either accepted that services provided by a lighthouse is a 'public good'; however, in case a lighthouse is operated by a private agency, how will it recover dues from the users of its services remains an issue that debunks the concept of 'public goods'.

Be that as it may, the lighthouse is an important component of sea-based navigation and serves several purposes including maritime security. Besides, it is used by commercial, military and state-owned vessels (deployed for scientific research, oceanographic surveys and underwater exploration). Lighthouse services are enjoyed by many users of the state and private agencies such as shipping.

Another good example of 'public goods' can be counter-piracy operations. It is widely known and acknowledged that pirates are the enemy of all and labeled as *hostis humani generis* under public international law. For Joseph Nye, "maintaining open international commons such as freedom of the seas and the suppression of piracy" constituted one of the three classic public goods provided by the British Empire."[4]

Under international law, a ship may be stopped or boarded and subjected to verification of its flag provided there is a reasonable ground for suspecting that it is engaged in piracy, the slave trade, unauthorized broadcasting, without nationality, or is flying a false flag. The 1982 United Nations Convention on the Law of the Sea (UNCLOS) provides significant powers to states to prosecute pirates, and several grounds and reasons for ships to intercept vessels engaged in piracy.[5]

Counter-piracy operations can therefore be understood within the framework of public goods under which navies and marine law enforcement forces ensure safety of merchant shipping irrespective of their flag state. Also, the ICC International Maritime Bureau (IMB), a specialised division of the International Chamber of Commerce (ICC) and a non-profit making organisation is focused on fighting all types of maritime crime and malpractice, set up a Piracy Reporting which offers a 24-hour free service to shipmasters to report any piracy, armed robbery or stowaway incidents.[6]

Closely related is an issue currently resonating in the strategic literature is about free and open Indo-Pacific (FIOP) which has appeared in the 2017 US National Security Strategy. Michael Mandel Baum states that the "British navy patrolled the sea lanes along which much of the world's commerce passed;"[6] and that in "the second half of the twentieth century, the United States succeeded Britain, assuming the responsibility for providing secure geopolitical conditions for trade." As a result, the United States retains the dominant "responsibility for quasi-governmental tasks that are vital to global order," including "furnishing security for international economic activity."[7]

China too has promoted the idea of 'public goods' at sea by setting up maritime safety services for the ships passing through the South China Sea and to local fishermen. It is important to mention that China claims all the islands and features in the South China Sea and on many of these, it has built lighthouses and set up weather satellite monitoring and radar stations. The Chinese have assured that "Countries alongside the South China Sea and vessels sailing through the waters will receive better service."[8] It has set up a maritime rescue centre on the Fiery Cross Reef, one of the reclaimed islands.[9]

Sustainable exploitation of fisheries in the high seas is also a useful explanation for public goods at sea. Globally, nearly 58 per cent of the ocean is legally defined as high seas (characteristically free for all) and the balance are appropriated as Exclusive Economic Zones (EEZs). The high seas are overfished, and a study has warned that "by 2050, 88% of fish stocks will be overfished if current trends continue."[10] A motion supported by 140 in the UN has been initiated for a High Seas Treaty and by 2020, it is hoped, new rules governing fish quotas and conservation areas on the high seas will be operational.[11]

Disaster Diplomacy

Natural catastrophes such as Tsunamis, cyclones and storm surges can occur in any part of the world and impact on national economies of developed and developing countries alike. For instance, Hurricane Katrina hit United States and cyclone Nargis Myanmar, and both disasters left a massive destruction of infrastructure and lives and livelihoods of large populace were lost. It is fair to say that disasters know no boundaries and are not bound by religion, culture, society or political systems.

Natural disasters have also been occasions for political and diplomatic exchanges. For instance, India accepted material aid from Pakistan after the 2001 earthquake in Gujarat and a C-130 transport plane of the Pakistan Air Force, with 200 tents 2,000 blankets landed at Ahmedabad in Gujarat.[12] However, in 2003, in response to the 67,000 tonnes crude oil spill from tanker Tasman Spirit after it ran aground off Karachi, Pakistan, sought assistance from UK instead of India that had significant capacity to respond to the disaster.[13]

In the case of Myanmar, it initially refused to accept aid from the US after the country was hit by Cyclone Nargis. The US had "two aircraft carrier groups (led by the USS Kitty Hawk and the USS Nimitz), both of which had more helicopters on board, as well as medical teams and personnel that could be deployed to the affected areas",[14] but the Myanmar government was "reluctant to accept any foreigners in the country to assist in responding to the disaster. It took extensive discussions and a personal visit to Burma by PACOM Chief Navy ADM Timothy J. Keating and Director of Foreign Assistance and USAID Administrator Henrietta Fore for the United States to be allowed to fly supplies into Burma."[15] Further, the US military personnel were not allowed to distribute supplies.

Unlike the above incident, after Iran was hit by an earthquake in 2002, the US Government provided humanitarian aid and President George W Bush stated, "Human suffering knows no political boundaries.'[16] The Iranian leadership stated that aid had "no political character" even though Iran had been labelled as member of the "axis of evil".

These discussions are highlighted to argue that disaster diplomacy is an important tool of international relations to help states, international organizations and communities to deliver humanitarian aid by overcoming stubborn political positions, open new channels of communication.

Bay of Bengal: Humanitarian Aid and Disaster Relief (HADR)

According to the Indian Metrological Department (IMD), occurrence of cyclones in Bay of Bengal is a near continuous feature. These are rare during January to March and those between April and May strike the Arakan coasts and Andhra-Orissa-West Bengal-Bangladesh coasts. During monsoon (June–September) they affect Andhra-Orissa-West Bengal coasts and in the post monsoon period, (October-December) affect Tamil Nadu-Andhra Orissa-West Bengal-Bangladesh coasts.[17]

There is a history of catastrophic weather and natural events in the Bay of Bengal and the region has witnessed numerous cyclones and at least one Tsunami. Further, on an average "five to six tropical cyclones form every year, of which two or three could be severe".[18] According to an assessment, "Over the past two centuries, 20 out of the 23 major cyclone disasters in the world have occurred bordering the Bay of Bengal, particularly in India and Bangladesh."[19] Further, of the 35 deadliest tropical cyclones (lives in excess of 100,000 people were lost) in world history, 24 of these occurred in the Bay of Bengal (See Table 8.1).[20]

In recent times, Cyclone Nargis in 2008 left over 138,000 people dead and affected 2.4 million others. Ships and aircraft carrying humanitarian assistance were dispatched by many countries including the US and France.[21] Under Operation Sahayata, two Indian warships delivered relief materials, and these were supplemented by two India Air Force AN-32 aircraft which carried medicines and tents.[22]

Table 8.1

Name / Areas of Largest Loss	Year	Area	Deaths
Great Bhola Cyclone, Bangladesh	1970 (Nov 12)	Bay of Bengal	300,000-500,000
Hooghly River Cyclone, India and Bangladesh	1737	Bay of Bengal	300,000
Coringa, India	1839	Bay of Bengal	300,000
Backerganj Cyclone, Bangladesh	1584	Bay of Bengal	200,000
Great Backerganj Cyclone, Bangladesh	1876	Bay of Bengal	200,000
Chittagong, Bangladesh	1897	Bay of Bengal	175,000
Super Typhoon Nina, China	1975 (Aug 5)	West Pacific	171,000
Cyclone 02B, Bangladesh	1991 (May 5)	Bay of Bengal	138,866
Cyclone Nargis, Myanmar	2008 (May 3)	Bay of Bengal	138,366

The Bay of Bengal also witnessed the fury unleashed by the 2004 Tsunami. On 24 December, high tidal waves hit the shores of eleven countries of which six are in the Bay of Bengal-Bangladesh, Myanmar, India, Indonesia, Malaysia, Sri Lanka, and Thailand. Among these Indonesia and Sri Lanka were hit the hardest, and extensive damage was experienced along the coastal areas in Thailand, Tamil Nadu, Andhra Pradesh, and the Andaman and Nicobar Islands.[23]

Search and Rescue

According to Safety and Shipping Review 2018, total ship losses in 2018 was 94 as against 98 the previous year which is a significant improvement from an average figure of 113 losses in the last ten years.[24] These are promising signs of high levels of ship safety and can be attributed to modern ship design, advances in technology and improvements in risk management.

In terms of the geographical areas that were spared of these losses, according to the report, "South China, Indo-China, Indonesia and Philippines maritime region" accounted for 32% of losses occurred here and this was due to dense shipping activity (…ships transit through the South China Sea) and the area is prone to bad weather. For instance, Typhoon Damrey in 2017 contributed to several losses. The other areas that recorded losses were: (a) East Mediterranean and Black Sea region (17), British Isles (8), and the Arabian Gulf (6). It is evident from the report above natural events such as typhoons and cyclones can result in loss of shipping. Although Bay of Bengal is not mentioned in the above report, but the region is prone to extreme cyclonic activity and the probability of such accidents is not improbable.

Be that as it may, three accidents—Malaysian Airlines flight MH 370 in the southern Indian Ocean, loss of Air Asia flight QZ 8501 in the Java Sea and the sinking of the Korean ferry Seawol—have exposed the limitations of SAR operations at sea. The mysterious loss of MH 370 brought ships, submarine, aircraft and satellites from several countries into the Indian Ocean clearly showcasing that SAR is a 'public good'. But the operations were constrained too wherein some countries refused to allow PLA Navy ships to carry out SAR fearing the Chinese might engage in suspicious activities including surveillance. Contested boundaries, mutual suspicion, lack of trust, and lack of agreements on SAR are fertile grounds to undermine SAR efforts challenging the concept of public goods at sea.[25]

Bay of Bengal is witness to shipping, and fishing activity. Also, turbid waters make the underwater domain opaque resulting in immense challenges for SAR operations. However, there are no boundary issues which can potentially preclude timely SAR and above all littorals enjoy good relations and are amenable to joint SAR.

As far as SAR for submarines is concerned, most modern submarines are have inbuilt rescue equipment/chambers and submarine rescue tenders and other portable arrangements can facilitate evacuation of the crew. It is also a practice among navies that they do not share many details of the platforms and therefore their operations are generally shrouded in secrecy. No navy discloses submarine accidents and under such circumstances international efforts are unacceptable. Among the Bay of Bengal littorals, submarines are in the inventory of the Indian and Bangladesh navies; Thailand is acquiring submarines from China, and Myanmar is contemplating acquisition of submarines. In the event of a submarine accident, the regional capacity to respond to the event is limited.

Regional Capacity to Respond

As argued elsewhere, "Successful SAR operation is dependent on surveillance assets such as ships, aircraft, satellites and underwater systems. It is important to mention that most Indian Ocean littorals lack surveillance assets and proper equipment to conduct SAR operations, and only a few can undertake deep sea rescue. Similarly, training and enhanced planning is critical for SAR. It involves detailed organisational structures and strategies for mobilisation of the SAR resources for a quick response."[26] Further, it is true that some nations possess inherently larger maritime and naval capacity than others to deal with the disasters internally and across their border, while others may require assistance. The strains will be higher on weaker nations who wish to focus their resources on national development and may not have developed enough maritime capability. In such cases a multilateral response from both within the region and outside will have to be marshalled to respond to the crisis. With crucial assets like helicopters, support ships, hospital ships and organizational skills, the US military possesses enormous capacity to respond to natural disasters. In 2009, it responded to multiple disasters (Tsunami, earthquakes and a severe storm) simultaneously. Likewise, India too possesses similar capacity but not of that scale, to respond to disasters as was showcased during the 2004 Indian Ocean Tsunami.

SAR capacity of the Bay of Bengal littoral is quite limited barring India which has massive capabilities to respond and it can put to operations ships and aircraft with little reaction time. Besides, several Indian Navy ships are deployed in the Bay of Bengal region and can be mobilized at short notice and can potentially provide SAR support to all the littorals. Besides, Bay of Bengal littorals are signatory to international conventions concerning SAR. These are: (a) 1974 Convention for the Safety of Life at Sea (SOLAS), (b) 1979 International Convention on Maritime Search and Rescue (SAR), (c) 1982 United National Law of the Sea (UNCLOS) Convention, and (d) International Aeronautical and Maritime Search and Rescue (IAMSAR) and these have been adopted by regional countries.

Conclusion

It is an acknowledged fact that natural disasters can happen anywhere on land. In the air, on the sea and underwater The international community have taken upon themselves to provide assistance for HADR and SAR and these services are rendered free of charges. Several agencies, government and NGOs, respond to catastrophes with a variety of assets both human, material and fiscal. The militaries are in the forefront in operations relating to HADR and SAR in the Bay of Bengal, and the 2004 Indian Ocean Tsunami and other cyclonic disasters in the Bay of Bengal are good examples. These agencies have developed strategies that are focused on cooperative response to natural disasters. Natural catastrophes in the Bay of Bengal will increase in the future and cyclonic activity will witness an increase in intensity and frequency and that context, humanitarian assistance operationalised through the maritime forces is both symbolic as well as substantive display of the 'soft power' of the state. It is not surprising then that government has chosen to deliver 'public goods' at sea as an important tool for diplomacy.

In the previous chapters and the present, regional challenges emanating from manmade and natural causes were discussed. The following three chapters will deal with economy. Also, regional connectivity is an essential element of growth and development and will be examined in the subsequent chapter.

NOTES

1. Maxime Desmarais-Tremblay, "On the Definition of Public Goods Assessing Richard A. Musgrave's contribution", https://halshs.archives-ouvertes.fr/halshs-00951577/document (accessed 23 January 2019).
2. "What are Public Goods?" http://www.sanandres.esc.edu.ar/secondary/economics%20packs/microeconomics_sl/page_115.htm (accessed 23 January 2019).
3. "The Light House as a Public Good – Theory, History and Policy", https://lighthouse.hypotheses.org/files/2015/01/lighthouse-Aims-20141217.pdf (accessed 23 January 2019).
4. Edward R Lucas, "Public Goods, Club Goods, and Private Interests: The Role of Business Elites in British Counter-Piracy in the South China Sea, 1921-1935", Security Studies, 2019, p.7.
5. "Piracy under International Law", https://www.un.org/Depts/los/piracy/piracy.htm (accessed 28 January 2019). Articles 100 to 107 and 110 specifically relate to repression of piracy under international law. "The Security Council has repeatedly reaffirmed "that international law, as reflected in the United Nations Convention on the Law of the Sea of 10 December 1982 ('The Convention'), sets out the legal framework applicable to combating piracy and armed robbery at sea, as well as other ocean activities" (Security Council resolution 1897 (2009), adopted on 30 November 2009). Article 100 of UNCLOS provides that "[all] States shall cooperate to the fullest possible extent in the repression of piracy on the high seas or in any other place outside the jurisdiction of any State." The General Assembly has also repeatedly encouraged States to cooperate to address piracy and armed robbery at sea in its resolutions on oceans and the law of the sea. For example, in its resolution 64/71 of 4 December 2009, the General Assembly recognized "the crucial role of international cooperation at the global, regional, sub regional and bilateral levels in combating, in accordance with international law, threats to maritime security, including piracy."
6. Edward R Lucas, "Public Goods, Club Goods, and Private Interests: The Role of Business Elites in British Counter-Piracy in the South China Sea, 1921-1935", Security Studies, 2019, p.7.
7. Ibid.
8. Richard Macauley, " Countries alongside the South China Sea and vessels sailing through the waters will receive better service", https://qz.com/527289/chinas-south-china-sea-island-building-is-for-the-public-good-says-china/ (accessed 23 January 2019)
9. "China Opens 'Rescue Center' in West Philippine Sea", https://www.rappler.com/nation/222353-china-opens-maritime-rescue-center-fiery-cross-reef-west-philippine-sea (accessed 14 February 2019)
10. "As Catch Reduces, Should Nations Close the High Seas to S\Fishing?", https://scroll.in/article/878380/as-catch-reduces-should-nations-close-the-high-seas-to-fishing (accessed 28 January 2018)
11. Ibid.

12. "Rival Pakistan Offers India Help", http://news.bbc.co.uk/2/hi/south_asia/1139807.stm (accessed 28 January 2018).
13. Vijay Sakhuja, "Offshore Energy Exploration: Risky, Yet Vital", https://icwa.in/pdfs/IBBP_Oil_spill.pdf (accessed 28 January 2018).
14. Jennifer D. P. Moroney, Stephanie Pezard, Laurel E. Miller, Jeffrey Engstrom and Abby Doll, "Lessons from Department of Defense Disaster Relief Efforts in the Asia-Pacific Region", RAND Corporation, 2013, https://www.jstor.org/stable/pdf/10.7249/j.ctt4cgdkv.10.pdf (accessed 28 January 2018).
15. Ibid.
16. "222 Believed Dead in Iran Earthquake", https://www.telegraph.co.uk/news/worldnews/middleeast/iran/1398270/222-believed-dead-in-Iran-earthquake.html (accessed 28 January 2018).
17. "Cyclones in Indian Seas", http://www.imdmumbai.gov.in/scripts/detail.asp?releaseId=E0000CY3 (accessed 15 February 2019).
18. For more details see http://vikaspedia.in/social-welfare/disaster-management-1/natural-disasters/cyclones (accessed 15 February 2019).
19. Pardeep Sahni, Alka Dhameja and Uma Medury, *Disaster Mitigation: Experiences and Reflections* (PHI Learning Pvt. Ltd., 2001) cited in Aparana Roy, "BIMSTEC and climate change: Setting a common agenda", https://www.orfonline.org/research/bimstec-climate-change-setting-common-agenda/#_edn13(accessed 15 February 2019).
20. For more details see https://www.wunderground.com/hurricane/deadlyworld.asp (accessed 15 February 2019).
21. "Angry France diverts Myanmar aid to Thailand", https://www.reuters.com/article/us-myanmar-cyclone-france/angry-france-diverts-myanmar-aid-to-thailand-idUSL254340520080525 (accessed 15 February 2019).
22. "India launches 'Operation Sahayata' in Nargis-hit Myanmar", https://www.oneindia.com/2008/05/07/india-launches-operation-sahayata-in-nargis-hit-myanmar-1210161790.html (accessed 15 February 2019).
23. Vijay Sakhuja, "Indian Naval Diplomacy: Post Tsunami", http://www.ipcs.org/focusthemsel.php?articleNo=1640 (accessed 15 February 2019).
24. For more details see "Safety and Shipping Review 2018", https://www.agcs.allianz.com/insights/white-papers-and-case-studies/safety-and-shipping-review-2018/(accessed 15 February 2019).
25. Vijay Sakhuja, " The Indian Ocean in 2015", http://www.ipcs.org/issue_briefs/issue_brief_pdf/SR167-Forecasts-IndianOcean.pdf (accessed 15 February 2019).
26. Vijay Sakhuja, "Indian Ocean and the IORA: Search and Rescue Operations", http://www.ipcs.org/comm_select.php?articleNo=4724 (accessed 15 February 2019).

9

Connectivity:
Shipping, Ports, Tourism and Digital

This chapter expounds on connectivity in the Bay of Bengal built around trade, tourism including culture, and the role of cutting-edge digital and disruptive technologies to augment connectivity. It begins by discussing very briefly the concept of 'connectivity ecosystem' relating to ships, ports, supply chain infrastructure including digital systems and processes that facilitate the use of the medium of sea for commerce, trade, people-to-people connection including transmission of culture and ideas. The chapter highlights connectivity projects that BIMSTEC can augment to harness the economic, strategic, social and cultural potential of the region.

Connectivity Ecosystem

A 'connectivity ecosystem' is a process which facilitates movement of goods and services that are transported onboard carriers which move on road, on the rails, in the air, over the seas, and through digital platforms including fibre optic cables. It is dynamic in nature and lies at the core of globalization which is the highpoint of current state of the global economy marked by economic prosperity.

A vibrant 'connectivity ecosystem' involves at least three stakeholders. First are the humans who travel using a variety of transports and facilitate people-to-people contacts which form the bedrock of cultural exchanges and interactions for sharing ideas and thoughts. These include numerous stakeholders such as cinema and television artists, musicians and dancers, media, sportspersons, etc. Furthermore, opinion makers and personalities too are important to facilitate interactions among civil society, educationists, intelligentsia, and people at large. It is useful to mention that professional bodies such as the bar councils, chambers of commerce, industry associations and business houses transact ideas and perspectives thus creating an ecosystem that positively impacts on decision making, opinion exchanges, business transactions and relations.

Second is the movement of goods, services and industries. In the maritime domain, globalization is best represented by the complex relationship between businesses which use the medium of the seas to deliver prosperity to states and its people. In this context, a maritime connectivity ecosystem involves infrastructure such as ports and shipping which facilitate trade, transfer and delivery of commodities and cargoes create a dynamic link between different stakeholders such as factories, logistics management firms, consolidators, truckers, tour operators, rail-road-air carriers, port terminal operators, ocean carriers, customs agents, financial and information services, and final recipient of goods and services to people. A complex interaction among these, individually or collectively, enables a booming maritime ecosystem.

Third is the use of digital technologies to enhance the efficiency and the productivity of the maritime trading systems. The marine-digital ecosystem built around physical infrastructure and cyber facilities provides the foundation for conduct of various activities and operations in the oceanic domain. The consolidated physical and cyber dimensions, referred to as Cyber-Physical System (CPS), are facilitated through a system of sensors or actuators and consist of diverse constituents that collaborate, i.e. the physical world with the virtual world of information processing through software systems, communications technology, and sensors/actuators including embedded technologies.

Another significant feature of the future trends in maritime infrastructure is characterized by cutting-edge science and technology in their operations through digital connectivity in which disruptive technologies (Big Data, Marine Cyber Physical Systems (MCPS), Artificial Intelligence (AI), Autonomous Systems, etc.) are upscaling the efficiency of the maritime connectivity ecosystem built around ships, ports and associated supply chains that connect the production hubs in the heartland to the oceans.

Bay of Bengal Physical Maritime Connectivity

Container Ports

In modern times, shipping containers have transformed the way goods are carried onboard ships. These boxes (20 feet and 40 feet) are multimodal and can be easily shifted to land-based transport. According to an estimate, transport of goods in container, by sea, accounts for almost 60 per cent of the total sea-borne trade in the world (in terms of value), and this represents the high usage of containers in the sea freight transportation.[1] There have also been improvements in the size of the container ships and some larger-sized vessels can carry over 10,000 containers. For instance, the OOCL Hong Kong can carry 21,413 TEU.[2] This has necessitated new ports with modern container handling capacity. Among the top 50 container ports, 13 are in China.[3] Among these, Singapore, Malaysia (Port Kelang and Tanjung Pelepas), Colombo, Sri Lanka are major combiner ports and the Bay of Bengal littoral countries engage in international commerce by trans-shipping through these ports. This is so due to the absence of many major container ports in the Bay region. However, Chennai port in India can handle fifth generation (5000-8000 TEUs) container vessels and few shipping lines make direct calls.[4] In early 2017, a direct container shipping service from Chennai to the US east coast was launched, which would result in voyage savings of 10 days.[5]

Three river ports, i.e. Kolkata in India, Chittagong in Bangladesh and Yangon in Myanmar can handle container traffic but shipping services through these ports are not highly profitable due to constraints imposed by geography. Vessels calling at these ports must travel up the river which adds to costs due to extra time and fuel costs. Vishakhapatnam and Kattupalli in India and Mongla in Bangladesh handle only small volumes of container traffic. Vishakhapatnam, with deep draft is closer to other major ports in the Bay such as Paradip, Kolkata, Haldia, Chittagong and Yangon, is popular and larger container vessels make port calls. It also serves Nepal-based container cargo.[6]

India's Sagarmala Programme features port-led development and some of its important facets are: (a) Port Modernization and New Port Development including new Greenfield ports; (b) Port Connectivity Enhancement with the hinterland to optimize cost and time of cargo movement through multi-modal logistics solutions including inland water transport and coastal shipping; (c) Port-linked Industrialization and development of Coastal Economic Zones and industrial clusters to reduce logistics cost and time international and domestic seaborne trade; and Coastal Community Development promoting sustainable development of coastal communities through skill development and livelihood generation activities, fisheries development, coastal tourism, etc. These involve nearly 600 projects in different coastal states and as of 30 September 2018, a total of 522 projects (costing around Rs. 4.32 Lac Crore) were under various stages of implementation, development and completion.[7]

Short Sea Shipping

The Bay of Bengal primarily features Short Sea Shipping involving liquid bulk (crude oil and petroleum products) and dry bulk (coal, iron ore, grains, bauxite, fertilizer). As noted above, container trade (merchandised goods) is quite low due to lack of infrastructure as also the manufacturing capacity of the countries around the Bay of Bengal. The RoRo and general cargo constitute less than 5 per cent the total seaborne trade in the Bay region.[8] In 2017, a consignment of motor vehicles belonging to M/s. Ashok Leyland Ltd was shipped from Chennai Port in India to Mongla port in Bangladesh onboard a roll on roll off (RoRo) cum general cargo vessel. This resulted in saving nearly two-three weeks of travel time.[9]

Similarly, India announced plans to link Chittagong port with its North Eastern states (Tripura with Chittagong port which is about 90 miles).[10] Currently, "Goods to North East are taken by rail and road from Mumbai or Chennai through Kolkata to Guwahati. If we are going to connect to Chittagong port, it will be an excellent connectivity,"[11] In 2018, a senior Indian political functionary stated that "South West China can use North East as hub to go to Indian Ocean through Chittagong and "Chinese groups like e-bike manufacturers, software and hardware firms showed interest to go to Assam to explore the opportunities.[12] It is worth mentioning that the Bangladesh, Bhutan, India and Nepal (BBIN) sub-regional network too can benefit from the short sea shipping operating in the Bay region.

In this context, the India-Bangladesh Coastal Shipping Agreement (CSA) is an important regional initiative and ensures direct movement of goods between India and Bangladesh which otherwise were being routed through Colombo or Singapore adding to freight charges (between US$1700–2400) which now are as little as US$ 400, and reduce travel times to 8-10 days (transit time earlier was 30-40 days).[13]

Issues of Cabotage

Cabotage is a process under which goods are transported or passengers are ferried between two places in the same country by a transport operator from another country. States adopt restrictive policies and generally do not permit foreign carriers to operate on local routes. In India, under Cabotage law only Indian-registered ships can operate on local routes for carrying cargo. In 2016, the Government relaxed the Cabotage rules allowing foreign registered ships to deploy between Indian ports albeit with fewer conditions. However, the Bay of Bengal countries are yet to harmonize their Cabotage rules to give impetus to Short Sea Shipping.

Other Connectivity Projects

The Bay can also be connected through two strategic waterways, i.e. Sethusamudram Canal Project (SSCP) between Southern India and Sri Lanka and the Kra Canal to the Arabian Sea and Gulf of Thailand. The SSCP project can reduce shipping time between Arabian Sea to the Bay of Bengal and vice versa by about 36 hours resulting in a net saving of over 400 nautical miles in terms of distance. This will also add to the growth of several minor ports along the passage. Similarly, the Isthmus of Kra or the Kra Canal can link Bay of Bengal to Gulf of Thailand. It envisages a channel across southern Thailand which will cut the shipping distance by at least 1,000 km but the project has been under discussion for several decades.[14]

The economic benefits of these connectivity projects are quite understandable but the impact on the fragile ecosystem in the Gulf of Mannar and the adjacent sea areas of the Kra canal in the Bay of Bengal and Gulf of Thailand are major issues of concern. Also, Kra has witnessed intense debate and discussion on issues relating to environment, economic as also on account of dividing Thailand on religious ground, i.e. Buddhist in the north of the canal and Muslims in the south have further precluded interest in Thailand.

Digital-Cyber Maritime Connectivity

At the heart of digital connectivity is fibre optic cable which crisscross across the seas and the oceans and carry large volumes of digital data to different destinations. The Bay of Bengal Gateway (BBG) is an 8,000 km long cable network which connects UAE, Oman, India, Sri Lanka, and Malaysia[15] and is operated by a consortium of AT&T, China Telecom, Dialog Axiata, Etisalat, Omantel, Reliance Jio Infocom, Telekom Malaysia, Telstra, Vodafone.[16] Although it passes through the Bay of Bengal, it does not make landfall in majority of the Bay littorals to provide services.

The Indian government has drawn plans to lay 2,300 km of optical fibre cable (OFC) across the Bay of Bengal linking Chennai in the Indian mainland and Port Blair in the Andaman and Nicobar (A&N) islands.[17] This 'Chennai

Andaman Nicobar Island' (CANI) cable system will have a speed of 100 Gigabit per second and "the primary purpose of the project is to support e-governance, e-commerce, education and socio-economic development in the A&N islands under 'Digital India', a flagship initiative announced by Prime Minister Modi to provide digital services across the country."[18] The project involves the state-owned Bharat Sanchar Nigam Limited (BSNL) and Japanese IT major NEC Technologies will implement the project,[19] and will "manufacture the optical submarine cable and provide technical assistance during the turnkey implementation" and the network will cover Long Island, Rangat, Havelock, Hut Bay in the Andaman group of islands, and Car Nicobar, Kamorta and Great Nicobar.

Energy Connectivity

Transmission of power (Direct Current (DC) and Alternate Current (AC)) is an important issue for energy connectivity and involves transmission of current through cables that lie on the seabed. First, AC is converted into DC and the High Voltage Direct Current (HVDC) can be transmitted over longer distance with less transmission losses as compared with the AC. There are several HVDC lines in operation across the globe and are in operation between surplus energy to deficient energy areas.[20] The current underwater HVDC market is small and such types of cables could grow in length, depth and capacity which can then be linked to other energy networks. India had proposed a South Asian power grid and a modest attempt was made to send HVDC from India's eastern electrical grid to Bangladesh's western grid, a project partly financed by the Asian Development Bank.[21]

Marine Leisure Industry

Coastal states harness natural geographic advantages of the seas and oceans and invest in the development of coastal and marine tourism. Bay of Bengal littoral countries are endowed with long coastlines, island territories with pristine beaches and their natural scenic beauty has resulted in several marine tourist destinations. Some of these have now been developed into modern recreational sites to include water sports, marine resorts and subsea recreation.

The Andaman & Nicobar (A&N) islands are an excellent tourism destination but have been selectively opened for tourism due to environmental and security concerns. India constituted the Islands Development Agency (IDA) in 2017 and in the first phase four islands, i.e. Smith, Ross, Aves, Long and Little Andaman, have been identified for holistic development which would add to the tourism potential of the in Andaman and Nicobar.[22]

Ecotourism is fast gaining popularity in Bangladesh. There are a number of popular beaches—Cox's Bazar beach and Kuakata beach; Neval beach, Patenga beach, Halishahar beach and Parki beach in Chittagong; and St. Martin's and Nijhum Deep in Sonadia are established tourist destinations.[23] Further, cruise shipping, recreational eco-diving, surfing, fishing, boating, mangrove ecotourism, etc., are potential growth sectors under the sector.[24] It has been noted that "Sustainable tourism around ecological sites can aim to trickle down funds to protect our rivers, coastlines and communities whose livelihood depends on a healthy marine ecosystem."[25]

Similarly, scuba diving, snorkelling and marine safaris are popular in Sri Lanka.[26] In 2015 costal tourism contributed US$ 2.2 billion to the national economy. The Bar Reef Marine Protected Area is estimated to provide livelihood options to over 15,000 people through tourism activities.[27]

Cruise Tourism

It is a neglected and overlooked industry in the Bay of Bengal and therefore most Cruise Liners bypass the region either to Southeast Asia (Malaysia, Singapore and Indonesia) or the Middle East. However, this is changing quite quickly, and the Indian government is conscious of infrastructure inadequacies and has a vision and plan for promotion of cruise tourism and increase sea arrivals to 1.2 million tourists by 2030-31.

Bangladesh is also finding mention in the international cruise destination map. In 2017, "Silver Discoverer", owned by Monaco-based luxury cruise line Silversea, with 95 foreign holidaymakers called at Cox's Bazar's Maheshkhali in Bangladesh. The voyage was titled "Colombo to Kolkata Asia Expedition Cruise,"[28] Major advancements in terms of facilities for immigration clearance of cruise tourists faster, e-permits for tour operators, so that the tourist can spend quality time on the shore are being developed. This will also encourage established cruise lines to dispatch more ships to these destinations as part of the sailing itinerary.

The Andaman and Nicobar Islands are closer to popular tourist destinations such as Phuket in Thailand and Langkawi in Malaysia, and by linking these tourist destinations through either air or cruise liners would add to the tourism potential of the Bay of Bengal.[29] For instance, the flying time between Port Blair, Andaman and Nicobar Islands is (a) to Bangkok: 2 hours; (b) to Phuket: 1.5 hours; (c) to Singapore: 3.5 hours; and (d) to Kolkata and Chennai: 2 hours.[30]

Marine Heritage Tourism

While marine tourism and recreation business is an established growth industry, an innovative initiative in the marine sector is marine heritage tourism. As noted in previous chapter, the Bay of Bengal has a rich maritime history which witnessed intermingling of cultures and shaped the destiny of the countries in the region. Port of call at destinations in Bangladesh, Myanmar, Thailand, Malaysia, Indonesia, and Sri Lanka Vietnam can potentially boost the domestic hospitality industry and services. These destinations need not be limited to the coastline itself but can be expanded to the hinterland to form a cultural heritage trail in the Bay of Bengal for experiencing cultural and natural heritage including UNESCO World Heritage Sites and Monuments.

Marine archeology, which may seem like an innocuous enough field, but underwater cultural sites such as shipwrecks or other sunken structures of ancient cities such as Poompuhar, the port capital of the Chola dynasty, can help to understand rich social, cultural and trading connections between India and Southeast Asia over the seas. Besides, the spinoffs for such an initiative would lead to technology cooperation in areas such as underwater imaging, satellite-based mapping of the ocean floor and carbon-dating submerged temples, port cities and ship wrecks. A dialogue among BIMSTEC members on marine archaeology and possibility of setting up a Monument and Archeology Fund could be a useful initiative.

Culture Tourism

Since ancient times, the waters of Bay of Bengal have facilitated cultural and religious exchanges among China, India and Southeast Asia. As noted in an earlier chapter of this volume, travellers and Buddhist Monks travelled to and from India by the sea route. Likewise, the Bay was also a maritime gateway for the east-west trade and ships from Rome, Egypt, Arabia, Persia, Malaya, Sumatra and China across the Bay.[31] Most of the shipping took the easterly/westerly route finally making land fall on the western shores of the Malay Peninsula at Kedah. Ships also sailed south from Nagapattinam along eastern shores to Ceylon before setting course south of Sumatra and making call at Palembang in Sumatra.

Landlocked Member Countries

Geography bestows coastal states several opportunities to participate in global seaborne trade. However, landlocked countries are deprived of such an opportunity and it is one of the several reasons for the low share of Landlocked Developing

Countries (LLDC) in world trade which adversely affects their development goals. In November 2014, the United Nations General Assembly adopted the Vienna Programme of Action (VPoA) for the sustainable development of LLDCs keeping in mind their geographical challenges and development needs.[32]

There are currently 48 countries designated by the United Nations as "least developed countries" (LDCs) and one Bay of Bengal littoral, i.e. Myanmar is an LDC. In the context of India, its northeast region, is also landlocked and accesses the port of Kolkata/Haldia for sea-based commercial activity. Besides, Bhutan and Nepal, benefit from access to Indian ports. The 1971 Transit Treaty between India and Nepal allows the latter to engage in international sea borne commerce through the port of Kolkata/Haldia.

Bay of Bengal maritime connectivity projects and initiatives serve as a maritime bridgehead and help overcome the tyranny of geography particularly for Nepal and Bhutan and hinterland areas of Northeast India that are far from the ports and are unable to participate in seaborne commerce and contribute to national growth. In this context, it will be useful to include the ongoing connectivity projects such as the Mekong-India Economic Corridor (MIEC), the India-Myanmar-Thailand Trilateral Highway, Kaladan Multi-Modal Transit Transport Project (KMMTTP) connecting Sittwe Port in Myanmar with Kolkata port in India, road connectivity from Zorinpuri, Mizoram, India to Sittwe port, Myanmar. Other connectivity initiatives such as the 2800-km long Bangladesh-China-India-Myanmar (BCIM) that connects Kolkata, Silchar, Imphal (India), Dhaka (Bangladesh), Mandalay (Myanmar), Boashan and Kunming (China) are good candidates for the BIMSTEC Maritime Connectivity initiatives. These can be integrated into the BIMSTEC initiatives on transport and logistics infrastructure to enable BIMSTEC Member States the access to external markets including identification of relevant "hard" and "soft" infrastructure projects whose realization would enhance BIMSTEC connectivity and trade.[33]

Port Cities Cooperation Network and Sister Port

Another important feature of maritime connectivity in the Bay of Bengal can be through Port Cities Cooperation Network. This can be built around 'memorandums of understandings' which serve as a fertile ground for promoting tourism, cultural exchanges and people-to people contacts. Such an arrangement can potentially create conditions for a mutually beneficial exchange of best business practices and exposure to modern technology; above all it could be the trigger for capacity building to enhance port productivity and contribute to technology development.

Conclusion

Bay of Bengal littoral countries possess enormous geographical advantages to participate in international commerce but are constrained due to technological capabilities. A regional maritime infrastructure development plan merits attention and which can be built through sharing technological knowledge and engaging in collaborative capacity-building projects. Unlike infrastructure, the littoral countries enjoy cultural advantages to pursue people-to-people connection through transmission of culture and ideas. A common region-wide digital development plan to improve connectivity across the Bay of Bengal by sharing knowledge and technical capacity through collaborative ventures would also be advantageous. A regional governance framework for short sea shipping and port development projects can help harness the potential of the commercial value of the Bay of Bengal.

The study would now discuss economic regionalisation in the Bay of Bengal.

NOTES

1. "Shipping Containers Market - Segmented by Size, Type, and Geography - Growth, Trends, and Forecast (2018–2023)", https://www.mordorintelligence.com/industry-reports/shipping-containers-market (accessed 31 March 2019).
2. "Top 10 World's Largest Container Ships In 2019", https://www.marineinsight.com/know-more/top-10-worlds-largest-container-ships-in-2019/ (accessed 31 March 2019).
3. "Top 50 World Container Ports", http://www.worldshipping.org/about-the-industry/global-trade/top-50-world-container-ports(accessed 31 March 2019).
4. Vijay Sakhuja, "Short Sea Shipping in Bay of Bengal Takes Baby Steps", http://www.ipcs.org/comm_select.php?articleNo=5386(accessed 31 March 2019).
5. "Chennai-U.S. direct container shipping service launched", https://www.thehindu.com/todays-paper/tp-national/tp-tamilnadu/Chennai-U.S.-direct-container-shipping-service-launched/article14735265.ece (accessed 19 January 2019).
6. "Indian Container Market Report 2017", http://www.containersindia.in/pdf/CI%20REPORT-2017.pdf (accessed 12 January 2019).
7. Ibid. (accessed 31 March 2019).
8. Vijay Sakhuja, "Short Sea Shipping in Bay of Bengal Takes Baby Steps", http://www.iorgroup.net/new-blog/2017/12/4/short-sea-shipping-in-bay-of-bengal-takes-baby-steps-vijay-sakhuja (accessed 25 November 2018).
9. Press Release, "Shri Nitin Gadkari digitally flags off RORO Ship carrying trucks from Chennai Port to Mongla Port in Bangladesh; Transport by Sea to Save 15-20 Days of Travel Time", Press Information Bureau, Government of India, Ministry of Shipping, 28 October 2017.
10. K J M Varma, "India Plans to Connect North East with Bangladesh's Chittagong Port: Madhav", http://www.businessworld.in/article/India-plans-to-connect-North-East-with-Bangladesh-s-Chittagong-port-Madhav-/15-08-2018-157922/ (accessed 16 January 2019).
11. Ibid.
12. Ibid.

13. Rahul, Karan, "Acting Beyond Borders - An Action Plan for Reorienting BIMSTEC", https://www.c3sindia.org/wp-content/uploads/2018/10/Acting-Beyond-Borders.pdf (accessed 18 January 2019).
14. Vijay Sakhuja, "Chinese New Infrastructure Projects Worry India", *South Asia Defence and Strategic Review*, Volume 9, Issue 1, Mar - Apr 2015, p. 32.
15. "The Bay of Bengal Gateway (BBG) ", https://www.bayofbengalgateway.com/ (accessed 25 January 2019).
16. Ibid.; also see http://www.fiberatlantic.com/system/wprWw (accessed 25 January 2019).
17. T K Rohit, "Andamans to get undersea cable", https://www.thehindu.com/news/national/tamil-nadu/andamans-to-get-undersea-cable/article25815283.ece (accessed 25 January 2019).
18. Vijay Sakhuja, "Digital Connectivity in the Andaman and Nicobar Islands", https://www.eurasiareview.com/18072018-digital-connectivity-in-the-andaman-and-nicobar-islands-analysis/ (accessed 25 January 2019).
19. "BSNL, Japanese IT Major NEC Ink Submarine Cable Deal to Connect Chennai, Andaman", http://www.newindianexpress.com/business/2018/jul/11/bsnl-japanese-it-major-nec-ink-submarine-cable-deal-to-connect-chennai-andaman-1841899.html (accessed 25 January 2019).
20. For instance, Italy and Greece (160 kilometers), Victoria-Tasmania (300 kilometers), New Jersey – Long Island (82 kilometers) and the Transbay cable (Pittsburg, California – San-Francisco) are good examples of HVDC. The NorNed cable runs for about 580 kilometers and the Dutch consumers receive hydropower generated in Norway during daytime peak demand hours and there is a reverse process too in which Norway can draw power from Dutch coal-burning power plants. According to cable maker ABB, the increased efficiency produced by the linkage reduces carbon dioxide emissions by nearly 1.7 million tons annually.
21. "India Electricity Flows to Bangladesh in First South Asian HVDC Cross-border Link", https://www.adb.org/news/india-electricity-flows-bangladesh-first-south-asian-hvdc-cross-border-link (accessed 31 March 2019).
22. "Union Home Minister Chairs First Meeting of Islands Development Agency (IDA)", *Press Information Bureau*, Ministry of Home Affairs, Government of India, 24 July 2017.
23. "The Role of Marine Tourism in IORA: The Pathways Ahead", https://www.iora.int/media/23919/cios-prof-attri-presentation.pdf (accessed 31 March 2019).
24. Ibid.
25. Samia Tamrin Ahmed, "Global Goals and Greener Travel", https://www.thedailystar.net/opinion/environment/global-goals-and-greener-travel-1468096 (accessed 28 February 2019).
26. Ibid.
27. Ibid.
28. "International cruise ship arrives in Cox's Bazar", *Dhaka Tribune*, 22 February 2017.
29. "Incredible Islands of India: Holistic Development", http://niti.gov.in/writereaddata/files/document_publication/IslandsDev.pdf (accessed 28 February 2019).
30. Ibid.
31. Radha Kumud Mookerji, *Indian Shipping: A History of the Sea-borne Trade and Maritime Activity of the Indians from the Earliest Times*, (Bombay: Longmans, Green and Co, 1912).
32. "UN Office of the High Representative for the Least Developed Countries, Landlocked Developing Countries and Small Island Developing States", http://unohrlls.org/about-lldcs/programme-of-action/ (accessed 23 March 2019).
33. "Infrastructure And Logistics Study Final Report Updating And Enhancement: Final Report", https://think-asia.org/bitstream/handle/11540/8660/updating-bimstec-transport-logistics-study.pdf?sequence=1 (accessed 23 March 2019).

10

Economic Regionalisation:
Trends and Challenges

Bay of Bengal Initiative for Multi-Sectoral Technical and Economic Cooperation (BIMSTEC) is a regional organisation of seven nations hemmed around the Bay of Bengal that has shared bonds of culture, trade and heritage for over two millennia. At a time when Europeans were locked in Thucydides trap, building galleys for war, the Bay of Bengal community was riding the monsoon winds, prospering and enriching their civilisational ties. For most part of human history this region and East Asia were the centres of economic power. However, European colonisation erased the skills of its economic astuteness. As a result, despite possessing the critical mass by population (22.43 percent of the world), Bay of Bengal region contributes only 4 percent to the world's GDP. The prospects of re-emerging as an economic power will require these nations to bind their aspirations and blend their destinies, as it was in the past. The silver-lining is that today this region constitutes some of the fastest-growing economies; each prospering by their own esteem to integrate with the world, oblivious of the strength in their unified voice. This is partly due to the geo-economic eddies of our time, but largely attributable to sclerotic domestic systems that has fraught most nations from within. Intra-regional trade is often taken as a measure for economic integration. By that yardstick, States of the Bay of Bengal region is being allured more by the world outside, than by their intrinsic strengths.

Economic Regionalism

The role of regionalism in accelerating development is contentious. Between 1950s and 1970s theories of Customs Union provided analytical framework for regional integration, trade creation and diversion. Protective Regionalism was another dominant economic theory prevalent between 1950s and 1980s and practiced in Africa and Latin America. But the success of economic reforms in East Asia in the 1980s resulted from abandoning closed regionalism that used to be based on import substitution and trade barriers for development. It got replaced by the concepts of open regionalism based on openness of trade, knowledge and capital flows. In the end, trade theory prevailed upon development theory in defining regionalism. It also marked the victory of markets over command economy. The surge of regionalism post-1990 is reframing the global order. The debate about regionalism is less about integration and more about: (a) the kind of regionalism that is appropriate in the prevailing global regime; (b) rapid globalisation of markets, production and capital flows; and (c) breakdown of bipolarity that governed global security between 1945 and 1990. The troika of these related phenomena poses diverse challenges for developing regions in the twenty-first century. In developing countries, regionalism is not merely an adaptive response to globalisation, but also a mechanism to cope with hegemony and unilateralism. There is a growing sense that unless the developing world reshapes itself into powerful regional economic blocs, it is unlikely to have a say in the world order.[1]

Gains from Economic Regionalisation

Some of the major gains that motivate economic regionalisation are:[2]

(a) *Expands market size*: It offers opportunities to domestic firms for enlarging markets in neighbouring countries and harnesses the benefits of economy of scale. This is especially useful for landlocked and smaller countries that have small domestic markets of their own. Other attendant benefits are improvement of efficiency, infusion of new technologies for production and increase in competitiveness.

(b) *Elevates FDI flows*: It has the potential of attracting more FDI from within the region than from the outside. FDIs supplement domestic investments and improve the prospects of development and growth.

(c) *Escalates trade efficiency*: It allows formulation of better micro-policies and enhances trade efficiency, than is usually provided by the WTO regulations. It helps formulation of customised policies for local trade exchanges across the borders on issues related to trade tariffs, non-trade

tariffs, technological assistance, single window facilities and labour migration.
(d) *Ensures government credibility*: Credibility of governments can be enhanced by successful execution of economic elements of Sustainable Development Goals (SDGs), especially with respect to goals on mitigation of poverty (Goal 1), reduction of hunger (Goal 2), gender equality (Goal 5), decent work and economic growth (Goal 8), alleviation of inequalities (Goal 10) and partnership (Goal 17).
(e) *Enhances bargaining power*: Enhances the capacity of contiguous countries to deal with common challenges with regard to resources. For example, water and environment issues can be collectively taken up by countries to oppose unilateral developments undertaken by upper riparian states like China or bring international pressure for transparent norms. These have direct and indirect consequences on economic well-being. It also helps exact better visibility and bargain for the region in international trade negotiations.
(f) *Enables security*: Any increase in trade, investments and people-to-people (P2P) contact fosters deeper trust and increases opportunity cost for conflict. Consequently, it enhances peace, stability and security of the region.

Economic Trends in Bay of Bengal Region

To understand economic trends in Bay of Bengal region, it is necessary to determine the economic parameters and ratio of trade within the region, *vis-à-vis* the aggregate trade of individual countries. According to UN's 'Comtrade' data for 2017, the seven states of the region had an aggregate trade of US$ 1.35 trillion with the world, which has grown steadily year-on-year (y-o-y). However, trade within the region has been quite insignificant, i.e. US$ 38.39 billion, amounting to barely 2.8 percent of their overall trade.[3] In contrast, according to a World Bank estimate, the intra-regional trade of other regions is significantly higher and stands at 60, 35 and 25 percent for European Union, Asia Pacific and ASEAN respectively.[4] It is evident from this analysis that the Bay of Bengal region lacks basic drivers of economic interdependence and barely satisfy the parameters of regionalisation.

It is essential to understand the economic structure of each of these countries to decipher their cross-linkages. Accordingly, data sets were drawn from the Asian Development Bank (ADB) and country-wise UN 'Comtrade' database for analysis (Appendix A). Relevant inferences on the economic trends of the Bay of Bengal region are as below:

(a) Workforce in most countries is gravitating from agricultural sectors to the services sector. There is greater emphasis on removal of trade restrictiveness on the service sector. The industrial sector has been stagnant in most countries since 2001, which is a cause for concern, but also provides windows of opportunity.

(b) Barring a few exceptions, regional countries are not the top import source or export destination amongst themselves. Their low trade volumes can be attributed to causes such as tariff barriers, non-tariff barriers (NTB), transaction cost, and trust deficit. Some of these challenges have been elaborated later in this chapter.

(c) The nature of major goods exchanged between the Bay of Bengal countries (tabulated at Appendix A) reveal that there exists immense potential for structuring multiple regional value chains (RVC). This would result in economic prosperity and provide better bargaining power to the region in the international market. A few options will be examined in the Chapter.

Challenges of intra-regional Trade between Bay of Bengal States

When WTO member countries enter into a regional trade agreement (RTA), they grant more favourable conditions to their respective region at the expense of other WTO members. Such departure is permitted by WTO, provided they are conducted within the framework of Article XXIV of GATT 1994 and Article 5 of GATS. Regions are also permitted to form RTAs under free trade agreements (FTA), partial trade agreements (PTA), customs union, (CU) and economic integration agreement (EIA).[5] RTAs provide opportunity for unlocking the untapped trade potential and dismantling trade barriers. As on 18 December 2018 there were 308 RTAs in force worldwide.[6] The current volume of Bay of Bengal intra-regional trade is barely 2.8 percent of its overall trade with the world and is in itself an indicator of the immense gap between its potential and practice. This trend is not unusual, given the discriminatory barriers imposed by countries on each other. As a result, high levels of informal trade persist, causing losses to the exchequer. Another hurdle for intraregional trade has been the disproportionately high cost of trade, which leads to substitutions of exports outside the region.[7] Various challenges faced by traders for conducting intra-regional trade are:

Tariff barriers: Bay of Bengal countries had agreed to adopt FTA way back in 2004, with Bangladesh being the last country to consent. Formal institutions have already been set up under the framework of Trade Negotiations Committee

(TNC) and two working groups, i.e. Working Group on Rules of Origin (WGRoO) and Working Group on Dispute Settlement Mechanism (WGDSM). Nonetheless, it is unlikely that Bangladesh, Bhutan, Nepal and Myanmar will consent to a regional FTA regime till they enjoy the concessions of Least Developed Countries (LDC). LDC rate of tariffs accrue considerable advantage to them over others in the region when trading with the large western markets.

Five out of the seven Bay of Bengal countries (excluding Myanmar and Thailand) are also covered under the South Asian Free Trade Agreement (SAFTA), which came into effect in 2006. However, SAFTA has been largely unsuccessful in liberalizing trade due to multitude of denial regimes like Sensitive List and para-tariffs imposed by most countries. In Bangladesh and Sri Lanka, 44–45 percent imports from South Asian states fall under the sensitive list and 39 percent of India's exports to South Asia fall under the sensitive list. In effect para-tariffs are import duties by other name. For example, if para-tariffs are included, the average tariff in Bangladesh would double to 25.6 percent and in Sri Lanka the overall tariffs increase from 10.8 percent to 22.4 percent. In contrast, the ASEAN FTA has managed to eliminate intra-regional trade duties to over 89 percent of products.[8] In other words, BIMSTEC is a melting pot of both the extremes. While, Myanmar and Thailand enjoy the benefits of ASEAN FTA between them, the balance five nations are victims of sensitive list and para-tariffs.

High Cost of Trade

Competitiveness of products is adversely affected by high costs of trade as a result of poor transportation, ineffective logistical infrastructure, inefficient customs, and poor border administration. These are disproportionately high in South Asian countries of the BIMSTEC grouping. For example, the average cost of trade between South Asian countries is 20 percent higher than the ASEAN nations.[9] Interestingly, trading with some countries within BIMSTEC is costlier than that with Brazil. The unit of measurement for plotting the histogram below is the ad valorem equivalent trade costs in percent, which includes transport costs, tariffs, costs at customs, and so on.[10] It can be deducted from Figure 10.1 that the average trade cost between Bangladesh and Nepal is 326 percent, which is higher than the trade cost between Bangladesh and Brazil of 243 percent. Similarly, the average cost of trade between Sri Lanka and Nepal is 332 percent. In contrast the trade cost between Sri Lanka and Brazil is 269 percent.

Figure 10.1: Average cost of Intra and Inter-regional trade cost 2010–15

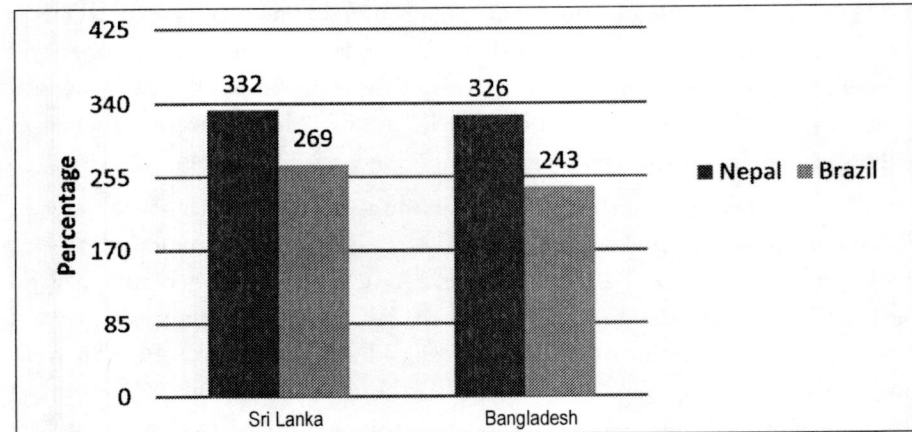

Source : Author, based on UNESCAP-WB trade cost data. (Accessed on 18 December 2018) https:// www.unescap.org/resources/escap-world-bank-trade-cost-database

Connectivity

Connectivity is a major contributor to trade cost. Inefficient air travel can impact freight of high-value/low-volume goods, health care, education travel and tourism. Services sector has become an important element of regional trade and investment. The World Bank (WB) has developed logistics performance index (LPI) of 180 countries. It constitutes both quantitative and qualitative measures to determine logistics friendliness of a country. A graph at Figure 10.2 has been generated based on WB data on LPI of the BIMSTEC countries from 2010 to 2018.[11] The graph shows that India and Thailand are more logistically friendly for trade than other members of BIMSTEC.

Non-Tariff Measures

Non-tariff measures (NTMs) are defined by United Nations Conference on Trade and Development (UNCTAD) as policy measures other than ordinary customs tariff that can potentially have an economic effect on international trade, changing qualities of trade or price or both. NTMs are legitimate tariffs to protect customers, plants and animal lives and are broadly categorised into three classifications: (a) import non-technical measures; (b) import technical measures; and (c) exports. Technical measures include issues such as sanitary and phytosanitary standards (SPS) and pre-shipment inspection. Non-technical measures include intellectual property rights (IPR), distribution restrictions, subsidies, rules of origin (RoO) etc.[12]

Figure 10.2: Logistics Performance Index Ranks 2010-2018

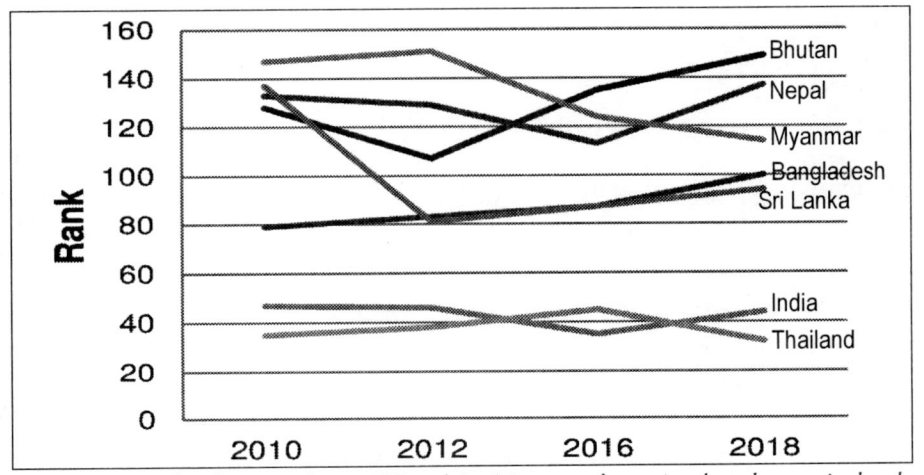

Source: Author, based on LPI date on WB website (Note: two data points have been arrived at by averaging to normalise the graph and no data was available for 2014)

According to a report, technical measures account for 85 percent NTMs in South Asia. Port restrictions is another NTM that traders often face in South Asia, especially when restricted list of items are not allowed through certain ports due to lack of adequate testing facilities with the port customs. For example, Bangladesh does not permit export of vulcanized rubber, yarn, milk powder, fish, sugar and potatoes through its check post at Agartala-Akhaura corridor. Similarly, India does not permit Bangladesh to export ceramics and electronic goods through Dawki-Tamabil corridor.[13] Several public and private laboratories have been accredited by National Accreditation Board for Testing and Calibration Laboratories (India) (NABL) to test food items in India. However, due to lack of awareness, traders only approach Central Food Laboratory, Kolkata, leading to backlogs and delays. Ad hoc and inconsistent testing measures are being adopted at various customs posts at the borders and ports. Such NTMs encourage illegal trade, resulting in loss to exchequer and affect businesses of small and medium enterprises (SME).

Trust Deficit

Trade creates economic interdependencies between countries and increases stakes in peace and stability, thus lowering the risks for conflict and war. Absence of geopolitical reasons is an advantage in BIMSTEC. However, India's large size and economic clout is an overbearing reason for trust deficit and concomitant tariffs. This can be overcome by P2P contact through trades at the 'border haats'.

Prospects

Use of tariffs quotas, non-tariff measure, sensitive lists, strict rules of origin, restrict liberalisation of intra-regional trade. In the backdrop of the aforesaid, a concerted effort has to be made by the BIMSTEC Senior Trade/Economic Officials Meeting (STOEM) and the Senior Officials Meeting (SOM) to address the following:

(a) Time bound schedule for reduction of sensitive lists.
(b) Para-tariffs to be eliminated to the extent possible.
(c) Tariffs of non-sensitive items to be progressively eliminated.
(d) Reduce logistics costs.
(e) Increase people to people contact through border haats.
(f) Awareness should be generated on accredited labs by NABL.
(g) Interpretation of rules by the customs department across borders need to be standardised.
(h) Electronic data exchange to be installed at border points through single window system.
(i) ROO negotiations need to be expedited by the BIMSTEC working group.

Conclusion

The Bay of Bengal region registered an aggregate trade of US$ 1.35 trillion with the world in the year 2017. However, the intra-regional trade has been an insignificant US$ 38.39 billion, amounting to barely 2.8 percent of the overall trade. In contrast, the levels of intraregional trade in other regions are quite high. Despite the lack of integration between Bay of Bengal countries, they are one of the fastest growing economies. Global economic linkages benefit big and medium businessmen. But, smaller businessmen, capable of doing cross-border trade get left out from the growth story. Regional economic integration can be achieved only when smaller businessmen in border states succeed alongside big business houses. Border trade between Ireland and North Ireland (UK) provides a salutary example.

Having examined the trends and challenges of economic regionalisation in the Bay of Bengal in this Chapter, the next Chapter will examine the aspects of economic corridors, regional value chain and gender sensitivity in border trade.

APPENDIX A

Trends and Structure of Economy – Bay of Bengal Countries

Bhutan

Bhutan has a GDP of US$ 2.512 bn[14] and a total population of 727145 as on 2017. 332099 are employed as labour force, with an employment rate of 97.6 percent. While 43 percent of the labour force is employed in agriculture, the percentage contribution of this sector has declined steadily from 26 percent in 2001 to 17.3 percent in 2016. On the other hand, 66036 people employed in the industrial sector correspond to 19.8 percent of the country's population and contributes 43 percent to the GDP. There has been a sudden spurt in employment in the construction sector and concomitant reduction in other sectors. The Agriculture sector had witnessed an average growth of 2.5 percent, Industry sector at 9.4 percent and Services sector at 8.4 percent, in comparison to GDP growth of 7.7 percent for a period of 16 years between 2001 and 2016.[15] India, Bangladesh and Germany are three major export destinations and the top exports of Bhutan in 2017 have been electricity, ferro-silicon, cardamoms, cement, dolomite, carbides, boulders and plastics. The major import sources have been India, Korea, Japan, Thailand and China and the top imports have been fuel, cars, transport parts, ferrous products, hydro-turbine parts, rice, machinery and coke.

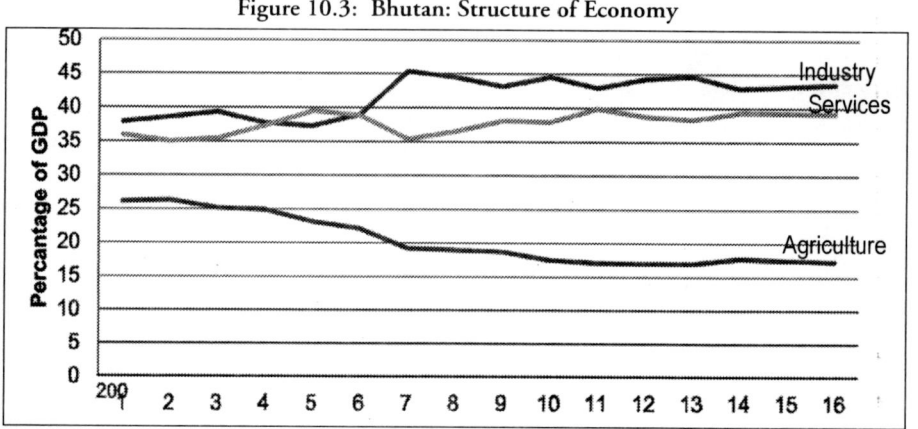

Figure 10.3: Bhutan: Structure of Economy

Source: Author, based on ADB[16]

The detailed breakdown is available on the Ministry of External Affairs site.[17]

The breakdown of major products traded intra-regionally with Bhutan for the year 2017 is tabulated as follows (Table 10.1).

Table 10.1: Major products traded intra-regionally with Bhutan in 2017

Country	Exports to	Value Nu M	Imports from	Value Nu M
India	Electricity, ferro-silicon, cardamoms, cement, dolomite, carbides, boulders, plastics	31618	Fuel, cars, transport parts, ferrous products, hydro-turbine parts, rice, machinery, coke	53973
Bangladesh	Boulders, pebbles, cardamom, oranges, ferro-alloy, lime stone, dolomite, steel, plasters	3486.27	Fruit juice, garments, confectionaries, table ware, rice, soap, sugar, aluminum structures	329.18
Thailand	Corecycep Senensis, natural honey, assorted tea	33.63	(87) Vehicles & spares, ovens, polymers, machinery & spares, laptops, milk, polymer,	1295.97
Nepal	Gypsum products, coal, limestone, Incense poe,	321.21	Garments, pasta, registers, calculators, metal statutes & gongs, footwear, silk fabric, sails & boards, coffee, electrical transformers and converters	64.58
Sri Lanka[18]	Beverage, spirits, vinegar	0.47	Metal products, aluminum, furnishing, lamps, prefab buildings, rubber articles, electric equipment, TV, recorder parts	0.47
Myanmar	-	0.08	-	0.08

Bangladesh

Bangladesh population is of 167.2 million as on 2017 and its GDP is US$ 249.724 billion.[19] Nearly 40 percent of the labour force is employed in agriculture, the percentage contribution of this sector has declined steadily from 24.1 percent in 2001 to 14.2 percent in 2017. On the other hand, people employed in the industrial sector and the services sector corresponds to 12.4 and 46.6 percent of the country's population and contributes 29.3 and 56.5 percent to the GDP respectively. The agriculture sector had witnessed an average growth of 3.7 percent, industry sector at 8.5 percent and services sector at 5.9 percent, in comparison to GDP growth of 6.1 percent for a period of 17 years between 2001 and 2017.[20]

The United States, United Kingdom and Germany were the three major export destinations in 2018 and the top export goods to 185 countries in the Q3 of 2018 included products of fish, vegetables, rice, edible oil, confectionaries, medicaments, plastic, leather, paper, cotton, meat, dairy, tea, coffee, spices, cotton, cereals, nuts, chemicals and garments.[22] Q3 export data of Bangladesh provides a fair insight into the trends in its exports. The gross export of goods and services for the year

Figure 10.4: Bangladesh: Structure of Economy

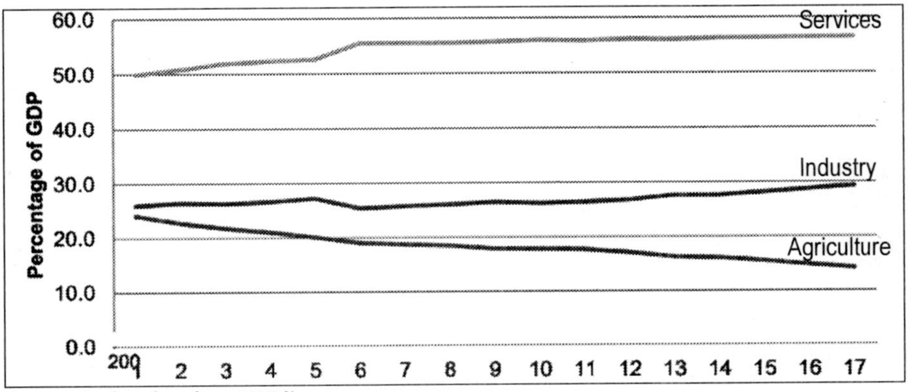

Source: Author, based on ADB[21]

ending June 2017 was Tk 2691.6 bn and gross imports in goods and services were Tk 3441.0 billion.[23] Twenty-six item codes have been declared as controlled goods and are prohibited from importing into Bangladesh.[24] The import sources were China, India and Singapore. The breakdown of major categories of products traded intra-regionally with Bangladesh for the year ending June 2017 is tabulated as follows (Table 10.2).

Table 10.2: Major products traded intra-regionally with Bangladesh in June 2017

Country[25, 26]	Export to	Value[27] US$ M	Imports from	Value[16] US$ M
India	Vegetable textile fiber, paper yarn, apparels, lead product, fish	591	Cotton, (87) vehicles and spares, (84) boilers, machinery, cereals, mineral fuel	7210
Bhutan*	Fruit juice, garments, confectionaries, table ware, rice, soap, sugar, aluminum structures	5.17	Boulders, pebbles, cardamom, oranges, ferro-alloy, lime stone, dolomite, steel, plasters	54.73
Thailand#	Apparels, fertilizer, textile, leather	56.22	Plastics, salt, sulphur, lime, cement, tanning extracts, (84) boilers, machinery	932.77
Nepal	Vegetable preps, textile fiber, sugar, confectionaries, electric equipment, TV, recorder, pharma products	9.77	Vegetables, roots, food industry, textile, miscellaneous edible preps, oil seeds, industrial or medical lants, straw, fodder	38.88
Sri Lanka	Pharma products, (84) boiler machinery, machinery, Vegetable roots, electrical machinery, textile fiber, paper yarn	43.57	Plastic, cotton, mineral fuel, fabric, soap, organic agents, wax, bituminous substances	127.71@
Myanmar	Pharma products, tools, implements, cutlery, Vegetable fiber, textile, apparels	23.8	Cereals, fish products, vegetable, tuber roots, iron or steel articles, lead articles	128.85

Notes: (*) conversion rate of US$1 = 63.74 Bhutan Nu on December 07, 2017
(#) Data of year 2016
(@) Includes re-exported data

Nepal

Nepal has a GDP of US $ 24.472 bn[28] and a total population of 28.7 million as on 2017. Contribution of the agriculture sector to the GDP in 2017 was 29.4 percent, a decline from 36.6 percent in the year 2001. The contribution of the industry sector also has depreciated from 17.3 percent in 2001 to 14.6 percent in 2017. On the other hand, the services sector has appreciated from 46.1 percent to 56 percent in 2017. India, the Unites States, and Germany were the three major export destinations of 2017 and India, China and UAE were the major source of imports.[29]

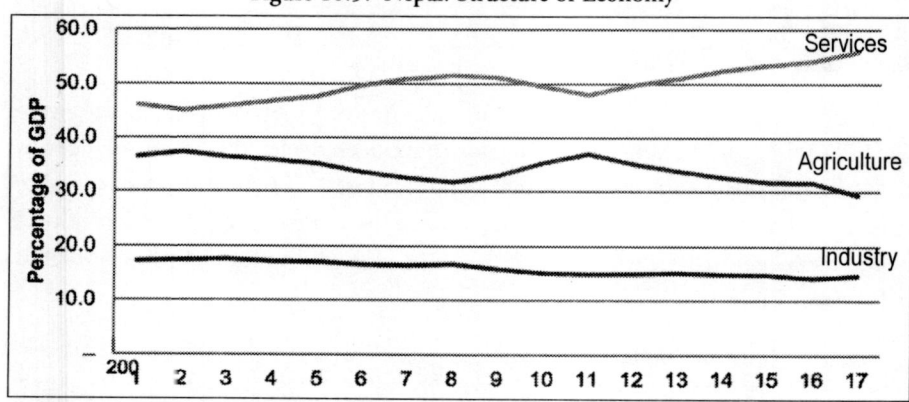

Figure 10.5: Nepal: Structure of Economy

Source: Author, Based on ADB[30]

The breakdown of major categories products traded intra-regionally with Nepal for the year ending June 2017 is tabulated as follows (Table 10.3):

Table 10.3: Major products traded intra-regionally with Nepal in June 2017

Country[31, 32]	Export to	Value[33] US $ M	Imports from	Value[22] US $ M
India	Coffee, tea, spices, preps of vegetables, fruits, nuts, iron, steel, man-made filaments, textile, fibers	420.18	Mineral fuel, iron, steel, bituminous, wax, (87) vehicles, rail & tram stocks, (84), boiler, machinery, cereals	6519.7
Bhutan	Gypsum products, coal, limestone, Incense poe,	8.258	Boulders, pebbles, cardamom, oranges, ferro-alloy, lime stone, dolomite, steel, plasters	0.538
Thailand	Meat, apparel, edible preps, hides and skins, carpets	0.42	Plastics, beverage, vinegar, fiber, (87) vehicles, rail, tram parts, (84) boilers, machinery	107.96

Country[31, 32]	Export to	Value[33] US $ M	Imports from	Value[22] US $ M
Bangladesh	Vegetables, roots, food industry, textile, miscellaneous edible preps, oil seeds, industrial or medical plants, straw, fodder	38.88	Vegetable preps, textile fiber, sugar, confectionaries, electric equipment, TV, recorder, pharma products	9.77
Sri Lanka	Measuring, checking, optical & cinematography, medical & surgical instruments, art work, textile, musical instrument, appeals	0.097	Chemical products nec, electrical equipment, TV and recorder parts, aluminum & articles, coffee, tea, spices, paper & products	2.05
Myanmar	Pharma products, fiber, textile, rags	0.009	Vegetable, tuber roots, wood & articles, coffee, tea, spices, ships, boats, electrical machinery, TV and recorder parts,	32.55

Sri Lanka

Sri Lanka has a GDP of US $ 87.175 billion[34] and a total population of 21.4 million as on 2017. Contribution of the agriculture sector to the GDP in 2017 was 8.5 percent, a decline from 16.8 percent in the year 2001. The contribution of the industry sector has remained almost steady at 30 percent between since 2001 and 2017. On the other hand, the services sector has appreciated from 52.5 in 2001 to 61.5 percent in 2017. The United States, India and United Kingdom remained the three major export destinations for the year 2017 and India, China and UAE were the major source of imports.[35]

Figure 10.6: Sri Lanka: Structure of Economy

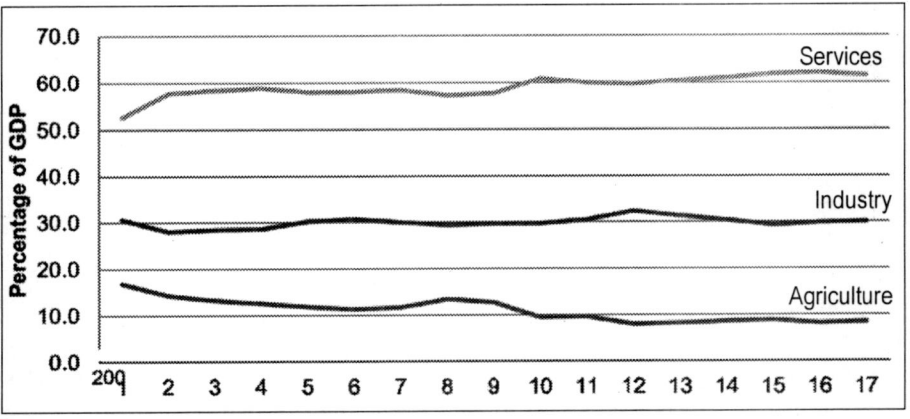

Source: Author, based on ADB [36]

The breakdown of major categories of products traded intra-regionally with Sri Lanka for the year ending June 2017 is tabulated below (Table 10.4):

Table 10.4: Major products traded intra-regionally with Sri Lanka in June 2017

Country[37, 38]	Export to	Value[39] US$ M	Imports from	Value[28] US$ M
India@	Coffee, tea, spices, mineral fuel, food industry, prep animal fodder, arms and ammunition, fruits, nuts, peel of citrus fruit or melons	889.63	Mineral fuel, iron, steel, bituminous, wax, (87) vehicles, rail & tram stocks, salt, sulphur, lime, cement, cereals	4494.06
Bhutan	Metal products, aluminum, furnishing, lamps, prefab buildings, rubber articles, electric equipment, TV, recorder parts	0.305	Beverage, spirits, vinegar	0.000013
Thailand@	Pearls, semi-precious stones, precious metals, (84) boiler, machinery, milling industry products, malt, starch, inulin, gluten, Fish, mollusks, aquatic invertebrates, electric equipment, TV, recorder parts	55.39	Fish, mollusks, aquatic invertebrates, salt, sulphur, earths, stone, lime, cement, (84) boiler, machinery, rubber articles, sugar & confectionaries	518.322
Bangladesh@	Plastic articles, cotton, mineral fuel, wax, fabric, soap, lubricants, dental wax	127.71	Vegetable, tuber, textile fiber, electric equipment, TV, recorder, pharma products, (84) boiler, machinery, paper yarn	43.57
Nepal	Measuring, checking, optical & cinematography, medical & surgical instruments, art work, textile, musical instrument, appeals	2.05	Chemical products nec, electrical equipment, TV and recorder parts, aluminum & articles, coffee, tea, spices, paper & products	0.097
Myanmar	(84) boiler, machinery, tanning dyes, pigments, varnish, mineral fuel, wax, bituminous, furniture, beddings, prefab buildings, electrical equipment, TV and recorder parts	3.363	Cereals, vegetable, tuber roots, wood & articles, coffee, tea, spices, apparels	79.972

Note : (@) Re-exports included

Thailand

Thailand has a GDP of US$ 455.221 billion[40] and a total population of 67.7 million as on 2017. Contribution of the agriculture sector to the GDP remained constant from 2001 to 2017 at 8.7 percent. The contribution of the industry sector also saw minor changes between 2001 and 2017 and hovered between 35 and 39 percent. The services sector has marginally appreciated from 54.8 in 2001 to 56.3 percent in 2017. The United States, China and Japan remained the three major export destinations, as also the major source of imports.[41]

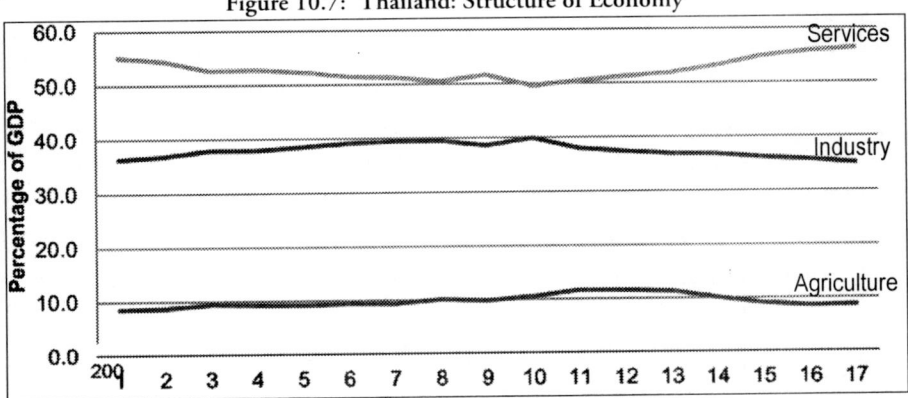

Figure 10.7: Thailand: Structure of Economy

Source: Author, based on ADB[42]

The breakdown of major categories of products traded intra-regionally with Thailand for the year ending June 2017 is as follows (Table 10.5):

Table 10.5: Major products traded intra-regionally with Thailand in June 2017

Country [43, 44]	Export to	Value[45] US $ M	Imports from	Value[34] US $ M
India	(84) boiler, machinery, electric equipment, TV, recorder parts, plastic articles, organic chemicals, (87) vehicles, railway, tram rolling stocks	6456.382	(84) boiler, machinery, electric equipment, pearls, semi precious stones, precocious metals, iron, steel, (87) vehicles, railway, tram rolling stocks, fish, molluscs, aquatic invertebrates	3588.643
Bhutan#	Metal products, aluminum, furnishing, lamps, prefab buildings, rubber articles, electric equipment, TV, recorder parts	24.039	Beverage, spirits, vinegar	0.123
Sri Lanka	Fish, mollusks, aquatic invertebrates, salt, sulphur, earths, stone, lime, cement, (84) boiler, machinery, rubber articles, sugar & confectionaries	518.322	Pearls, semi-precious stones, precious metals, (84) boiler, machinery, milling industry products, malt, starch, inulin, gluten, Fish, mollusks, aquatic invertebrates, electric equipment, TV, recorder parts	55.39
Bangladesh	Plastics, salt, sulphur, lime, cement, tanning extracts, (84) boilers, machinery	932.77	Apparels, fertilizer, textile, leather	56.22
Nepal	Plastics, beverage, vinegar, fiber, (87) vehicles, rail, tram parts, (84) boilers, machinery	107.96	Meat, apparel, edible preps, hides and skins, carpets	0.42
Myanmar@	(84) boiler, machinery, (87) vehicle, railway, tram, rolling stocks, sugar, confectionaries, mineral fuel, wax, bituminous, plastics	2718.883	(84) boiler, machinery, mineral fuel, wax, bituminous, copper, fish, aquatic invertebrates, oil, seeds, nuts, grains, medical plants, fodder	2166.677

Note: (@) Re-imports included
(#) 2016 data

Myanmar

Myanmar has a GDP of US $ 69.322 billion[46] and a total population of 53.4 million as on 2017. Contribution of the agriculture sector to the GDP was 23.7 percent in 2017, a sharp decline from 57.2 percent in 2001. The contribution of the industry sector improved steadily from 10.6 percent in 2001 to 36.2 percent in 2017. The services sector rose consistently from 32.4 percent in 2001 to 40.1 percent in 2017. The major destinations of its exports have been its neighbours India, China and Thailand and the three major sources of imports have been China, Singapore and Thailand.[47]

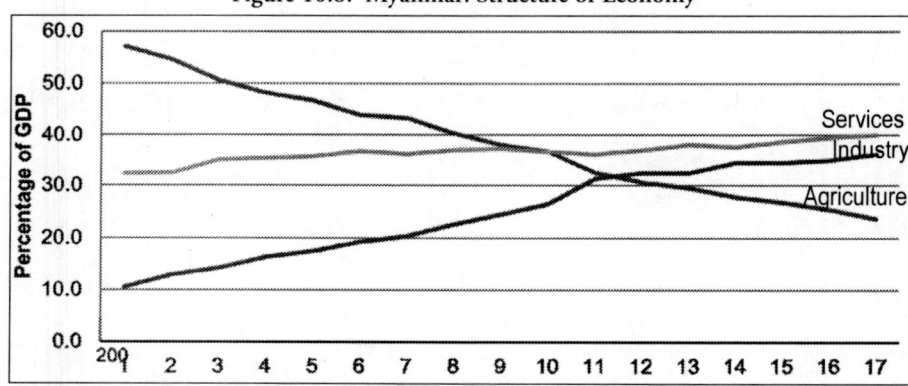

Figure 10.8: Myanmar: Structure of Economy

Source: Author, based on ADB[48]

The breakdown of major categories of products traded intra-regionally with Myanmar for the year ending June 2017 is tabulated as follows (Table 10.6):

Table 10.6: Major products traded intra-regionally with Myanmar in June 2017

Country[49,50]	Export to	Value[51] US$ M	Imports from	Value[40] US$ M
India	Vegetable, roots, wood & articles, lead & products, iron & steel, (09) coffee, tea, spices	708.115	(72) Iron, steel, (87) (87) vehicles, railway, tram rolling stocks, pharma, iron & steel, (85) electrical equipment	975.107
Bhutan#	-	-	(84) Machinery, (82) tools & implements, (39) plastics, (90) optical, cinematography	0.007811
Sri Lanka	Cereals, vegetable, tuber roots, wood & articles, coffee, tea, spices, apparels	79.972	(84) boiler, machinery, tanning dyes, pigments, varnish, mineral fuel, wax, bituminous, furniture, beddings, prefab buildings, electrical equipment, TV and recorder parts	3.363

Country[49,50]	Export to	Value[51] US$ M	Imports from	Value[40] US$ M
Bangladesh	Cereals, fish products, vegetable, tuber roots, iron or steel articles, lead articles	128.85	Pharma products, tools, implements, cutlery, Vegetable fiber, textile, apparels	23.8
Nepal	Vegetable, tuber roots, wood & articles, coffee, tea, spices, ships, boats, electrical machinery, TV and recorder parts,	32.55	Pharma products, fiber, textile, rugs	0.009
Thailand@	(84), boiler, machinery, mineral fuel, wax, bituminous, copper, fish, aquatic invertebrates, oil, seeds, nuts, grains, medical plants, fodder	2166.677	Nuclear reactor, boiler, machinery, (87) vehicle, railway, tram, rolling stocks, sugar, confectionaries, mineral fuel, wax, bituminous, plastics	2718.883

Note: (@) Re-exports included
(#) 2016 data

India

India has a GDP of US$ 2.597 trillion[52] and a total population of 1316 million as on 2017. Contribution of the agriculture sector to the GDP was 17.1 percent in 2017, a minor decline from 22.9 percent in 2001. The contribution of the industry sector improved gradually from 26.0 percent in 2001 to 29.1 percent in 2017. The services sector rose marginally from 51.0 percent in 2001 to 53.9 percent in 2017. The major destinations of its exports have been its neighbours the United States, UAE and Hong Kong and the three major sources of imports have been China, Saudi Arabia and UAE. [53]

Figure 10.9: India: Structure of Economy

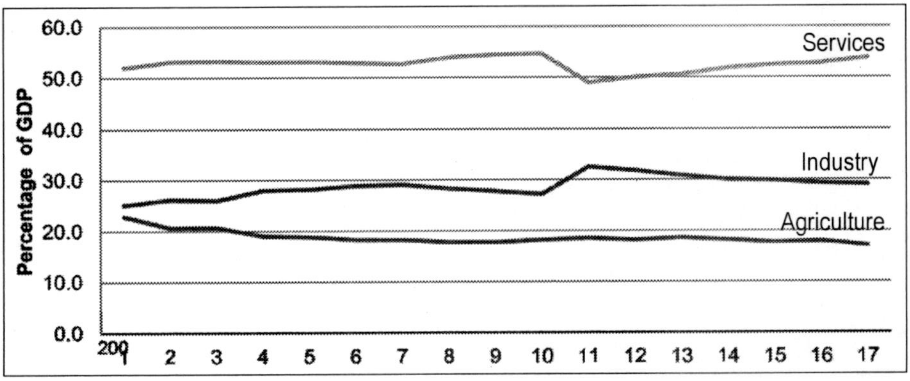

Source: Author, based on ADB[54]

The breakdown of major categories of products traded intra-regionally with India for the year ending June 2017 is available in tables of other BIMSTEC countries above.

NOTES

1. Percy S Mistry, "*New Regionalism and Economic Developmen*t", (ed) Fredrik Soderbaum and Timothu M Shaw *Theories of New Regionalism* (New York :Palgrave Macmillan Ltd, 2003), pp.117-119.
2. Sanjay Kathuria, "*Glass Half Full*", World Bank Group, pp.32-34 (accessed 18 December 2018) https://openknowledge.worldbank.org/bitstream/handle/10986/30246/9781464812941.pdf?sequence=8&isAllowed=y.
3. Department of Economic and Social Affairs, The United Nations (accessed 15 December 2018), https://comtrade.un.org/data/
4. World Bank, "*One South Asia*", (accessed 17 December 2018) http://www.worldbank.org/en/programs/south-asia-regional-integration?cid=EXT_WBEmailShare_EXT
5. World Trade Organisation, "*Regional Trade Information System*", https://rtais.wto.org/UserGuide/User%20Guide_Eng.pdf (accessed 18 December 2018)
6. World Trade Organisation. " List of RTAs", https://rtais.wto.org/UI/PublicAllRTAList.aspx (accessed 18 December 2018)
7. Sanjay Kathuria, "*Glass Half Full*", World Bank Group, pp.39-53
8. Ibid., p.40.
9. Ibid., p.41.
10. UNESCAP data and methodology, https://www.unescap.org/resources/escap-world-bank-trade-cost-database (accessed 18 December 2018)
11. World Bank, "International LPI", (accessed 19 December2018) https://lpi.worldbank.org/about
12. UNCTAD, "International Classification on NTMs, 2012 Version", (accessed 18 December2018) https://unctad.org/en/PublicationsLibrary/ditctab20122_en.pdf?user=46
13. Op cit, Sanjay Kathuria, p.43.
14. World Bank, "IBRD-IDA Data", https://data.worldbank.org/country/bhutan (accessed 16 December 2018)
15. Extracted from Asian Development Bank (ADB), https://data.adb.org/dataset/bhutan-key-indicators (accessed 16 December 2018)
16. Ibid.
17. Ministry of External Affairs, Bhutan, https://www.moea.gov.bt/wp-content/uploads/2017/10/ANNUAL-TRADE-STATISTICS-2017.pdf, (accessed 16 December2018)
18. UN "Comtrade", https://comtrade.un.org/db/ce/ceSnapshot.aspx?cc=all&px=HS&r=144&y=2017&p=64&rg=1,2&so=9999&rpage=dqBasicQuery&qt=n (accessed 17 December 2018)
19. World Bank "IBRD-IDA Data", (accessed 16 December 2018) https://data.worldbank.org/country/bangladesh
20. Extracted from Asian Development Bank (ADB), (accessed 16 December 2018) https://data.adb.org/dataset/bangladesh-key-indicators .
21. Ibid.
22. Export Promotion Bureau of Bangladesh, http://www.epb.gov.bd/site/files/51916ae6-a9a3-462e-a6bd-9ef074d835af/Statistic-Data-2016-2017 (accessed 16 December 2018)
23. Asian Development Bank, https://data.adb.org/dataset/bangladesh-key-indicators (accessed 16 December2018)
24. Ministry of Commerce, Bangladesh, https://www.bangladeshtradeportal.gov.bd/kcfinder/

upload/files/List%20of%20Controlled%20goods.pdf (accessed 16 December2018)
25 United Nations, "Comtrade", https://comtrade.un.org/db/dqBasicQuery.aspx (accessed 16 December 2018)
26 United Nations, "Comtrade", https://comtrade.un.org/db/ce/ceSnapshot.aspx?cc=all&px= HS&r =699&y=2017&p=50&rg=1,2&so=9999 &rpage= dqBasic Query&qt=n (accessed 16 December 2018)
27 United Nations, "Comtrade", https://comtrade.un.org/data/ (accessed 16 December 2018)
28 World Bank, "IBRD-IDA Data", https://data.worldbank.org/country/nepal (accessed 16 December 2018)
29 Extracted from Asian development Bank, https://data.adb.org/dataset/nepal-key-indicators (accessed 16 December 2018)
30 Ibid.
31 The United Nations, "Comtrade", https://comtrade.un.org/db/dqBasicQuery.aspx (accessed 16 December 2018)
32 The United Nations, "Comtrade", https://comtrade.un.org/db/ce/ceSnapshot.aspx?cc=all&px= HS&r= 524&y=2017&p=699&rg=1,2&so=9999&rpage=dqBasicQuery&qt=n (accessed 16 December 2018)
33 The United Nations, "Comtrade", https://comtrade.un.org/data/ (accessed 16 December2018)
34 WB, IBRD-IDA data, https://data.worldbank.org/country/sri-lanka (Accessed on December 17, 2018)
35 Extracted from ADB, https://data.adb.org/dataset/sri-lanka-key-indicators (Accessed on December 17, 2018)
36 Ibid.
37 The United Nations, "Comtrade", https://comtrade.un.org/db/dqBasicQuery.aspx (accessed 16 December2018)
38 The United Nations, "Comtrade", https://comtrade.un.org/db/ce/ceSnapshot.aspx?cc=all&px= HS&r= 144&y=2017&p=699&rg=1,2&so=9999&rpage=dqBasicQuery&qt=n (accessed 17 December2018)
39 The United Nations, "Comtrade", https://comtrade.un.org/data/ (accessed 16 December2018)
40 World Bank, "IBRD-IDA Data", https://data.worldbank.org/country/thailand (accessed 17 December2018).
41 Extracted from Asian Development Bank Data, https://data.adb.org/dataset/thailand-key-indicators (accessed 17 December2018).
42 Ibid.
43 The United Nations, "Comtrade", https://comtrade.un.org/db/ce/ceSnapshot.aspx?cc=all&px= HS&r= 144&y=2017&p=699&rg=1,2&so=9999&rpage=dqBasicQuery&qt=n (accessed 17 December2018).
44 The United Nations, "Comtrade" https://comtrade.un.org/data/ (accessed 16 December 2018).
45 World Bank, "IBRD-IDA Data", https://data.worldbank.org/country/myanmar (accessed 17 December 2018)
46 Extracted from ADB, https://data.adb.org/dataset/myanmar-key-indicators (accessed 17 December2018)
47 The United Nations, "Comtrade", https://comtrade.un.org/db/dqBasicQuery.aspx (accessed 16 December 2018).
48 Ibid.

49. The United Nations, "Comtrade", https://comtrade.un.org/db/dqBasicQuery.aspx (accessed 16 December 2018).
50. The United Nations, "Comtrade", https://comtrade.un.org/db/ce/ceSnapshot.aspx?cc=all&px=HS&r=144&y=2017&p=699&rg=1,2&so=9999&rpage=dqBasicQuery&qt=n (accessed 17 December 2018)
51. The United Nations, "Comtrade", https://comtrade.un.org/data/ (accessed 16 December2018)
52. World Bank, "IBRD-IDA Data", https://data.worldbank.org/country/india (accessed 17 December2018)
53. World Bank, "IBRD-IDA Data", https://data.worldbank.org/country/india (accessed 17 December2018)
    Extracted from Asian Development Bank, https://data.adb.org/dataset/india-key-indicators (accessed 17 December2018).
54. Ibid.

11

Economic Corridors, Regional Value Chain and Gender Sensitivity in Border Trade

Diversity of Bay of Bengal provides ample opportunity for trade, investments and economic growth yet economic integration between the states of the Bay of Bengal has not gained momentum. This can be attributed to fragmented hardware and software of cross-border infrastructure which affect trade costs and efficiency. Economic corridors can fill these gaps as well as promote socio-economic development. Although there is no clear definition of economic corridor, but the concept has become popular through the Asian Development Bank (ADB) and Greater Mekong Sub-region (GMS). In general, economic corridors are networks of infrastructure that helps facilitate economic activities. It can include transportation networks, human resource, communication facilities, energy grids and institutional infrastructures.[1]

Economic Corridors

Lack of economic corridors in the Bay of Bengal region is a major constraint for growth. Inadequate infrastructure causes congestion, resulting in diminishing returns for industries. Low rates of return act as disincentive to investments that leads to low rate of labour absorption, which then perpetuates a vicious cycle of poverty. Economic corridors are different from transport corridors in three specific ways. First, they ease the demand for infrastructure; second, they encourage regional cooperation, lower tariffs, facilitate trade and investments and foster regionalisation;

and third, better supply links lead to distribution of job (fragmented) for production and enhanced regional and global trade.[2]

Economic corridors are essential for the Bay of Bengal region so that countries can get their goods to markets efficiently, cheaply and quickly. But progress has been slow due to social, political, economical and technical reasons. Technical factors include absence of integrated railway networks; absence of adequate trade facilitation policy measures (in the interior of countries); and absence of transit trade.[3] India's Act East policy has expedited connectivity projects in the region, however, much more needs to be done.[4] Some of the issues which merit attention are:

(a) *Accession to International Conventions:* As goods begin to move along the international transport corridors, there is a need to harmonise laws and processes amongst countries. The region requires a legal framework to define the rights of goods, people and vehicles and then decide on the permits, licenses, and mechanisms of dispute settlement.

(b) *Intermodal transport:* The goal of intermodal transport is to get the whole region interconnected. Specific projects like the Kaladan multi-modal transport are being progressed. But, a project akin to 'Sagarmala' needs to be commissioned for the region for landlocked countries like Bhutan and Nepal, as also for interior areas of other countries, so that they get access to the global market at low cost.

(c) *Strengthening rules, regulations and standards:* For the economic corridors to function effectively, rules and regulations must meet common regional benchmark, and if possible international also. The Cross-Border Transport Agreement (CBTA) of the Greater Mekong Sub-region (GMS) can be adopted and customised. This will enable seamless integration with Southeast Asia in the future. CBTA is also an important step for harmonising software-related cross-border infrastructure. To make these agreements effective, they have to be incorporated into national laws, regulations and standards. In addition, there is a requirement to coordinate with agencies like customs, immigration and quarantine authorities and make them single stop, single window throughout the region.

(d) *Financing cross-border transport project:* Trans-border railways, metros, roadways have to be achieved by the Bay of Bengal region like the EU. This will require financing and political will. Without such seamless facilities "*we-ness*" cannot be achieved in the region.

(e) *Security coordination:* Regional security cooperation will be required along the economic corridor for transport network, goods and other facilities. Automated technologies like the bar codes, wireless communication, radio frequency identity tags, GPRS-enabled cargo movement. tamper-proof seals, will enhance security as also accelerate trade. Airports, land ports, sea ports, customs, immigration, border security, shippers would need to be networked for real-time connectivity.

(f) *Investments:* There are several reports on how regionalism had improved investments within a region. But there was no evidence found on the reverse trend. Influence of investments on regionalism is an unexplored area and needs detailed investigation that is beyond the scope of this project.

Regional Value Chain

Michael Porter was the first to use the term 'value chain' in his book entitled *Competitive Advantage: Creating and sustaining superior Performance.* Value chain analysis aims to maintain competitiveness at every stage of manufacturing. Porter classified inbound logistics, operations, outbound logistics, marketing and sales, and service as primary activities of a company. Procurement, technology development, human resource management, and infrastructure were described as secondary activities. Porter's value chain model is illustrated in Figure 11.1.[5]

Figure 11.1: Porter's Value chain model

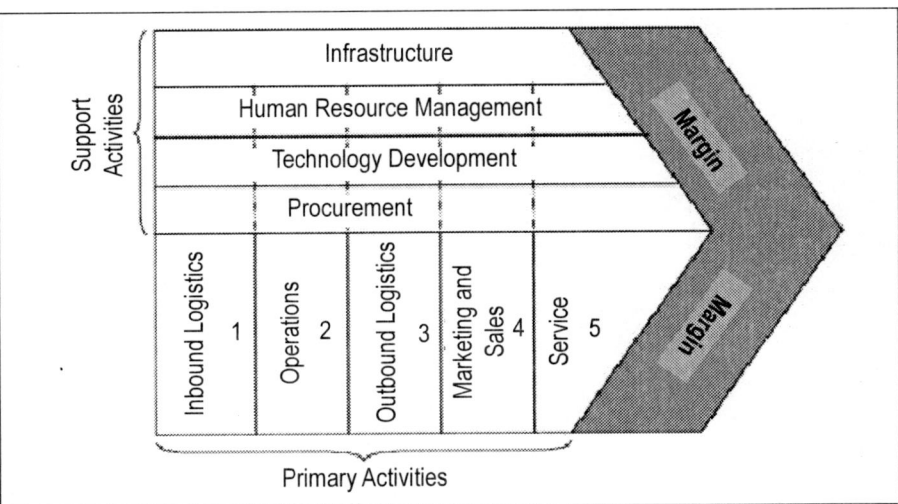

Source: Food and Agriculture Organisation, UN

From the country graphs on 'structure of economy' (Appendix A, Chapter 10) it can be deduced that barring Myanmar, the percentage of industrial sector as component of GDP has remained stagnant in all countries of BIMSTEC since 2001. Industry is not only an engine of growth, but also promises proliferation of large volumes of jobs. Current spell of stagnation in the industrial sector could be broken by Regional Value Chains (RVCs) and can create thousands of jobs in the region. Success of Global Value Chains (GVCs) is already well known. For GVCs to succeed in say mobile and automobile industry, an array of technologies needs to be aggregated by a large number of countries.

BIMSTEC can take a leaf out of the GVC concept and aggregate their strengths to create successful RVCs. Most countries in BIMSTEC are small and do not have large domestic markets, which prevents them from reaping the benefits of economy of scale. Also, limited scope for specialisation in a single country can exacerbate technological and production constrains.[6] RVCs also align well with India's 'Act East' and 'neighbours first' policies. It can eliminate the trust deficit in the smaller countries of the region that are fearful of India capturing their markets. Being the largest country by size, Indian government would have to take the initiative as a facilitator and allow the private sectors to shape the market. In addition, the BIMSTEC working group on Rules of Origin (ROO) needs to conclude its negotiations expeditiously.

Potential RVCs for BIMSTEC can be arrived through various mathematical models, which is beyond the scope of this paper. However, based on major products being exported by BIMSTEC countries (Appendix A, Chapter 10) and Porter's stages at Figure 11.1, an *indicative list* of potential RVCs has been tabulated in Table 11.1.

Table 11.1: An Indicative list of potential RVCs

Stages	*Operations/Logistics*	*Country*
Textile Industry		
Stage 1	Cotton	India
Stage 2	Spinning, weaving, dyeing and finishing, fabric, textile	India, Bangladesh, Nepal
Stage 3	Designing, cutting, sewing, finished apparels	Bhutan, Bangladesh
Stage 4	BBIN transport network	Dhaka Port
Leather		
Stage 1	Animal skin	Bangladesh
Stage 2	Hide processing, Tanning products footwear and garment	Bangladesh, Thailand, Nepal
Stage 3	Multi-modal transport	Dhaka/ Phuket

Stages	Operations/Logistics	Country
Food		
Stage 1	Raw grain, fruit, vegetable, fish	Bhutan, Nepal, Bangladesh, Thailand
Stage 2/ Support activity	Processing, drying Note: Research and development of international brand	Bhutan, India, Bangladesh, Thailand
Stage 3	BBIN + Multi-modal transport	Ports in India, Bangladesh, Thailand
Chemicals		
Stage 1	Raw organic and inorganic components	India, Thailand
Stage 2	Pharmaceutical products	Myanmar, India, Bangladesh
Stage 3	Other chemical products, fertilizer	Bhutan
Stage 4	BBIN+ Multi-modal	Ports in India, Bangladesh

Border Trade

In April 2015, the Indian government announced Foreign Trade Policy (FTP) 2015–20. In April 2016, India ratified the WTO Agreement on Trade Facilitation (TFA), and subsequently unveiled the National Trade Facilitation Action Plan (NTFA) 2017–20. NTFA seeks to transform the trade ecosystem by reducing the time and cost of doing business. To achieve economic integration with the region, the Government of India has emphasised on 3Cs—Commerce, Connectivity and Culture. Act East Policy and the Neighbours First Policy are the two primary drivers for improving connectivity with countries in the region.[7]

India's northeast region is geographically central to the Bay of Bengal region and BIMSTEC. Presently, border trade with neighbouring countries is quite small and to improve trade, the Government of India had promulgated a policy shift in December 2015 from Barter/Border trade to Normal trade.

In 2017-18, northeast region border trade was US$ 197 million, which was only 0.002 per cent of the region's total trade with its neighbouring countries. Notwithstanding that, bilateral trade between India and Myanmar has grown from US$ 994.45 million in 2007-08 to US$1.6 billion in 2017-18. Similarly, Myanmar's border trade is almost 46 percent of its total trade in 2017-18.[8] Bangladesh too is an important border trading partner accounting for 87 percent of the border trade followed by Bhutan with a share of 11 per cent. The others account for only 1 percent (Table 11.2).[9]

To promote border trade, improving connectivity, easing non-tariff barriers, upgrading Land Custom stations and creating financial instruments need to be undertaken. In addition, checking of informal transaction and prohibiting diversion of third country goods need to be enforced.

Table 11.2: India's Northeast Region trade with neighbours in US$ million (2017-18)

Country	Total Bilateral Trade	Bilateral Border Trade	Share of Bilateral Border Trade in Total Border Trade (%)
Bangladesh	9300	172	87.4
Bhutan	924	23	11.6
China	89714	2	0.99
Myanmar	1606	0.02	0.01
Nepal	7051	0.0	0.0
Total	108595	197.02	100

Source: Directorate General of Commercial Intelligence and Statistics (DGCI&S), Government of India

Gender Sensitivity in Border Trade

Challenges of economic integration have been discussed in Chapter 9. The governments of the Bay of Bengal region have been actively engaged in consultation with BIMSTEC Headquarters located in Dhaka, Bangladesh, to resolve trade bottlenecks between states. But an area that remains largely unexplored is the importance of gender sensitivity in trade facilitation. Oversight of this aspect not only impacts women empowerment but also economic growth.

A January 2018 study report by Indian Council for Research on International Economic Relation (ICRIER) examined the issues of gender mainstreaming on Bangladesh-Bhutan-India-Nepal (BBIN) region.[10] BBIN countries scores poorly on gender sensitivity in trade and in fulfilling obligations under WTO's trade facilitation agreement (TFA) and SDG targets.

Trade in the northeastern region of BBIN takes place mainly by roads and can be broadly categorised into: (a) formal trade through land customs stations (LCS); (b) formal trade through border 'haats'; (c) and informal trade.[11] Despite the 136 LCSs, border trade management at BBIN is suboptimal due to lack of support infrastructure and single coordination authority between the customs, immigration and other regulatory agencies. This is further compounded by restrictions in seamless transport, size of trucks and entry schedule restrictions. All this adds to the cost of trade and adds to inefficiency. In this backdrop women participation in logistic services such as transport, handling, compliance and clearance remains negligible. Some of the impediments faced by women are common to men too but worthy of mention:[12]

(a) *Starting business:* Obtaining licenses for export can be cumbersome, even though the system is online, poor internet can be a hindrance. Lack of

information—Information on trade procedures, rules and regulations on international trade is not easily accessible.
(b) *Dealing with officials:* Women face considerable difficulty in dealing with male customs and officials. A system where cross-border bribing is quite common, women need to be aware of the rules and rights to reduce costs of trade.
(c) *Accessing cross-border markets:* Marketing goods and processing payments across the border can be tedious for women.
(d) *Women traders are not organised:* Women are not represented in the business and trade associations.

Women Sensitivities in Border Haats

Border haats are another means of licensed trade. Traders are required to use legal permits to trade at the border haats. Haats Management Committees (HMC) have been mandated to select vendors for haats on rotation. In three out of the four HMCs, there is no woman representation. Poor connectivity, bad roads, lack of toilets, unreliable mobile network and no electricity, erratic banking facilities deter women vendees to the haats. Absence of women police and officials further complicate the participation of vendees in these haats.[13] A comparison of haats from gender perspective is tabulated at Table 11.3.[14]

Women engaged in informal trade mostly function as carriers taking advantage of the duty free trade worth Rs 25000.[15] To circumvent the cumbersome LCS and border haat procedures, small entrepreneurs engage in suitcase trade. It is estimated that there are 16 informal border haats at Bangladesh-Mizoram border. One survey indicates that almost 80-90 percent women residing close to Dawki LCS are involved in informal trade. Cattle trade is also informal across India-Bangladesh and is believed to be worth US$ 500 million.

To instill gender sensitivity in border trade, the border crossings have to be made women friendly. This will require measures like creation of women-friendly infrastructure, helpdesks for women, digitization of single window interface. Information outreach needs to be targeted towards women for spreading awareness on rules, procedures and rights. Women need to be supported with access to cross border markets. Governments should collect gender disaggregated database at regular interval for feedback purposes.

Table 11.3: Comparison of haats from gender perspective

	Kamalasagar	Srinagar	Kalaichar	Balat
	Manual registrations at time of entry and exit by customs and the BSF officials. Women personnel from the local police and BSF deployed only for physical frisking of female entrants.			
Other Female Government Personnel	None	None	Currently the District Administration Supervising Official is a woman.	One customs staff at the entry gate is a woman.
Access to haat	Transportation is available up only till the first gate of the haat. From mere on goods have to be carried manually.	Brick soiled access road.	Poor condition of access road leading to Haat.	Poor condition of access road leading to Haat.
Separate Toilet for Women	No	No	No	Separate toilet for women but without water supply and no roof.
Common Facility Centre	Yes but used primarily for HMC meetings.	Yes but used primarily for HMC	No	Yes but used primarily for HMC meetings.
Running Water supply	Available.	Available	Not available	Not available
Electricity Supply	No	Available only in the common facility centre	Limited banking and foreign exchange facilities	No
Storage/Warehouse Facility	No	No		No
Banking Facilities	No	Manual banking service is provided by Bangladesh in common facility centre	Limited banking and foreign exchange facilities	Limited banking and foreign exchange facilities
Phone and Internet Connectivity	Poor mobile phone connectivity.	Poor mobile phone connectivity.	Poor mobile phone connectivity.	Poor mobile phone connectivity.
	No internet connectivity.	No internet connectivity	No internet connectivity	No internet connectivity

Source: ICRIER Survey 2017

Conclusion

India's Act East policy has expedited connectivity projects in the region. But much more needs to be done to establish efficient business corridors. It would require accession to international conventions, improving intermodal transport, strengthening rules, regulations and standards, financing cross-border transport project, and security coordination. In addition, implementation of Michael Porter's value chain model needs to be explored and customised for the unique manufacturing and production capabilities of each country. Lastly, to improve border trade, improvement of connectivity, easing of non-tariff barriers, upgrading of Land Custom Stations, and creation of financial instruments need to be undertaken. In addition, checking of informal transaction and prohibiting diversion to third country goods need to be enforced. Gender sensitivity in border trade also needs attention to facilitate women to actively participate in the economic initiative. Having examined the dynamics of regional economic integration, the study would move on to discuss Blue Economy in the next chapter.

NOTES

1. Prabir De, "*Economic Corridor and Regional Economic Integration*", (ed) Prabir De and Kavita Iyengar *Developing Corridors in South Asia*, ADB, India, 2014, pp.15-16.
2. Ibid., pp.17-18.
3. Ibid pp. 37.
4. Ibid pp. 38-41
5. Food and Agriculture Organisation, United Nations (accessed 19 December 2018), http://www.fao.org/fileadmin/user_upload/fisheries/docs/ValueChain.pdf
6. Ram Upendra Das, "*Towards Make in South Asia, Evolving Regional Value Chains*", Discussion Paper No. 199, RIS, July 2015, p.2 , (accessed 19 December 2018), http://ris.org.in/newasiaforum/towards-%E2%80%98make-south-asia%E2%80%99-evolving-regional-values-chain-ram-upendra-das-2015
7. Nisha Taneja, et al, "*Trade facilitation measure to enhance women's participation in cross-border trade in BBIN*", Working paper 350, January 2018, ICRIER, p.2, (accessed 19 December 2018), http://icrier.org/pdf/Working_Paper_350.pdf
8. Ibid, pp. 3-6.
9. Ibid, p 7.
10. Ibid.
11. Ibid.
12. Ibid, p. 11.
13. Ibid, pp. 12-16.
14. Ibid, p. 15.
15. Ibid, p. 16.

12

Blue Economy:
Regional Approach Takes Roots

It is an acknowledged fact that there is a symbiotic relationship between mankind and the sea. Since time immemorial, sea has been an important source of food and livelihood, and has facilitated commerce. It has also been the trigger for globalization and contributed to integration of the global economy and human development. In this context, this chapter illustrates the concept of Blue Economy and its development among the Bay of Bengal littoral countries. The chapter argues that Blue Economy is not just limited to national boundaries, it also transcends to neighbouring countries and contiguous sub-regions and regions which necessitate multilateral initiatives under the BIMSTEC where the concept has debuted recently.

What is Blue Economy?

In the past, concepts related to the seas and the oceans such as 'Seapower' and 'Maritime Power' have been debated, discussed and theorized; the new understanding of the oceans is led by the idea of Blue Economy. Gunter Pauli was the first to coin the term Blue Economy through his book *Blue Economy—10 Years, 100 Innovations, 100 Million Jobs*. However, his understanding of Blue Economy has undergone trans-mutation leading to a number of terms such as 'ocean economy', 'coastal economy', 'Blue Economy' and 'Greening the Blue economy'.

Among these terms, Blue Economy is most popular and is finding reference and relevance in international relations, geopolitics, geostrategic issues, safety and security discourse, environment and ecological debates, financing, legal implications and in entrepreneurship and technological innovation. Some countries have appointed ministers for Blue Economy and some have introduced Blue Bond's, a pioneering financial instrument designed to support sustainable marine and fisheries projects.[1] Further, it is also resonating in the SDG 2030 discourse given that Goal 14 focuses on the oceans and calls for sustainable development of the sea-based resources.[2]

The World Bank has defined Blue Economy as "sustainable use of ocean resources for economic growth, improved livelihoods, and jobs while preserving the health of ocean ecosystem."[3] The Center for Blue Economy makes a distinction between 'ocean economy' and 'coastal economy' and states that "it is now a widely used term around the world with three related but distinct meanings: the overall contribution of the oceans to economies, the need to address the environmental and ecological sustainability of the oceans, and the ocean economy as a growth opportunity for both developed and developing countries."[4]

In India, FICCI Task Force Report titled "Blue Economy Vision 2025: Harnessing Business Potential for India Inc and International Partners", a pioneering effort, defines Blue Economy as "encompasses a wide range of economic activities pertaining to sustainable development of resources and assets in the oceans, related rivers, water bodies and coastal regions in a manner that ensures equity, inclusion, innovation and modern technology."[5] There is no common definition of Blue Economy and the two terms, i.e. 'Blue Economy' and 'Ocean Economy' are often used interchangeably; however, it is generally agreed that Blue Economy is related to the seas, water bodies including inland water bodies.

The United Nations has pegged the commercial value of various activities related to the oceans between US$ 3 trillion to US$ 6 trillion.[6] This is accrued from goods such as food (fisheries and aquaculture feed 4.3 billion people with more than 15 per cent of annual consumption of animal protein), oil and gas (over 30 per cent is produced from offshore), and services such as marine transport (90 per cent of global trade moves over the seas), global telecommunications (submarine cables carry 95 per cent of all digital data across the globe), marine tourism [5 per cent of the global Gross Domestic Product (GDP) and 6-7 per cent of global employment], shore-based commercial activity (13 of the world's top 20 megacities and over 40 per cent, or 3.1 billion, of the world population lives within 100 km of the sea in about 150 coastal cities located along the coast and in island nations).7

Embracing Blue Economy

The Bay of Bengal littoral countries are well-aware of the economic potential of the seas and look upon this medium as a source of wealth to leverage socio-economic development of their people. A large population in these countries is dependent on the seas for livelihood as also for food. The respective governments have internalized the concept of Blue Economy and the policies and pronouncements acknowledge their national commitments to use the resources of the sea in a sustainable manner.

Blue Economy has also entered the politico-diplomatic, socio-economic, environment-ecology, techno-scientific and safety-security discourses of the Bay of Bengal littoral at various levels. The member countries have made financial investments and are committed to marshalling technological innovation to develop Blue Economy. There is also a desire to cooperate for capacity building through partnerships, joint development programmes, and collaboration in scientific research and human resource training. This has necessitated blending national coastal development frameworks into regional sustainable development initiatives. Perhaps the critical necessity is to share with each other the scientific knowledge and data accumulated over the years, and help develop scientific models to study and harness the Blue Economy.

Bangladesh

According to World Bank Country Director for Bangladesh, Bhutan and Nepal, "In the last decade, the fisheries sector accounted for around 4 per cent of the Bangladesh's economy and is the country's second largest export earning sector after garments."8 As a developing country, it is quite natural for Bangladesh, to see the Bay of Bengal as a major source for its socio-economic development. It has been noted that for a country with "710 km long coast line extending from the tip of St. Martin's Island in the southeast to the west coast of Satkhira and 121,110 km² sea area" there are enormous "employment opportunities and other income-generating activities, develop other social services, security services as well as the overall standard of life for the local people at coastal areas."9

Bangladesh has been leading the regional discourse on Blue Economy. It has not only internalized Blue Economy, but has been championing and leading the contemporary understanding of the Blue Economy as also promoting the concept at international level through communiqués, regional growth strategy documents, bilateral agreements, and national development plans. In 2014, Prime Minister Sheikh Hasina outlined her country's vision of Blue Economy; speaking at the first-ever seminar on the subject, she described Bay of Bengal as the 'third neighbour' (India and Myanmar being the others) and observed that "sea-related subjects like expansion of international trade, use of marine mineral resources for long-term energy security, proper management of marine fish resources and protecting marine environment and bio-diversity" are critical for Bangladesh's future development and economic growth.[11]

Another fact that encouraged Bangladesh to explore and develop Blue Economy was the 8 July 2014 award of 19,467 square kilometres of the disputed 25,602 square kilometres area in the Bay of Bengal,[10] following the settlement of maritime dispute with India. Earlier, in 2013, it had settled the dispute with Myanmar over its maritime boundary. The delimitation of maritime boundary between India and Bangladesh and between Bangladesh and Myanmar through international arbitration has opened a number of opportunities to exploit marine resources in their respective EEZs and harness the economic potential of the Bay of Bengal. This has opened the flood gates for the three countries develop partnership to advance Blue Economy in the northern Bay of Bengal.

Bangladesh has hosted several major national and international conference and workshops and has finally identified 26 promising sectors for Blue Economy.[11] Furthermore, a Blue Economy Cell (BEC) under the Energy and Mineral Resources Division of the Ministry of Power, Energy and Mineral Resources has been set up.[12]

During the 2014 Blue Economy conference in Dhaka, Bangladesh's foreign minister AH Mahmood Ali proposed the idea of 'Bay of Bengal Partnership for Blue Economy' based on the principles of engagement through 'mutual trust, respect, mutual benefits, and equitable sharing of benefits' as also be 'inclusive and people-centric'; he argued for cooperation and stated "let us move together and ahead with a 'Bay of Bengal partnership for Blue Economy' to secure sustainable development among the coastal or littoral States".[13]

India

India is the largest among the Bay of Bengal littorals and is endowed with 7,516 kilometres long coastline and 2.3 million square kilometres of EEZ which is a repository of huge wealth of living and non-living resources. The sea is also an important source of livelihood and employment and contributes to the national economy. Marine and ocean studies have been a priority area and Indian has made significant scientific and technological advances in this domain. It has established a number of research and development laboratories and institutions for the technological advancements to study and exploit sea-based resources in sustainable ways.

In India, the NITI (National Institution for Transforming India) Aayog which is the think tank of the Government on policy has positioned Blue Economy high on its agenda.[14] Prime Minister Narendra Modi has been vocal about the Blue Economy and has likened the "Blue chakra or wheel in India's national flag represents the potential of Blue Revolution or the Ocean Economy." His vision for the seas is "Security and Growth for All in the Region" (SAGAR) and the national Saga-mala Project focused on 'port led development' resonate in Indian policy for development of the Blue Economy.[15] Further, "Maritime India Summit 2016 in Mumbai witnessed investment commitments of nearly US $13 billion in the maritime sector which is expected to create nearly 10 million jobs over the next ten years under the Sagarmala project."[16] The priority sectors for India's maritime ecosystem include shipping, ports, special economic zones, and coastal freight zones, road, rail and coastal connectivity, leisure industry including cruise and lighthouse tourism.

Prime Minister Narendra Modi, during his visit to Bangladesh in June 2015, signed a 'Memorandum of Understanding on Blue Economy and Maritime Cooperation in the Bay of Bengal and the Indian Ocean'. The India-Bangladesh joint statement reads "The two Prime Ministers expressed satisfaction at the amicable settlement of the maritime boundary between the two countries. To harness the vast economic opportunities this has opened up, they agreed to work closely on the development of ocean-based Blue Economy and Maritime Cooperation in the Bay of Bengal and chart out the ways for future cooperation."[17]

Sri Lanka

The country is surrounded by the seas, and waters of the Indian Ocean wash its shores. It has a coastline of 1785 kilometres which generates an EEZ of 517,000 square kilometres which is 7.8 times its land area. The Sri Lankan government has promoted Blue Economy both at the national and international levels. Professor G.L. Peiris, Sri Lanka's External Affairs Minister, highlighted Blue Economy at the 2011 Galle Dialogue and stated that the "vast economic resources of the ocean and methods for exploiting this potential for the benefit of humankind without inflicting grave damage on the environment, has been an integral part of the current international discourse, and that the discussion has included reference to practical means for conservation of fisheries resources, new arrangements for regional and international co-operation to enhance benefits, regulation of new technology and a fresh look at principles of international maritime law and practice, including suitable changes to the United Nations Convention on the Law of the Sea (UNCLOS)."[18]

Similarly, in his address at the Blue Economy Summit in Abu Dhabi, United Arab Emirates, Professor G.L. Peiris, Sri Lanka's External Affairs Minister, reiterated the importance of Blue Economy to Sri Lanka. In 2014, the country set up Centre of Excellence on Ocean Sciences to promote Blue Economy among Indian Ocean countries.[19] Another Sri Lankan initiative for the promotion of Blue Economy was under the 'Sri Lanka NEXT' programme announced in October 2016 and it has been noted that for Sri Lanka, "adopting a Blue Economy strategy is not optional but mandatory for Sri Lanka" [20]

Sri Lanka has identified a number of key areas under Blue Economy: (a) fisheries for food security and sustainable livelihoods; (b) tourism to support jobs; (c) renewable energy from wind and biomass sources for energy security; and (d) shipping and ports for the growth of the economy and the well-being of the people of the country. The country is also partnering with Norway Blue Economy and Norwegian research vessel *Dr Fridtjof Nansen* (owned by NORAD and jointly operated by the Norwegian Institute of Marine Research (IMR) and the University of Bergen (UIB)) *conducted* resource mapping survey for the Sri Lankan Government.[21] There are plans to jointly work in the field of maritime innovation and ocean-technology, fisheries and aquaculture, and sustainability of fish resources.[22]

Similarly, Sri Lanka has chosen to partner with France and under the FOCUS-LK "Managing the Oceans and Boosting the Blue Economy", a multi-stakeholder initiative focused on 'sustainable and innovative solutions for ocean's sustainable management'. A Declaration of Intent between Sri Lanka and France on " bilateral cooperation and exchanges regarding the Blue Economy" focusing on "coastal cities sewerage, fisheries and strategic investments in coastal cities facing rapid expansion due to tourism." Further, Sri Lanka has also indicated its willingness to join the International Coral Reef Initiative, with purpose to protect coral reefs, alongside France and 80 other members.[23]

Myanmar

Myanmar's plans for the development of Blue Economy were announced in 2017 at the World Ocean Summit in Bali, Indonesia. The government in partnership with the Wildlife Conservation Society (WCS) put out the "Marine Spatial Planning for Myanmar: Strategic Advice for Securing a Sustainable Ocean Economy", a coordinated plan for a sustainable ocean economy. Its primary purpose is to help preserve Myanmar's biodiversity spanning 486,000 square kilometres sea areas, protect marine life (finless porpoise, several species of sea turtle, and the dugong) and ensure the livelihoods of the 1.4 million citizens who rely on fishing.[24] U Hla Kyaw, Deputy Director of the Ministry of Agriculture, Livestock and Irrigation (Department of Fisheries) has noted that the strategy would provide Myanmar "a robust structure through which to develop our ocean economy," and ensure sustainable development of marine resources keeping their economic, ecological and social outcomes in mind.[25] The report lists 'primary threats' to the coastal and marine environment, issues related to "overfishing and destructive fishing; coastal development; watershed degradation; marine pollution from extractive industries and, climate change."[26]

Myanmar's fishing fleet has improved considerably (over 2,700 vessels), and according to the ILO, fishery sector was the fourth largest contributor to Myanmar's GDP during 2010–15 as also the fourth largest source of foreign exchange (USD 605 million). The fisheries sector employs nearly 3.2 million people (0.15% of total employment) and according to the State of the Basin Assessment, the Ayeyarwady River ecosystem output ranges between US$ 350 to US$ 530 million in freshwater capture and US$ 380 to 600 million aquaculture.[27]

Myanmar has nine ports (Yangon, Sittwe, Kyaukphyu, Thandwe, Pathein, Mawlamyine, Dawei, Myeik and Kawthaung)[28] and Yangon handles nearly 85 per cent of the country's trade. A river port, Yangon is constrained due to high sediment build-up from the Yangon River and requires continuous dredging. Mandalay is an important inland waterway transport hub and supports trade water routes to other regions of Myanmar. Port modernization is a high priority area and Kyaukphyu port in the Rakhine region is worth over €1 billion.

Myanmar also sought Norwegian assistance and the research vessel Dr. Fridtjof has carried out survey for Myanmar to study the marine biodiversity and oceanography in Myanmar's waters.

Thailand

For Thailand, its maritime interests span both in the Bay of Bengal. It has coast line of approximately 2,815 kilometres, 316,118.3 square kilometres of territorial waters and an EEZ of 420,280 square kilometres.[29] The estimated value of marine resources (living and non-living) is 24 trillion Baht ($685.7 billion). The country is rich in biodiversity and has healthy Mangroves (244,154 hectares), Sea Grass (20,524 hectares) and Coral reefs (18,986 hectares). Its Marine National Parks are spread over 4,79,068 hectares, coastal zone of 3.3 million hectares and sea area of 350,00 square kilometres[30] which generate enormous ecosystem services.[32] Thailand exports nearly 90 per cent of marine and coastal fisheries production and the sector employs over 650,000 workers.[31] Besides, marine transport and marine tourism industry are major industries.

The Thai government is committed to the development of Blue Economy and at the 2nd Indian Ocean Rim Association (IORA) Ministerial Blue Economy Conference in Jakarta in May 2017, Virasakdi Futrakul, Deputy Minister of Foreign Affairs of the Kingdom of Thailand[32] stressed the importance of a number of issues such as maritime infrastructure and connectivity, financing the Blue Economy through financial institutions, investments in MSMEs' for the development of the Blue Economy and sharing Thailand's experience on Sufficiency Economy Philosophy for sustainable growth and responsible to the environment of coastal communities.

Thailand's long-term vision is to invest in improving economic governance for promoting the Blue Economy in each of the Bay of Bengal littorals and play a role in conservation and utilization of marine resources such as mangrove forests. At the Bay of Bengal level, carry out and coordinate a systematic scientific review and economic analysis of the coastal marine ecosystem integrity in the Bay of Bengal region, resource mapping exercise in both the aquatic and marine environments, including mangrove ecosystems and resources, raise people's awareness and facilitate a good understanding of the Blue Economy resource base, including both natural and human capital.[33]

Blue Economy in Multilateral Construct

At another level, political leaders from the Bay of Bengal countries have promoted Blue Economy at multilateral forums and urged member states to place the issue high on global agenda. It is their belief that multilateral approaches help identify and develop cooperative strategies and actions plans to support sustainable development of marine resources.

Reference to Blue Economy in speeches at national and international levels has led to a greater awareness among the global community. This has encouraged several multilateral and regional organisations to promote the concept among the partners. For instance, the 2014 Perth Communiqué of the Indian Ocean Rim Association (IORA) of October 2014 impresses upon the member states to 'strengthening the Blue Economy' through sustainable development of resources and services offered by the seas. Likewise, the IORA Summit in March 2017, the Jakarta Concord and the IORA Action Plan identified six working groups including a Working Group on Blue Economy. There are examples of the vision and action plans adapted by the IORA countries pursue the development of the Blue Economy.

The issue is slowly percolating into other groupings such as the South Asian Association for Regional Cooperation (SAARC) and at its Eighteenth Summit meeting in Kathmandu, Nepal in November 2014 it was agreed that Blue Economy offers "manifold contributions" to the SAARC Region and therefore the need for collaboration and partnership among the member countries.

The Partnerships in Environmental Management for the Seas of East Asia (PEMSEA) is an intergovernmental organization operating in East Asia to foster and sustain healthy and resilient oceans, coasts, communities and economies across the region. The PEMSEA report *"Blue Economy for Business in East Asia towards an Integrated Understanding of Blue Economy"*, [34] identifies nine marine industries and notes that, "while the discussion has remained largely the domain of government, the private sector is showing more interest in the potential that blue economy holds. Indeed, business will play a critical role as its development unfolds." Another important facet of the report is the observation that companies can provide "marine technology and environmental services to cover oil spill response, wastewater treatment, marine scientific services, information technology and data solutions and more."

The BIMSTEC member countries have endorsed Blue Economy and the 2016 Leaders' Retreat Outcome Document states " We recognize the enormous potential that the development of the blue economy holds for our region, and agree to explore ways to deepen our cooperation in areas such as aquaculture (both inland and coastal), hydrography, seabed mineral exploration, coastal shipping, eco-tourism and renewable ocean energy with the objective of promoting holistic and sustainable development of our region."

Further, the BIMSTEC has identified 14 sectors for cooperation: trade and investment, transport and communication, energy, tourism, technology, fisheries, agriculture, public health, poverty alleviation, counter-terrorism and transnational crime, environment and natural disaster, people-to-people contact, culture and climate change. These are closely associated with the development of Blue Economy.

Blue Economy and Maritime Security

There is a symbiotic relationship between Blue Economy and security. The 1982 UNCLOS III establishes a comprehensive framework for the regulation and management of the ocean space and addresses a spectrum of issues relating to 'order at sea' in terms of management of the boundaries, marine resources, environment, scientific research and seabed mining. The Blue Economy is being securitized and it is a challenge for States to balance and manage different maritime interests and strategies and resource and environmental arguments. In essence, it is incomprehensible to think of resource and environmental compulsions without maritime safety and security. In the above context, Blue Economy is fast gaining currency among law enforcement agencies and is finding reference in national maritime strategies and policies.

In March 2017 the National Security Advisors (NSAs) of BIMSTEC had met for the first time and had agreed to formulate a common security regime for the Bay of Bengal. The second meeting of the NSAs was held in Dhaka on 28 March 2018. Therefore, there appears to be consensus on building a structure on maritime security for Bay of Bengal. The question however, is that what should be the terms of reference for such a security framework?

Conclusion

It merits emphasis that Blue Economy cannot be developed, even partially, without cooperation, collaboration and mutual trust among neighbours. As one of the authors of this book has argued elsewhere, "there is an opportunity for Bangladesh, India and Myanmar to develop partnership to advance Blue Economy in the Bay of Bengal. This would require the integration of each others' coastal development frameworks into respective national sustainable development initiatives. Further, they would need to share with each other the scientific knowledge accumulated over the years, and help develop scientific institutions and human resource to study the seas."[35]

The Bay of Bengal littorals have individually or collectively endorsed Blue Economy and keen to harness the seas in a sustainable manner. The pan-regional initiative to pursue collectively the Blue Economy is in early stages. It is fair to say that BIMSTEC would require the integration of each other's coastal development frameworks into respective national sustainable development initiatives. Further, they would need to share with each other the scientific knowledge accumulated over the years, and help develop scientific institutions and human resource to study the seas. This framework has the potential to include other Bay of Bengal littorals such as Thailand, Malaysia, Indonesia and Sri Lanka.

Having explored regional dimensions of Blue Economy, the study will examine the implications of Sustainable Development Goals in the context of BIMSTEC.

NOTES

1. "Seychelles launches World's First Sovereign Blue Bond", https://www.worldbank.org/en/news/press-release/2018/10/29/seychelles-launches-worlds-first-sovereign-blue-bond (accessed 12 January 2019).
2. "Sustainable Development Goal 14 : Conserve and sustainably use the oceans, seas and marine resources for sustainable development", https://sustainabledevelopment.un.org/sdg14 (accessed 12 January 2019).
3. "What is Blue Economy", http://www.worldbank.org/en/news/infographic/2017/06/06/blue-economy (accessed 12 January 2019).
4. "Our History and Methodology", https://www.middlebury.edu/institute/academics/centers-initiatives/center-blue-economy/about/history (accessed 12 January 2019).
5. "Blue Economy Vision 2025: Harnessing Business Potential for India Inc and International Partners", http://ficci.in/spdocument/20896/Blue-Economy-Vision-2025.pdf (accessed 12 January 2019).
6. "Ocean Assets Valued at $ 24 Trillion, but Dwindling Fast", http://www.worldwildlife.org/stories/ocean-assets-valued-at-24- trillion-but-dwindling-fast (accessed 10 November 2016)
7. "Goal 14—Conserve and Sustainably Use Oceans, Seas and Marine Resources for Sustainable Development", https://unchronicle.un.org/article/goal-14-conserve-and-sustainably-use-oceans-seas-and-marine-resources-sustainable (accessed 20 January 2019).
8. "Bangladesh: World Bank Helps Improve Coastal and Marine Fisheries", http://documents.worldbank.org/curated/en/308831538969417996/pdf/Bangladesh-Sustainable-Coastal-and-Marine-Fisheries-PAD-P161568-2-09182018.pdf (accessed 20 January 2019).
9. Md. Monjur Hasan et al., " The Prospects of Blue Economy to Promote Bangladesh into a Middle-Income, Country", https://file.scirp.org/pdf/OJMS_2018052116151033.pdf (accessed 24 January 2019).
10. "Potentials of Blue economy still untapped", https://www.bangladeshpost.net/potentials-of-blue-economy-still-untapped/ (accessed 24 January 2019).
11. Shipping, coastal shipping, seaports, passenger ferry services, inland waterway transports, shipbuilding, ship recycling industries, fishery, aquaculture, coastal aquaculture and mariculture, marine acquaintance products, marine biotechnology, oil and gas, sea salt production, ocean renewable energy, tidal energy, blue energy (osmosis) and biomass, aggregate mining (sand, gravel, etc), marine mineral mining, coastal tourism, recreational water sports, yachting and marines, cruise tourism, coastal protection/artificial islands/greening coastal belts, human resource development, marine surveillance and marine special planning.
12. "Promising sectors under blue economy identified", https://www.thedailystar.net/city/news/

promising-sectors-under-blue-economy-identified-1709323 (accessed 02 March 2019).
13. "Bangladesh seeks 'Bay of Bengal partnership' for blue economy", https://bdnews24.com/economy/2014/09/02/bangladesh-seeks-bay-of-bengal-partnership-for-blue-economy (accessed 24 January 2019).
14. "Niti Ayog Constitutes Working Group on National Blue Economy", http://portways.in/shipping/niti-ayog-constitutes-working-group-on-national-blue-economy/(accessed 24 January 2019).
15. "Text of Shri Nitin Gadkari's Address the Indian Ocean Conference in Singapore", *Press Information Bureau*, Ministry of Shipping, Government of India, 01 September 2016.
16. Vijay Sakhuja, "Blue Economy: Expanding India-US Maritime Cooperation", http://www.maritimeindia.org/View%20Profile/636094238574342172.pdf (accessed 24 January 2019).
17. "Joint Declaration between Bangladesh and India during Visit of Prime Minister of India to Bangladesh", https://www.thedailystar.net/online/bangladesh-india-joint-declaration-93490(accessed 24 January 2019).
18. See http://www.slhcindia.org/images/Newsletter/Newsletter_November11.pdf (accessed 24 January 2019).
19. "Workshop on Establishing a Centre of Excellence on Ocean Sciences and Environment for the Indian Ocean Rim Countries", http://www.ips.lk/workshop-establishing-centre-excellence-ocean-sciences-environment-indian-ocean-rim-countries/ (accessed 12 February 2019).
20. "Oceans and Sri Lanka's future: Towards a blue economy" http://www.ips.lk/wp-content/uploads/2017/03/FT_07June_Oceans-and-Sri-Lanka%E2%80%99s-future.pdf (accessed 12 February 2019).
21. "Norwegian State Secretary for Development Cooperation Visits Sri Lanka",
22. "Joint Statement - Norway and Sri Lanka", https://www.regjeringen.no/no/aktuelt/dep/smk/nyheter/2018/sri-lankas-statsminister/joint-statement—norway-and-sri-lanka/id2614202/?selectLanguage=/se/id4/ (accessed 22 February 2019).
23. "France and Sri Lanka join hands for Oceans protection and Blue Economy", https://lk.ambafrance.org/France-and-Sri-Lanka-join-hands-for-Oceans-protection-and-Blue-Economy (accessed 22 February 2019).
24. "Govt Announces Plan to Protect Burma's Oceans", https://www.irrawaddy.com/news/govt-announces-plan-protect-burmas-oceans.html (accessed 16 January 2019).
25. Ibid.
26. Mads Barbesgaard, "A landscape of ocean and land-control grabbing in Northern Tanintharyi, Myanmar", https://www.tni.org/files/publication-downloads/workingpaper.pdf (accessed 16 January 2019).
27. "The Ayeyarwady River and the Economy of Myanmar", https://d2ouvy59p0dg6k.cloudfront.net/downloads/ayeyarwady_risks_and_ opportunties_ report_v1_en_web.pdf (accessed 16 January 2019).
28. For more details see https://www.netherlandswaterpartnership.com/sites/nwp_corp/files/2019-01/Country%20Update%20Myanmar.pdf (accessed 16 January 2019).
29. "Blue Economy Principle and Maritime National Interest of Thailand", https://tci-thaijo.org/index.php/rpu/article/view/144122 (accessed 16 January 2019).
30. Orapan Nabangchang and Nawarat Krairapanond, "Ocean Economy and Ocean Health in Thailand", http://eascongress.pemsea.org/sites/default/files/file_attach/PPT-S3W3-12-

Nabangchang%2BNawarat.pdf (accessed 18 January 2019).
31 Thana Yenpoeng, "Fisheries Country Profile: Thailand", http://www.seafdec.org/fisheries-country-profile-thailand/ (accessed 18 January 2019).
32 Press Release, " Deputy Minister of Foreign Affairs of the Kingdom of Thailand attended the 2nd Indian Ocean Rim Association (IORA) Ministerial Blue Economy Conference", http://www.mfa.go.th/main/en/news3/6886/77686-Deputy-Minister-of-Foreign-Affairs-of-the-Kingdom.html (accessed 20 January 2019).
33 "Blue Economy in the Bay of Bengal Context: The Way Forward", http://coastbd.net/wp-content/uploads/2015/11/BoB-Blue-Economy-Thailand-PPT.pdf (accessed 20 January 2019).
34 See http://www.pemsea.org/sites/default/files/PEMSEA%20Blue%20Economy%20 Report%2011.10.15.pdf, p.32.
35 Vijay Sakhuja, "Bay of Bengal: Exploring Partnership for Blue Economy", http://www.maritimeindia.org/Archives/BAYOFBENGALEXPLORING.html (accessed on 24 January 2019).

13

Towards a Sustainable Bay of Bengal

The contemporary discourse on sustainable development is led by the United Nations. Its global wing for development network, i.e. United Nation's Development Programme (UNDP) has noted that more than three billion people across the globe are reliant on the seas and the annual market value of marine and coastal resources and industries is estimated at US $3 trillion which corresponds to nearly 5 per cent of global GDP.[1]

Furthermore, oceans and seas are natural 'carbon sink' and absorb nearly 30 per cent of the carbon dioxide produced due to human activity. However, seas and oceans are experiencing acidification (26 per cent rise since the beginning of the industrial revolution), marine pollution from shore-based discharges (40 per cent of the ocean is heavily affected by pollution), and ocean plastic litter (13,000 pieces per square kilometre of ocean) is also a major concern for the international community. Further, there is a near continuous depletion in the world's fish stocks (nearly 30 per cent are over exploited). Besides climate change and the associated sea level rise is an ongoing phenomenon that impacts people across the globe.[2]

This chapter attempts to understand the role Bay of Bengal littoral countries play in the broader framework of the Sustainable Development Goals (SDG) 2030. It presents the narrative on the formulation of SDG 2030 in terms of its conceptualization, role of UN agencies and the schema of voluntary national reviews (VNRs). The chapter showcases the progress made by the Bay of Bengal littoral countries in support of their commitments to the SDG 2030.

Narrative of SDG 2030

In September 2015, the representatives of UN member states met in New York to discuss a global partnership and a blueprint for peace and prosperity for people across the globe. They labeled the initiative as Sustainable Development Goals (SDG) 2030 and identified 17 SDGs with 169 targets to be achieved by year 2030.[3] These Goals are aimed at eradicating poverty, addressing varied human deprivations, reduce economic inequality, making available good and affordable health and education, addressing climate change, conserving the oceans, and protecting forests.

To pursue the above goals and targets of SDG 2030, the UN set up the Division for Sustainable Development Goals (DSDG) and the United Nations Department of Economic and Social Affairs (UNDESA) was designated to act as the Secretariat for the SDGs.[4] The DSDG was mandated to be the nodal agency for the evaluation of implementation of the 2030 Agenda as also for advocacy and outreach activities relating to the SDGs.

The United Nations High-level Political Forum on Sustainable Development (HLPF) which emerged from the 2012 outcome document of the United Nations Conference on Sustainable Development (Rio+20), "The Future We Want", plays the central role in follow-up and review of the SDGs at the global level. The 2030 Agenda for Sustainable Development is a mechanism to encourage member states to 'conduct regular and inclusive reviews of progress at the national and sub-national levels, which are country-led and country-driven for the states' and the reviews are 'voluntary, state-led, undertaken by both developed and developing countries, and involve multiple stakeholders'.[5]

The voluntary national reviews (VNRs) facilitate sharing of experiences, including successes, challenges and lessons learned, with a view to accelerating the implementation of the 2030 Agenda. Furthermore, the VNRs are also a mechanism for states to 'strengthen policies and institutions of governments and to mobilize multi-stakeholder support and partnerships for the implementation of the Sustainable Development Goals'.

Environment, ecology and sustainable use of ocean-based resources have found reference in other SDGs and Goal 14, titled "Life Below Water", list 14 targets to be achieved over the next 15 years up to 2030 to help ensure good health of the oceans as also contribute to the sustainable use of marine resources for economic growth and human well-being.

It is worth mentioning that several other Goals under the SDG 2030 are closely connected to the Goal 14; for instance, SDG 1 (poverty), SDG 2 (food security), SDG 6 (water and sanitation), SDG 7 (energy), SDG 8 (economic growth), SDG 9 (infrastructure), SDG 10 (reduction of inequality), SDG 11 (cities and human settlements), SDG 12 (sustainable consumption and production), SDG 13 (on climate change), SDG 15 (biodiversity), and SDG 17 (means of implementation and partnerships).

There are several risks to the health of the oceans due to marine pollution, ocean acidification and damage to coastal and marine areas. Goal 14 calls on states to reduce marine pollution, address the impacts of ocean acidification, conserve coastal and marine areas, and facilitate transfer of technology to improve ocean health and to enhance the contribution of marine biodiversity.

The targets under Goal 14 can be placed into two closely connected baskets, i.e. health of the oceans and fisheries. As regards fisheries, SDGs call for regulated harvesting and to curb overfishing and prevent illegal unreported and unregulated (IUU) fishing. Further, efforts must be made to provide access to small-scale artisanal fishers to marine resources and markets.

Bay of Bengal Large Marine Ecosystem (BOBLME) Project

The Bay of Bengal Large Marine Ecosystem (BOBLME) Project involves eight member states—Bangladesh, India, Indonesia, Malaysia, Maldives, Myanmar, Sri Lanka, and Thailand. Under the project, these countries collaborate on the management of the Bay of Bengal environment and its fisheries to improve the lives of the people who live along the coastal areas and are dependent on the seas for their livelihoods. In September 2017, after thorough and constructive discussion spread over two years, the 8-member grouping endorsed the Strategic Action Program (SAP) which involves multi stakeholders from at least 16 national level Ministries that are associated with the management of fisheries and conservation of the environmental.[6] This was the Second Phase of the Project and now paves the way for implementation of the SAP.[7] Rudolf Hermes, an expert from the FAO has noted that it being an environment programme, the focus will be on fisheries as also on pollution and livelihoods.

However, there are worries about implementation of the Project given that there are long standing issues over the demarcation of boundaries. For instance, India and Sri Lanka are yet to resolve issues in the Palk Strait, and Myanmar-Thailand boundary dispute continues. Perhaps the biggest worry is "even when there is no conflict, it has been difficult to agree on a joint management plan, as with the Sundarbans – the world's largest mangrove forest, which straddles Bangladesh and India." Notwithstanding that, during the First Phase of the project, sufficient trust has been built and "now is the time to build on this start."[8]

Marine Protected Areas

The United Nations has been at the forefront and campaigned to preserve marine environment and supported the establishment of Marine Protected Areas (MPAs). Article 194 (1) of 1982 UNCLOS stresses the critical need to protect and preserve the marine environment and calls on the states to take measures to 'prevent, reduce and control pollution' and thus protect and preserve the rare or fragile ecosystems. It also involves responsibility to protect the habitat of 'depleted, threatened or endangered' species and other forms of marine life.

The UN Conference on Environment and Development (UNCED) adopted Agenda 21 in 1992 and "Chapter 17: Protection of the Oceans, all Kinds of Seas, including Enclosed and Semi-Enclosed Seas, and Coastal Areas and the Protection, Rational Use and Development of Their Living Resources". It urged the coastal states to preserve habitats of marine species and biological diversity, and judiciously harvested marine resources under their national jurisdiction.[9]

The Convention on Biological Diversity (CBD) focused on the use of protected areas or area-based closures and the World Summit on Sustainable Development (WSSD) placed MPAs at the top of the international agenda.[10] The Johannesburg Plan of Implementation "focused attention on MPAs by calling on nations to promote the conservation and management of important and vulnerable marine and coastal areas including …the establishment of marine protected areas consistent with international law and based on scientific information, including representative networks by 2012."[11]

At the regional and multilateral levels, Bangladesh, India, and Sri Lanka have promoted conservation and management of coral reefs and under the SAARC, a Regional Coastal Zone Management Centre has been set up based on the recommendations of a SAARC Study on the "Causes and Consequences of Natural Disasters and the Protection and Preservation of the Environment".[12]

The Government of Bangladesh declared the country's first ever MPA the 'Swatch of No Ground' (SNG) in November 2014.[13] It is spread over 1,738 square kilometres to protect whales, dolphins, sea turtles, sharks, and other marine species under the Wildlife (Conservation and Security) Act, 2012. The coastal waters in the mangrove forest in the Sundarbans are also included in the national MPA. Bangladesh has prohibited unplanned fishing and the access of ships to the area has been restricted to ensure safe habitat for the dolphins after reports of loss of 130 dolphins between January 2007 to April 2016 in the riverine, coastal and marine waters due to trapping in fishing nets or injury by propellers of ships.[14]

According to a study by the Indian Space Research Organization (ISRO), "there are a total of 128 marine Protected Areas in India. Out of these, there are four Marine National Parks, sixty-seven Marine Sanctuaries, National Parks and Wild Life Sanctuaries, three Marine Biosphere Reserves, three Ramsar Coastal Wetlands, one Tiger Reserve (Sunderbans), one National Mangrove Genetic Resource Centre and Gene Centre and the Coral Reefs of Lakshadweep (seventeen), thirty two Mangrove Notifies Forests. Four national parks (having area 130 square kilometres) and 16 wild life sanctuaries (185 square kilometres) have been identified for conservation measures. Apart from this, 17 parks and 28 wild life sanctuaries have been proposed/existing on the island territories of India."[15]

Sri Lanka has declared at least nine Marine Protected Areas across the country and these are unique and offer ambient habitat conditions for marine life, such as organisms, mammals, coral, and migratory and shore birds to not only survive but also flourish.[16]

The Bay of Bengal states have also established the Mangroves for the Future (MFF), an initiative for coastal sustainability for promoting coastal ecosystems for sustainable development. The programme is a recognition of the role of mangrove forests which had played a critical role in reducing the impact of the 2004 Indian Ocean tsunami. The MFF includes a variety of coastal ecosystems such as coral reefs, estuaries, lagoons, wetlands, beaches and sea grass beds.

Progress on SDG 2030 by Bay of Bengal Littorals

India
India's commitment to SDG 2030 is demonstrated by the national vision, key statements and articulations made by the political leadership at various international and nations forums. These have been supported by several policies including implementation plans that exhibit India's march towards achieving SDG 2030 goals and targets.

Among the many expressions that point towards India's commitment to SDG 2030, Prime Minister Narendra Modi's "Sabka Saath Sabka Vikas," i.e. "Collective Effort, Inclusive Growth" is the 'cornerstone of India's national development agenda'. The Government of India announced a draft Three-year Action Agenda covering years 2017-18 to 2019-20 which fits into the 15-Year Vision.[17] Perhaps what is noteworthy is the fact that these plans are prepared in close consultations with the State governments reflecting the 'inclusive' nature of India's approach even at the national level.

At the apex level, Speaker's Research Initiative aims to provide the Indian Parliamentarian deep insights into SDG-related issues[18] and the February 2017 South Asian Speakers' Summit was an opportunity to share India's efforts towards the elimination of poverty, gender equality, climate change and resource mobilization for SDGs.[19]

Yet another expression that is resonating among the policy makers is "SAGAR" an acronym for "Security and Growth for All in the Region". The English translation of the word SAGAR is "Sea" and has found reference in India's discourse on Blue Economy. According to the Indian Prime Minister, "The Blue chakra or wheel in India's national flag represents the potential of Blue Revolution or the Ocean Economy. That is how central the ocean economy is to us."[20] Another important initiative by India is the Sagarmala programme which focusses on port led development including, connectivity, industrialization and coastal community development.

According to India's Voluntary National Review 2017,[21] India has put in operations several strategies for the development of Blue Economy in the country. Some of the significant issues under active operations are: (a) strengthening marine research; (b) eco-friendly marine industrial and technology; (c) National Fisheries Action Plan; (d) Coastal Ocean Monitoring and Prediction System; (e) Online Oil Spill Advisory System; (f) National Oil Spill Disaster Contingency Plan; (g) Sustainable fisheries; etc.

Bangladesh

Bangladesh is proactive in its mission to meet the goals and targets of SDG 2030. At the structural level, it has 'integrated the 2030 Agenda in its 7th FYP (2016-2020) which helps the government to pursue and implement the Goals and Targets under the 2030 Agenda at the national level.[22] Perhaps what merits attention is that Bangladesh has adopted an inclusive approach labeled as "Whole of Society" which includes a variety of stakeholders that help in the process of formulation of the action plan and implementation of the SDGs. A 'SDGs Implementation and Monitoring Committee' in the Prime Minister's Office helps 'implementation of

SDGs Action Plan' and a 'Monitoring and Evaluation Framework for SDGs implementation' is in place.[23] Besides, specific ministries and agencies have been identified to pursue and accomplish the SDGs. Bangladesh has mapped out lead, co-lead and associate ministries against each target of the SDGs. Another noteworthy initiative is the Annual Performance Agreement (APA) which assesses the performance of individual and ministries/agencies.[24]

As far as Goal 14 is concerned, according to a government publication, 'Sustainable Development Goals: Bangladesh First Progress Report 2018', Bangladesh is rich in biodiversity that supports marine life and marine living resources such as fish (marine fish catch is 16% of the total catch and Hilsa is the largest and single most valuable specie with an annual catch of 395,000 tons).[25] The government has judiciously chosen in favour of sustainable fisheries and 'imposed a 2 months fishing ban in the Bay of Bengal during fish breeding season in order to conserve fish resources.[26]

The offshore oil and gas development has not been quite rewarding but offshore blocks adjacent to in the Arakan offshore of Myanmar are likely to of particular interest due to good prospects.[27] However, Bangladesh is conscious of the adversarial impact on the marine environment and fisheries. The fear of an oil spill near its coast is a major issue for Bangladesh and this could have "far-reaching impact on fishery, fishing grounds, fish breeding and nursery heavens, salt-marsh ecosystems, coral reef, mangrove ecosystems, coastal tourism, salt industry, peoples' livelihood and health'[28] The 'Bangladesh Delta Plan 2100' is another initiative of the Bangladesh government to "address climate change vulnerability and risk factors not only in short term but also in the longer term till next 100 years."[29]

Myanmar

Speaking at the United Nations Conference to Support the Implementation of Sustainable Development Goal 14, EiEi Khin Aye (Head of Delegation and Deputy Permanent Representative of the Republic of the Union of Myanmar) was categorical about her government's commitment and stated that Goal 14 "is one of the most crucial, cross cutting, inclusive in nature and indispensable for our combined efforts and potential to achieve the 2030 Agenda of SDGs, with our objective of leaving no one behind."[30]

For Myanmar, the fishery sector (particularly small-scale fisheries and aquaculture) is an important source of food for its people and contributes to the national food security, creates jobs and ensures livelihood for people and help the country to alleviate poverty. It is not surprising then that the national policy is to 'attain sustainability of fish stock and develop capacity in addressing issues of Illegal, Unreported and Unregulated Fishing'. The Myanmar government has aligned national policies on fisheries and aquaculture with those of the ' FAO Code of Conduct for Responsible Fisheries (CCRF) and Voluntary Guidelines for Securing Small Scale Fisheries (VGSSF), which are legally binding instruments, based on internationally accepted principles and guidance towards sustainable fisheries.' As a developing country, it seeks technical and technological assistance for 'capacity building through building multi stakeholder partnerships and partnership with financial and techno logical institutions'.

Sri Lanka

Since endorsement of the SDG 2030, the Sri Lankan government established a dedicated ministry 'as the focal point for coordinating, facilitating and reporting on the implementation of the SDGs; the establishment of a Parliamentary Select Committee for Sustainable Development to provide political leadership for the implementation of the SDGs; and the enactment of the Sustainable Development Act No. 19 of 2017 to provide the legal framework for implementing the SDGs.'[31] The strategic development framework (Vision 2025, its medium-term plan, the Public Investment Programme 2017-2020, and the 'Blue Green' Budget of 2018 align significantly with the SDGs),

The Sri Lanka Voluntary National Review on the Status of Implementing Sustainable Development Goals[32] list out in details national approach to SDG 2030 and as far as targets under Goal 14 are concerned, focus areas include protecting marine and coastal environments and harvesting marine resources on a sustainable basis (Targets 14.2, 14.4 and 14.7). The government has put in place 'legislative acts, national policies and plans that 'deal with different aspects of marine and coastal resource management'. The document identifies several challenges towards achieving Goal 14 such as (a) growing shipping close to Sri Lankan waters; (b) stresses to harness the potential of blue economy; (c) Illegal, Unreported and Unregulated (IUU) fishing operations; (d) poaching and unlawful fishing operations in Sri Lankan waters by Indian fishers; and (e) harmful bottom trawling. In the context of the latter, the fisheries sector constitutes nearly 1.8 percent of the GDP with a growth rate of 4.5 percent in 2014.[33]

However, the Voluntary National Review notes that though Sri Lanka has placed a comprehensive 'legal, policy and institutional framework for managing coastal and marine resources', there are inadequacies in implementation partly due 'limited capacity of implementing agencies for undertaking surveillance, monitoring and enforcement is a major factor responsible for this situation'.[34]

Thailand

Thailand presented its Voluntary National Review (VNR) at the High-level Political Forum on Sustainable Development (HLPF) in 2017.[34] There has been significant progress in Thailand towards Goal 14 and several agencies are engaged in the process. For instance, the Department of Marine and Coastal Resources has a programme to update national marine and coastal resources database, has developed techniques to monitor ocean acidification in the Gulf of Thailand and the Andaman sea, undertaken annual survey of coral reefs. The government also announced 4 marine and coastal protected areas and introduced new regulations to enhance partnership and participation of coastal communities and Local Administrative Organizations in marine and coastal resources management and this move resulted in the restoration of 'barren coral reefs in Mai Ton Island, Racha Yai Island and Patong Bay in Phuket province and Koh Khai Nai Island in Phang Nga province'. Other initiatives include "No Smoking Beach" program and 'beach cleanups' and it received 'positive cooperation from both tourists and local communities'. Another major issue confronting Thailand is plastic pollution in the Bay of Bengal. There have been instances of whales washing up on a southern Thai beach due to plastic pollution. Thailand's efforts to achieve SDG 14 would require a concerted effort by all stakeholders.[35]

Conclusion

The Bay of Bengal littoral countries have endorsed SDG 2030 and are working to achieve the stipulated targets. The Voluntary National Reviews are a testimony of their commitment to deliver economic well-being to their people. However, this is an example of localization of the SDGs wherein priority is given to national agendas. It is important to come out of silos and follow a horizontal approach to sustainable development. This can be achieved through collective strategies based on sharing of information, extending excess capacities among other regional countries and work towards a regional approach for the implementation of the SDGs.

In the last four chapters including this, economic perspectives of the region were examined. The study would now move on to the last Chapter and examine the emerging geopolitics of the Bay of Bengal region.

NOTES

1. "Goal 14: Life Below Water", https://www.undp.org/content/undp/en/home/sustainable-development-goals/goal-14-life-below-water.html (accessed 23 December 2018).
2. Ibid.
3. "Transforming our world: the 2030 Agenda for Sustainable Development", https://sustainabledevelopment.un.org/post2015/transformingourworld (accessed 23 December 2018).
4. For more details see "Division for Sustainable Development Goals", https://sustainabledevelopment.un.org/about (accessed 23 December 2018).
5. For more details see "Voluntary National Reviews Database", https://sustainabledevelopment.un.org/vnrs/ (25 December 2018).
6. "The Bay of Bengal Large Marine Ecosystem Project", https://www.boblme.org/ (accessed 23 February 2019).
7. "Eight countries come together to protect Bay of Bengal", https://www.downtoearth.org.in/news/environment/eight-countries-come-together-to-protect-bay-of-bengal-61018 (accessed 23 February 2019). Sevvandi Jayakody of Wayamba University, Sri Lanka, who was deeply involved in the first phase, said that when the project started, there was "inadequate dialogue, inadequate information on shared fish stocks, lack of transboundary dialogues. The first phase handled all this positively by increasing knowledge about the ecosystem, promoting regional coordination and cooperation and by starting to improve ecosystem health through transboundary demonstration activities."
8. Ibid.
9. "Agenda 21", UNCED, 1992, https://sustainabledevelopment.un.org/content/documents/Agenda21.pdf (accessed 23 February 2019).
10. "World Summit Calls for MPA Networks by 2012", https://mpanews.openchannels.org/sites/default/files/mpanews/archive/MPA34.pdf (accessed 23 February 2019).
11. Erik J. Molenaar & Alex G. Oude Elferink, "Marine protected areas in areas beyond national jurisdiction The pioneering efforts under the OSPAR Convention", file:///C:/Users/abcd/Downloads/92-92-1-PB.pdf (accessed 23 February 2019).
12. "SAARC Environment Action Plan", Adopted by the Third Meeting of the SAARC Environment Ministers, Malé, Maldives, 15-16 October 1997.
13. "Swatch of No Ground Marine Protected Area", http://www.mpatlas.org/mpa/sites/60009462/ (accessed 23 February 2019).
14. "Fishermen to turn dolphin saviours in Bangladesh", https://www.thethirdpole.net/en/2016/12/27/best-of-2016-fishermen-to-turn-dolphin-saviours-in-bangladesh/ (accessed 23 February 2019).
15. "Coastal Zones of India", http://www.moef.nic.in/sites/default/files/Coastal_Zones_of_India.pdf (accessed 23 March 2019).
16. "Sri Lanka represented at the SDG14: Oceans Conference", https://www.un.int/srilanka/news/sri-lanka-represented-sdg14-oceans-conference (accessed 23 March 2019
17. "Strategy for New India @ 75", http://niti.gov.in/writereaddata/files/Strategy_for_New_India.pdf (accessed 26 March 2019).
18. "Sustainable Development Goals (SDGs)", http://sri.nic.in/sustainable-development-goals-sdgs (accessed 26 March 2019).
19. "Voluntary National Review Report on the Implementation of Sustainable Development Goals",

http://niti.gov.in/writereaddata/files/India%20VNR_Final.pdf (accessed 26 March 2019).
20. "2nd ASEAN-India Blue Economy Workshop Keynote Address by Secretary (East)", https://www.mea.gov.in/Speeches-Statements.htm?dtl/30097/2nd_ASEANIndia_Blue_Economy_Workshop_Keynote_Address_by_Secretary_East (accessed 23 March 2019).
21. "Voluntary National Review 2017", https://sustainabledevelopment.un.org/memberstates/india (accessed 23 March 2019).
22. "Bangladesh: Voluntary National Review 2017", https://sustainabledevelopment.un.org/memberstates/bangladesh (accessed 13 March 2019).
23. Ibid.
24. Mohammad Mahmudul Islama1 and Md Shamsuddohab, " Coastal and Marine Conservation Strategy for Bangladesh in the Context of Achieving Blue Growth and Sustainable Development Goals (SDGs)", https://actascientific.com/ASAG/pdf/ASAG-02-0280.pdf (accessed on 08 December 2018).
25. "Sustainable Development Goals: Bangladesh First Progress Report 2018", http://www.bd.undp.org/content/dam/bangladesh/docs/Publications/Pub-2019/SDGs-Bangladesh_Progress_Report%202018%20(1).pdf (accessed on 28 December 2018).
26. "Sustainable Development Goals: Bangladesh Progress Report 2018", http://www.bd.undp.org/content/dam/bangladesh/docs/Publications/Pub-2019/SDGs-Bangladesh_Progress_ Report% 202018%20(1).pdf(accessed on 08 March 2019).
27. Ibid.
28. Ibid.
29. S. M. Anisul Haque, "Bangladesh in 2050: Aspiration, challenges & milestones", "http://saudigazette.com.sa/article/562005/World/Asia/Bangladesh-in-2050-Aspiration-challenges-amp-milestones (accessed 01 April 2019).
30. Statement by Mrs. Ei Ei Khin Aye Head of Delegation and Deputy Permanent Representative of the Republic of the Union of Myanmar United Nations Conference to Support the Implementation of Sustainable Development Goal 14: Conserve and sustainably use the oceans, seas and marine resources for Sustainable Development (New York, 8 June 2017) https://sustainabledevelopment.un.org/content/documents/24520myanmar.pdf (accessed 04 March 2019).
31. "Sri Lanka Voluntary National Review on the Status of Implementing Sustainable Development Goals" https://sustainabledevelopment.un.org/content/documents/19677FINAL_SriLankaVNR_ Report_30Jun2018.pdf (accessed 12 March 2019).
32. Ibid.
33. Remarks delivered by Dr. Anil Premaratne, Chairman, NARA on Making Fisheries Sustainable https://www.un.int/srilanka/news/sri-lanka-represented-sdg14-oceans-conference (accessed 14 March 2019).
34. "Thailand's Voluntary National Review on the Implementation of the 2030 Agenda for Sustainable Development, June 2018", http://www.mfa.go.th/sep4sdgs/contents/filemanager/images/sep/VNR%202018%20English%2010.07.18.pdf (accessed 12 March 2019).
35. "SDG 14 Life below water", https://thailand.opendevelopmentmekong.net/topics/sdg-14-life-below-water/(accessed 16 March 2019).

14
Geopolitical Underpinnings in the Bay of Bengal Region

In 2008, UNESCO recognised Georgetown (Penang) and Melaka as World Heritage Sites. The citation argues that they "bear testimony to the living multicultural heritage and traditions of Asia, where many religions and cultures met and coexisted".[1] Selective recognition of these two sites on the shores of the Bay of Bengal over others like Rangoon (Yangon) might underline the limitations of their acknowledgment. But, it also suggests that migration and movement of people, information and goods had much greater role in shaping the Bay's history than is often understood. Upsurge in such flows are now being fanned by globalisation and regionalisation, despite the limitations imposed by political boundaries of nation-states, nationalism, and identity politics. Aspirations of people are already transcending the imaginations of their governments. So the political map of Bay of Bengal no longer reflects its true nature.

However connected the coasts of the Bay have been, historically the littorals have seldom garnered a single regional political entity. Not even the imperial scaffolding of British Raj could hold the Bay together. Though the Bay has inspired many thoughts, it has never developed into a common identity. "What the region possesses richly is the practical ethics of coexistence".[2] A more modern BIMSTEC, yearns to knit the aspirations of its people together and build the bonds of *we-ness*.

In this as the backdrop, one is faced with the stark question—Who will eventually prevail up on the Bay? Will it be the great powers competing for geopolitical influence, markets and resources; or the self-serving capitalist; or the diverse inhabitants of the Bay united by common aspirations? These upwelling geopolitical dimensions of the Bay have been investigated in this Chapter from the perspective of core-periphery facets of regionalisation and maritime security dilemma.

Core and Periphery of Regionalisation

Regionalisation refers to those processes that deepen the integration of particular regional economic spaces. Conventional ways of measuring it are the flow of people, investments and trade. Regionalisation can develop before cultural or political unification may occur in a territory that has already achieved political unification. In the process, some areas of the region will be integrated and some will be marginalised. Unless the core of the regionalist project addresses the issue of inequality, the process of integration leads to further polarisation.[3]

The world order now has three cores—North America, the European Union and East Asia. The relations between the cores and their respective peripheries are complex and diverse.[4] The structural weight of each of these cores has created asymmetric relations in their respective regions. The core acts as a powerful magnet and drags other states in its orbit. This model becomes even more pronounced with the collapse of alternative models of development. Earlier in East Asia, this core used to be represented by Japan. The result was an economic structure where Japanese production was located in other parts of East Asia, but the technology and business strategies were in firm control with Japan. Maruti Udyog, HMT are examples of such collaborations between Japan and India. The mantle of core state has gradually shifted from Japan to China. Countries are eager to interact with the core to increase their rate of growth and social development, however unequal the relationship. These structural inequalities between the core and periphery continue to grow, due to the lack of alternative institutional mechanism for redistribution of wealth. The position is stark in the EU as well, with Germany, France and Benelux countries forming the core. Because of the difficulties in achieving convergence between the economies, those on the periphery are reduced to the status of being satellites. The potential hegemon in all the three areas does not endeavour to construct more permanent and inclusive frameworks.[5]

China is slowly inching towards a core nation based on economy, technological innovation and a desire to build an overseas identity through the Belt and Road Initiative (BRI). There are natural attractions that encourage other starts of Asia including those around the Bay of Bengal to gravitate to China for their own economic growth and development. This could be another form of imperialism with 21st century characteristics. Early signs of this are already palpable. BIMSTEC will have to turn the Bay of Bengal region into an economic and technological magnet to avert it from becoming a satellite of any power. To achieve that, it will require critical mass in terms of economy, diplomacy and military to uphold its integrity.

Belt and Road Initiative (BRI)

The concept of core-periphery can be examined under the BRI. It has already begun to transform the economic landscape of most of Bay of Bengal countries. India has not participated in the BRI on the grounds of Chinese insensitivity towards India's territorial integrity in the State of Jammu and Kashmir. Chinese investments have provided an alternative to smaller countries for development and growth which was otherwise unavailable to them. It has also spurred great-power competition for influence and hence attracted additional sources of investments. For the first time since the Great Wars, smaller countries in the Bay of Bengal are enjoying much political attention, investments, and strategic leverage. Besides, infrastructure developments under the BRI have succeeded in improving the legitimacy of the local governments albeit a few disappointments. China has also provided an alternative to these smaller states to balance an overbearing India. Hence, BRI appears to be a win-win scheme for the smaller states with immense incentives.

Adam Smith can be evoked here to understand the Chinese oft quoted concept of win-win. He avers "Whoever offers to other a bargain of any kind, proposes to do this. Give me that which I want, and you shall have this which you want; and this is the meaning of every such offer".[6] The Chinese propositions of BRI appear to be equitable transactions and one that is based on quid-pro-quo. It is especially attractive for governments as they can show visible development on the ground to their populace in much shorter timeframes, without having to shoulder the burden of repaying the debts, in their watch. However, attractiveness of BRI has started to wane.

Development projects commenced with Chinese investments by erstwhile head of states of Pakistan (Nawaz Sharif), Sri Lanka (Mahinda Rajapaksa) and Maldives (Abdulla Yameen) have left the succeeding governments, saddled with unmanageable debts. The ulterior motive of Chinese interest is often overlooked. This is eloquently captured by Adam Smith who notes, "It is not from the benevolence of the butcher, the brewer, or the baker that we expect our dinner, but from their regard to their own interest".[7] So, what are Chinese interests in the Bay of Bengal? What price are these small countries ready to pay? Are the political goals of their governments aligned with the country's long-term national interests?

China has emerged as the second largest economy which has led to significant military and political influence. This power has now become palpable across the Indo-Pacific region including the Bay of Bengal. It is however, unclear what the Chinese leadership wishes to do with this enhanced economic leverage and military muscle. The rise of East Asia in the 1980s had forced all to rethink the nature of economic development. China's ascent has transformed the very nature of power and influence in international relations of the 21st century.[8]

Post the Great Wars, the US created an international order that was conducive to its national interest. At stake were markets and ideological rivalry with the Soviet Union. In that context the Marshall Plan appeared as the right plan at the right time. The US was convinced that to sustain a dynamic economy at home, European economic recovery was essential. Incidentally, strategic interests piggyback the economic goals. European markets, resources, manpower, and industrial capacity were also strategic assets that needed to controlled and protected from hostile power or coalition. The defeat of Germany and British exhaustion after the Wars left a vacuum in Central and Western Europe into which the Soviet Union could have expanded, unless the US created a suitable balance of power in Europe.[9]

China insists that BRI is purely a benign economic project and should not be equated with the US Marshall Plan. But, it can be found that BRI's practical implications and significance are much greater. Edward Luttwak was the first to notice the changing dynamics of inter-state competition post-Cold war. He had noted that while armed conflicts would persist in unfortunate parts of the world, State actions will largely be represented by geo-economics, which is an admixture of conflict with the methods of commerce. In Clausewitzian parlance, it would mean logic of war in the grammar of commerce.[10]

Though the post-Cold war era did witness invasion in Iraq, it was Japan's economic success that epitomised the changing logic of international competition. It was the Japanese experience that provided policy models for China's leaders.[11] Two fairly recent incidents can be recounted to demonstrate China's propensity to exercise its economic leverage. When Norway awarded Chinese Liu Xiaobo the Nobel Peace Prize in 2010, Beijing froze relations with Oslo and dealt a serious blow to Norway's salmon market in China. As a result, the Prime Minister of

Norway refused to meet Dalai Lama when he visited Oslo in 2014. Beijing's message was received in Denmark as well. In 2012, countries that abstained, were absent, or voted against a resolution on violence in Syria, were under the Chinese geo-economic sway. So there is evidence that China has indeed flexed its geo-economic muscle to advance its geopolitical aims. It has also managed to foster asymmetrical economic dependence that enables China to exact congenial foreign policies from others. In other words, China uses geo-economics as deterrence by maintaining sufficiently credible threats of economic reprisal.[12] It would not be grossly inaccurate to view BRI from a similar prism.

BRI helps China draw nearby countries into its orbit, while bolstering diplomatic leverage and creating commercial opportunities for Chinese firms. These projects enhance China's access to natural resources. By addressing severe infrastructure shortfalls in the region, China curries political favour and brings these countries tightly under Beijing's influence. Foreign infrastructure also lessen China's dependence on vulnerable trade routes through the Malacca Straits.[13] For instance, a 793 kilometre long China-Myanmar gas pipeline became operational in 2017 and can transfer 22 million tons of gas at five stations. As on February 2019 it transferred 17.53 million tons. The project helped Myanmar collect 3.1 billion cubic meter of natural gas in February which goes to power stations in Kyaukpyu, Taneekam and Mandalay.

Kyaukpyu, once a deserted and dark port, now boasts of 24 hours of power supply.[14] CITIC, a Chinese state-owned company reached an agreement with Myanmar to build a deep water port at Kyaukpyu for US$7.3 billion and an industrial area in the Special Economic Zone at $2.7 billion. The oil and gas pipeline connecting the Bay of Bengal port of Kyaukpyu to Kunming in China is valued at US$1.5 billion. Dangers from such large-scale investments by China is both imagined and real. Assumption made by some that China will eventually use Kyaukpyu as a military base appears unfounded as both Myanmar's civilian and military leadership are jealous about their national sovereignty.

Perhaps a more worrying and realist possibility is the dangerous economic leverage that China might gain over Myanmar and use it to exact political and military concessions. Myanmar government has 30 percent stakes in the Kyaukpyu port amounting to $2.2 billion; if it takes 50 percent stakes in the SEZ, the net liability would be $3.5 billion, or 5 percent of the GDP. Loans of such magnitude from a Chinese company for just two projects cannot be considered economically prudent. It is unlikely that Myanmar government would be in a position to handle that level of financing, and would have to turn to Chinese loans,[15] which further increases Chinese leverage on Myanmar. There are five other projects that China plans to commence in Myanmar: Muse-Mandalay railway project, new Yangon development project, three border economic zones, Myitsone hydropower project and Kyaukphu-Kunming railway.

Nepal has formally joined the BRI and is progressing three major railway projects. Field study for Kyirong-Kathmandu has been concluded at an estimate of $2.75 billion. Kathmandu- Pokhara railway is estimated to be $3 billion. Feasibility of other projects from Aabukhaireni to Bharatput is also in progress.[16] Even if Nepal decides to have only 51 percent stakes in these project, it would entail an expenditure of $2.87 billion for just two projects whose budget estimates are known. This is 10.5 percent of Nepal's GDP ($27.27 billion as on 2018), which appears to be completely unsustainable. Nepal is contemplating to negotiate a deal with China in line with India-Japan Mumbai-Ahmadabad high-speed railways, for which India has obtained a loan of $14 billion at 0.1 percent rate of interest for 50 years. It is unlikely, that these BRI projects will materialize without Nepal making some serious strategic concessions to China, which could be detrimental to the region's security and are being closely monitored.

Quantum of Chinese investments vis-à-vis a country's GDP may not necessarily be an accurate representation of the actual debt accumulated. The temporal spread of a loan, amount of stakes, interest rates, commencement and completion of projects, impact on economy and growth, and are some of the many variables that will impinge on a country's ability to service its debt. Nevertheless, it provides a rough estimate of the dependence on China by any sovereign state. The following table (Table 14.1) compiles the volume of Chinese investments (including BRI) made in BIMSTEC countries since the launch of BRI in 2013 up until 2018. Total Chinese investments as percentage of their respective GDPs are quite intriguing.

From the table, it can be found that the highest Chinese investments made between 2013 and 2018 as percentage of GDP has been in Nepal. Investments in Sri Lanka, Bangladesh and Myanmar are also substantial and could lead to an irrecoverable debt trap. These countries could become vulnerable for future investments. Under these circumstances, it would be prudent for countries to exercise caution before investing for strategic considerations. Investing in these vulnerable countries is fraught with risk and balancing Chinese geo-economics may result in bad debts that India can ill afford. It is also quite possible that some countries are playing up Chinese investments to exact investments from other

Table 14.1: Volume of Chinese investments (including BRI) made in BIMSTEC countries since the launch of BRI in 2013–18

Country	Chinese Investments 2013-2018 (billion US$)*	GDP 2017 Constant (2010 billion USD)#	Chinese Investments as % of GDP	Major Sectors*
Sri Lanka	10.6	82.547	12.8	Transport, real estate, agriculture and logistics
India	13.63	2660.37	0.5	Energy, technology, metals and health
Nepal	4.6	21.463	21.43	Energy, transport & real estate
Bhutan	Nil	2.339	Nil	Nil
Bangladesh	24.2	179.99	13.4	Transport, energy, metals
Myanmar	4.03	79.495	5	Energy
Thailand	7.28	422.94	1.7	Transport, technology, energy, chemicals, agriculture

Sources: (*) AEI China Global Investment Tracker; (#) The World Bank.

major powers. So, investment should be made purely on firm business norms and market considerations and genuine desire of these countries to develop should be addressed through sound institutions like Asian Development Bank, the World Bank or AIIB. This entails the question as to why China is investing in countries that are unlikely to return such investments and loans.

Execution of BRI projects in the Bay of Bengal region point towards the possibility of China trying to establish a hierarchical patron-client relation in Asia, similar to one China has historically maintained with its neighbours (excluding undivided India). Theoretically, this conforms to the core-periphery concept of regionalisation, where countries of BIMSTEC on China's periphery are eager to interact with the core, in order to increase their rate of growth and social development, however unequal the relationship may be. This is also in agreement with China's Confucian hierarchical culture. Eventually, such inequality between the core and periphery only grows and makes the periphery strategically subservient to the core, like a vassal state. Such a hierarchical international system is different from US hegemony, which is premised on liberal values of political, economic and social equality and undergirded by consensus.

In other words, China's BRI project is creating so much gravitational pull that it is altering the geo-economic relations of the Indo-Pacific region into a one of strong hub and spokes with China in the centre and a weak rim on the periphery occupied by other regional organisations and States.

Figure 14.1: Hub and Spoke – with a Weak Rim

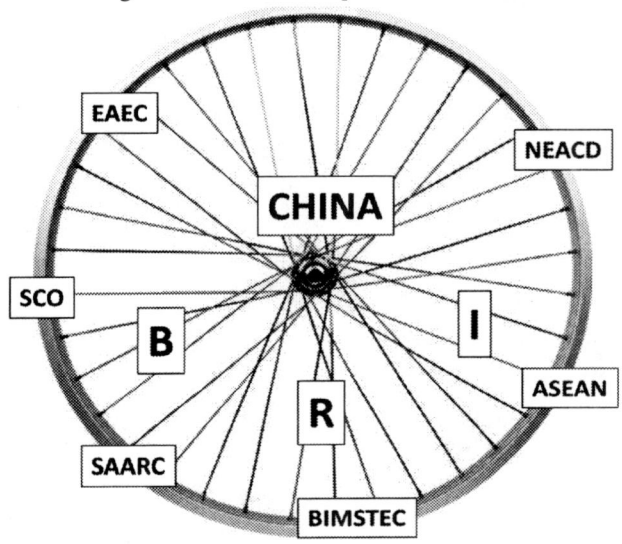

To stem the centrifugal forces created by Chinese BRI in the region, a multi-polar world order would have to be created with a stronger rim. This will require stronger linkages and intra-dependencies within each region and between the regions.

Figure 14.2: Multi-polar Regional Order needs a Strong Rim

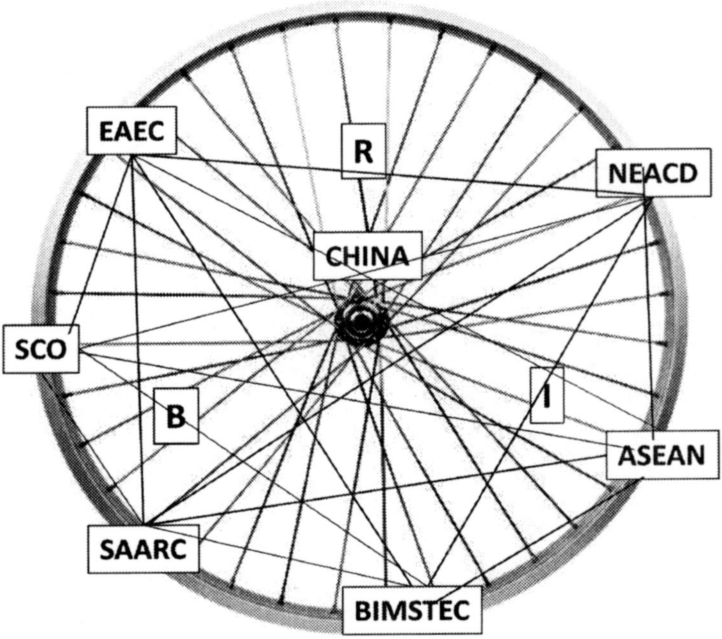

Maritime Security Dilemma in the Bay of Bengal

China has unsettled borders with India and Bhutan. This causes perpetual tensions and has the potential to snowball into an incident similar to the 73 days Doklam standoff between India and China in 2017. There are mechanisms to manage such border disputes through formal meetings of the Special Representatives co-chaired by the National Security Advisor of India and State Councilor from China.[17] However, security concerns are not limited to the land borders and have spilled over into the Indian Ocean, of which the Bay of Bengal is an integral part.

China's growing global economic and strategic footprints has made the Bay of Bengal vulnerable to international and regional turmoil. Besides, terrorism, piracy, natural disasters and epidemics also pose major challenges. Concomitantly, BRI investments have created substantial military advantages, should China require access to selected foreign ports for pre-positioning logistic support for military operations. In addition to the Anti-Access/Area Denial (A2/AD) in the Western Pacific, PLA Navy is developing power projection capabilities and concepts of operation for conducting offensive operations in the Indian Ocean. PLA Navy has the capabilities to conduct a variety of missions including, presence and sovereignty operations, as well as offensive missions. Its force structure continues to evolve in terms of versatility and power projection capabilities.

PLA Navy Maritime Corps (PLANMC) is expected to be a global maritime force capable of operating on land, at sea and in air by 2020. As of writing this chapter, two out of six PLANMC brigades are mission capable.[18] Regular deployment of the PLA Navy including its submarines in the Indian Ocean demonstrates China's operational reach and political intent. In the future, Chinese aircraft carriers will control the air and sea domains and participate in decisive missions like blockade and amphibious operations. Although China appears to be more than a decade away from achieving such capabilities, its modernisation portends intense militarisation of the Indian Ocean that gives rise to security dilemma for the regional countries of the Indian Ocean.

Security competition between India and China has grown and profoundly impacts the landscape of the Bay of Bengal. Maritime security contestation between the two is not marked by territorial claims but is profound and should be understood as a subordinate interaction in the larger mosaic of international system, alongside the shadows of the US power. China has vital strategic interests in the Bay of Bengal given that nearly 86 percent of its energy imports flow through the Straits of Malacca, whose northern edge straddles the Bay of Bengal.[19] This concern has been labeled as the 'Malacca Dilemma' in Chinese Defence White Paper 2015, which has doctrinally transcended China's military strategy from traditional offshore defence to open ocean protection.

Bangladesh, Myanmar, Thailand and Sri Lanka are highly dependent on Chinese military equipment. Bangladesh was recently supplied two Ming Class submarines and the PLA Navy participated in International Maritime Search and Rescue Exercise (IMMSARES) off Cox Bazar, Bangladesh under the Indian Ocean Naval Symposium (IONS).[20] Similarly, China has also been the leading supplier of arms to Myanmar, especially after the imposition of Western sanctions in 1989. It also conducted naval exercise for the first time in 2017 off Myanmar.[21]

Chinese naval engagements in Sri Lanka are noteworthy. Sri Lanka has prompted the idea of Indian Ocean Region as a Zone of Peace since 1971, and is now pursuing a disarmament Code of Conduct in the IOR. It maintains balanced relation with India and China and enjoys the larges of the competition between India and China who have been willing to provide it with military hardware.[22]

Thailand is fast gravitating towards China and would be receiving Chinese built submarines in the coming months. A China-Thailand-Malaysia military exercise in October 2018 was the first trilateralisation of a Chinese exercise. So, Chinese engagements with the States in the Bay of Bengal have graduated beyond armament sales to include regular port calls and bilateral naval exercises. This Chinese naval footprint is sufficient for it to set up military industrial complexes that could potentially be used for the PLA Navy, a concern which has been a recurring feature in Indian strategic discourse and cause security dilemma.[23]

Security dilemma exists when a states military posture creates an uncertainty. This depends not only on acquisition of offensive weapons but also on policy measures. Navy constitutes a substantial element of foreign policy that advances national interest on one hand and creates ambiguity by concealing intent. While China's maritime power has been coercive in the Western Pacific, it has been projected as benign power in the Indian Ocean and the Bay of Bengal. The primary reason for such a dichotomous stance is an acknowledgement of its vulnerabilities in the Indian Ocean that stems from India's maritime power. This could change in future when the PLAN is able to project power in the Indian Ocean autonomously with its carrier battle groups. China's propensity for coercion cannot be lost sight of.

The Maritime Silk Route (MSR) not only provides highway for new markets to China, but it also generates strategic vulnerabilities. The Vision for Maritime

Cooperation was unveiled under the BRI on 20 June 2017 and calls on MSR partner countries to join hands and protect maritime infrastructure and enhance security. Chinese power has manifested in the region through maritime capacity building, arms sales, port calls and joint exercises. Although India successfully lobbied with Sri Lanka to deny access to Chinese submarine in their ports, China has alternative ports in Pakistan and Djibouti for its submarines. Although the PLA Navy does not have military-related access to ports in Bay of Bengal, BIMSTEC has to cater to these factors of security dilemma and shape a regional order that is in the best interests of the littorals.

Conclusion

Henry Kissinger had avowed in his book World Order that no truly global order has ever existed. What passes for order in our time is the Westphalian system of sovereign states, refraining from interference in each other's affairs, and extensive network of international legal and organizational structures, designed to foster free trade and stable international financial system.[24] A regional order for the Bay of Bengal may have to be informed by similar principles, characterised by connectivity, trade, shared resources, communication, coordination on crimes, peaceful resolution of territorial disputes and internecine conflicts.[25]

Execution of BRI projects in the Bay of Bengal region point towards the possibility of China trying to establish a hierarchical patron–client relation in Asia. Debt traps could lead nations to become subservient to China. Sri Lankan port of Hambantota offers a peek into the future of China's dream and conforms to the core-periphery concept of regionalisation. Capacity building of states of the BIMSTEC by China through arms sales, port calls and joint exercises is also another manifestation of Chinese intent. It is in the interest of the sovereignty that debt traps have to be avoided and for tranquility in the Bay of Bengal that maritime security dilemma needs to be mitigated. It is also fair to argue that India's growing stature and maritime power also has become an issue of concern for some states in BIMSTEC. Such security dilemma cannot be escaped but can be transcended through transparency of strategic intent, equitable development in the region and respect for each other sensitivities.

NOTES

1. Sunil S Amrith, *Crossing the Bay of Bengal, The furies of Nature and Fortune of Migrants*, (Cambridge: Harvard University Press, 2013).
2. Ibid.
3. Ibid., p. 57.

4   Ibid., p. 51.
5   Ibid., pp.57–58.
6   Adam Smith, *Wealth of nations*, Mera Libri, digital edition, 2007, pp. 26, https://www.ibiblio.org/ml/libri/s/SmithA_WealthNations_p.pdf (accessed 11 June 2019,
7   Ibid.
8   Mark Beeson, *Geoeconomics with Chinese Characteristics: BRI and China's evolving Grand Strategy*, Economic and Political Studies, Routledge, 03 September 2018 (accessed 11 June 2019). https://www.tandfonline.com/doi/abs/10.1080/20954816.2018.1498988
9   Michael J Hogan, *The Marshall Plan: America, Britain and the Reconstruction of Western Europe, 1947–1952* (Cambridge: Cambridge University Press, 1987), pp.26–27.
10 Edward N Luttwak, *From Geopolitics to Geoeconomics,* The National Interest, No 20, (Summer 1990), pp.17–23.
11 Sebastian Heilmann and Oliver Melton, "The Reinvention of Development Planning in China 1993-2012", *Modern China*, (Sage Publication, 2013), pp.580–628.
12 Robert D Blackwell and Jenifer M Harris, *War by Other Means*, (Harvard : Harvard University Press, 2016), pp. 127–35.
13 Ibid, pp 115–18
14 Sun Guangyong, *China's pipeline project brings 24 hours electricity supply to Myanmar, Global Times*, 16 April 2019, Accessed on June 12, 2019, http://www.globaltimes.cn/content/1146125.shtml
15 Gregory Poling, *Kyaukpyu : Connecting China to the Indian Ocean, Asia Maritime Transparency Initiative*, 04 April 2018, https://amti.csis.org/kyaukpyu-china-indian-ocean/
16 Nandalal Tiwari, *The Talks of Kerung-Kathmandu Railways, The Rising Nepal*, June 12, 2019) http://therisingnepal.org.np/news/20618 (accessed 12 June 2019
17 Office of the Secretary the Defence, US, *Annual Report to Congress – Military and Security Developments of PRC 2019,* p.77. https://media.defense.gov/2019/May/02/2002127082/-1/-1/1/2019_CHINA_MILITARY_POWER_REPORT.pdf (accessed 14 June 2019).
18 Ibid.
19 David Brewster, "China and India at Sea: A Contest for status and legitimacy in the Indian Ocean" Australia India Institute, John D and Catherine T Mac Arthur Foundation September 2015
20 Shahidul Hasan Khokon, *Bangladesh President stresses on Indian Ocean Naval cooperation,* Times of India, Dhaka, November 28, 2017, (Accessed on 28 October, 2019) https://www.indiatoday.in/world/story/bangladesh-president-m-abdul-hamid-indian-ocean-naval-symposium-1095601-2017-11-28
21 Prashant Parmeshwaran, *Inaugural roles are yet another sign of Bejing's deepening security role in the subregion,* The Diplomat, May 25, 2017 (Accessed on October 28, 2019), https://thediplomat.com/2017/05/china-holds-first-naval-exercise-with-myanmar/
22 Shantanu Roy Chaudhury, *India-China-Sri Lanka Triangle: The Defence Dimensiion,* The Diplomat, July 12, 2019 (Accessed on October 28, 2019), https://thediplomat.com/2019/07/india-china-sri-lanka-triangle-the-defense-dimension/
23 Prashantha Parmeshwaran, *What's in China's Military Exercise with Malaysia and Thailand,* The Diplomat, October 17, 2018 (Accessed on October 28, 2019) https://thediplomat.com/2018/10/whats-in-chinas-military-exercise-with-malaysia-and-thailand/
24 Henry Kissinger, *World Order,* (London : Penguin Random House, 2014), pp. 2-7.
25 Richard Falk, "Regionalism and the World Order", (ed), Fredrik Soderbaum and Timothy M Shaw, *Theories of Regionalism* New York : Palgrave, 2003), pp. 69-79.

Conclusion and Policy Recommendations

This study has analysed the Bay of Bengal in the context of BIMSTEC wherein three different thematic, i.e. security, economic and geopolitics have been highlighted. These appear to shape the destiny of the people and countries that sit astride this water body. The study has argued that the Bay of Bengal, despite its modern cartographic delimitations, draws liberally from thousands of years of peaceful co-existence and harmony. The yesteryears were indeed epochal and the Bay was once a cauldron of multiple cultures, ethnicity and religion, facilitated by the movement of people who sailed through the ebb and flow of its water.

BIMSTEC is an attempt in the present times by the governments of the Bay of Bengal littorals and land locked States to once again tie the region into common bonds of identity. It holds the promise of catching the winds of change that are sweeping across Asia marked by maritime-based economic growth. It has provided impetus and enormous lateral potential for industrialization to enjoy the benefits of globalization through integration of trade, services, markets.

However, the region is faced with multiple serious threats and challenges, natural and human induced that have emerged in the form of environmental degradation, natural disasters, poverty, food and water security, migration, scarcity of resources, illegal activity, crime, radicalisation, terrorism, insurgency, to recount a few.

BIMSTEC has not been spared by the winds of change that has swept the world in the past two decades. These have tried to unravel the bonds that once tied the region into a cohesive entity. Its promise has been tempered by its intramural weaknesses and extraneous pressures. Hence, the interconnecting webs appear to be too few and too thin, and are being kept alive by the dint of periodic official parleys. As a result, BIMSTEC appears to be a boat weighed down to sail on an uneven keel in the choppy monsoons of the Bay of Bengal. BIMSTEC has the onerous responsibility of delivering on the aspirations of its people. In this backdrop, India's 'Act East' and 'Neighbours first' policies provides hope and seeks to revitalize the region.

Bay of Bengal as a region and BIMSTEC as its official vehicle is also being influenced by geopolitics of the Indo-Pacific, a formative concept linking the Indian and the Pacific Oceans. It is also being swayed by, the Quadrilateral Security Dialogue (QSD) involving Australia, India, Japan and the United States, confidence building measures of the ASEAN countries and varying perceptions of the Chinese Belt Road Initiative. These are being accentuated by the overarching rivalry between the US and China in the Indo-Pacific and, the ongoing trade war. There is also a lingering possibility that some Bay of Bengal littoral countries might gravitate towards opposite camps. It is worth mentioning that some countries are into the Chinese 'debt trap' that could potentially cause domestic political upheavals and social disruptions, financial stresses and at least in one case loss of sovereignty, which is particularly fundamental to any State. The spawning of neo-colonialism driven by geoeconomics in the immediate neighbourhood can be catastrophic. It also has the potential of causing deep fissures and exacerbating tensions within the region.

There is no one-solution-fit-all for infusing *we-ness* in the Bay of Bengal. Neither can regionalisation be achieved spontaneously, nor can it be forced by formal mechanisms. So, it is essential to comprehend the magnitude of complexities and multitude of forces that are influencing the ongoing project of regionalisation in the Bay of Bengal. It is fair to state that BIMSTEC has been evolving and has widened its scope into 14 sectors of cooperation. Yet, it seems to amble in search of regional consciousness. Even after two decades, the Bay of Bengal region remains one of the least integrated regions in the world.

Notwithstanding the above factors, the Bay of Bengal region already has the primary ingredient of territoriality. In addition, the absence of security competition between the constituent states makes it easier for an inclusive securitisation of the region. Existing cultural affinities and a sense of shared history in the Bay of Bengal region provides a readymade foundation for congealing a regional society. In order to actualise its full potential, BIMSTEC needs to facilitate its transition into a community by imbuing political coherence.

At this stage, a Bay of Bengal regional community appears to be a farfetched idea due to lack of adequate platforms for nurturing societal cross-linkages and rekindling common values. Countries will have to work harder to build enduring communication links, be responsive to each other's sensitivities, and avoid unilateral actions. In order to instill *we-ness,* the region will have to walk through the paces of *cooperative security, regional society, regional community* and *institutionalised polity.*

BIMSTEC has been facilitating the process of State-led regionalism. But, it needs to also focus on achieving the 'we-ness'. Often, the problem is about over centralisation and retention of excessive control by the governments. The project of regionalisation would require the involvement of non-state actors and participation of the people in equal measure. To achieve this, governments will have to remove the bottlenecks and act as background facilitators between regional economies and societies. BIMSTEC will have to turn the Bay region into an economic and technological magnet to preclude it from being a Chinese, Japanese or even ASEAN satellite. The region will need to generate a critical mass in terms of economy, diplomacy and military to keep its integrity intact. "BIMSTEC centrality" should drive the geopolitics of the "Eastern Indian Ocean", just as "ASEAN centrality" hopes to drive the Asia-Pacific agenda. It is our concerted belief that "BIMSTEC centrality" has equally promising potential like other regional anchors to strengthen peace, security and stability in the Indo-Pacific. It can supplement and complement ASEAN centrality in equal measure. In addition, BIMSTEC ++ architecture can also address the aspirations of external stakeholders like China, Japan, Australia, South Korea, ASEAN or the US.

Policy Recommendations

Flowing from the foregoing discussions and analysis and on the basis of consultations with policy makers, academia and experts, the study offers a set of recommendations that have been placed under three baskets. These can potentially encourage proactive and facilitative policy prescription to the growth of a number of vectors within the existing BIMSEC Working Groups.

Institutional

    (a) Commission focused studies under respective BIMSTEC Working Groups on issues of immediate and critical issues.
    (b) Map existing maritime infrastructure, port development projects, hinterland connectivity, including those under construction/development.
    (c) Identify the complementarities, convergences and similarities in maritime infrastructure development plans in the Bay of Bengal.

(d) Launch a 'Regional Blue Economy Forum' comprising representatives of government, business and private sector.
(e) Integrate stakeholders such as freight forwarders, shipping agents and supply chain managers on challenges and opportunities for enhancing regional maritime trade.
(f) Myanmar and Thailand can help share best practices of ASEAN into BIMSTEC, and create seamless inter-regional integration of capacities and capabilities.

Security

(g) *Information Centre for Crime Coordination*: The South Asia Regional Intelligence and Coordination Centre (SARICC) needs a full-fledged Headquarter where coordination of information on transnational organised Crime and terrorism is collated. SARICC would have to eventually network with the existing Central Asian Regional Information and Coordination Centre (CARICC) and Asia-Pacific Information & Coordination Center for Combating Drug Crimes (APICC) for inter-regional coordination.
(h) *Implementation of UN Resolution on Human Trafficking*: The UN General Assembly Resolution 55/25 was adopted in November 2000 against trafficking of persons, especially women and children. The Protocol deals with smuggling of migrants by land, sea and air. For coordination of regional efforts BIMSTEC Sub-group on trafficking needs to facilitate the following:
  (i) Adoption of legislative and other measures and harmonizing regional procedures to establish criminal offence (Article 5).
  (ii) Region-wide policy on protection of privacy and identity of victims of trafficking (Article 6).
  (iii) Permit victims of trafficking to remain in the territory, temporarily or permanently, as the case may be (Article 7) and resolution of safe extradition.
  (iv) Information exchange and training (Article 10).
  (v) Strengthen, border control to prevent and detect trafficking (Article 11).
  (vi) Security and Control of travel documents (Article 12).
(i) *Mitigation of Wildlife Trafficking:* International trade of over 30000 species of plants and animals is regulated by the Convention on International

Trade in Endangered Species of Wild Fauna and Flora (CITES), 1973. Due to the magnitude of this crime in Bay of Bengal region, commissioning a new Sub-Group on wildlife trafficking will be essential for effective implementation of the CITES guidelines with the following mandate:
- (i) Assist countries to comply with the Convention.
- (ii) Facilitate countries to create of national and local laws. Assistance to professional NGOs like the TRAFFIC and WWF could be sought for this purpose.
- (iii) Run regional training and exchange workshops for customs officers, border police, conservation officers and traders.
- (iv) Provide assistance and funding to countries for enforcement efforts.
- (v) Regional information sharing and coordination across the borders.
- (vi) Coordinate scientific and technical advice between states.
- (vii) Sri Lanka could provide leadership with its exceptional expertise in CTTC by setting up SARRIC HQ.
- (viii) Myanmar's domestic knowledge on CITES can be shared for wildlife protection.

(j) *Counter Terrorism:* The Convention on Counter Terrorism and Transnational Crime (CTTC) needs to be ratified and instrument on Mutual Legal Assistance in Criminal Matters (MCLACM), which can provide for measures to locate, freeze and forfeit or confiscate any funds or finances meant for the financing of all crimes in other's territory needs to be endorsed by the member countries.

(k) *Cyber-attacks and hacker warfare*: The threats and challenges arising from the cyberspace has added an entirely different dynamic to infrastructure. Cyber cooperation could be the new dimension of the larger regional security architecture including capacity-building initiatives which necessitates cooperation. A Cyber security Cooperation Strategy and the Critical Information Infrastructures (CIIs) cyber-attacks resilience plans can be developed.

Environment

(l) Response to oxygen depletion in the Ocean: The strategy to restore oxygen will require the following measures:
- (i) Reduction in Green Houses Gases.
- (ii) Reduction of nutrient infusion into the seas from the coast.

(iii) Adoption of marine spatial planning.
(iv) Unifying research, database collation and policies in BIMSTEC.
(v) Green House Gases – Bay of Bengal nations need to evolve national and regional strategies on GHG reduction, adaptation plan and adaptation taxes. Bangladesh's climate change strategy and action plan (BCCSAP) and national adaptation plan (NAP) could be used as a benchmark for these purposes. India's leadership in clean energy, especially in solar power can be leveraged by the policy makers. Nepal and Bhutan can provide lead role by expanding and exporting hydro energy to the region.

(m) *Marine Pollution*: Programmes like Swachh Bharat Abhiyan, Clean Ganga and Smart Cities initiated by the Government of India to control litter and build a sustainable environment need to be replicated region wide. Countries need to steer actions under the sustainable developmental goals (SDGs) targets 6.3, 11.6, 12.3, 12.4, 14.1, 14.2 and 14c. In addition, States need to promulgate National Marine Litter policies.

(n) *Plastics in the Bay waters*: Setting up an appropriate regional organisation, which should take the lead for policy formulations, identify, assess, monitor and response to marine litter, and promote management techniques for effective response and recovery of litter.

(o) *Pollution from Agriculture, Industry, Sewage and Waste*: Mitigation will require effective industrial planning and the safe disposal of ship oil, industrial and urban waste. Reducing high levels of pollutants need similar priority as air pollution for preserving coastal ecosystem and saving marine resource for the Bay.

(p) *Sea Level Rise (SLR)*: There are varying estimates of economic impact due to SLR. Adaptive strategies against SLR include retreat, accommodation and protection. Retreat strategy involves planned relocation or migration and needs to cater for loss of property, resettlement cost and rebuilding infrastructure. Accommodation strategies include optimal usage of vulnerable areas by converting agricultural lands to fish farming, growing salt tolerant crops, limiting damages by building piles, improving drainage systems, and positioning alarm and evacuation systems. Protection strategy would entail erecting barriers and sea walls. Most governments are yet to cater to these scenarios in their national plan.

Economics

(q) India's Act East policy has expedited connectivity projects in the region. But much more needs to be done to establish efficient business corridors. It would require accession to international conventions, improving intermodal transport, strengthening rules, regulations and standards, financing cross-border transport project, and security coordination. In addition, implementation of value chain needs to be explored customised for the unique manufacturing and production capabilities of each country. Improvement in border trade, easing of non-tariff barriers, upgrading of Land Custom Stations, and creation of financial instruments also need to be undertaken. In addition, checking of informal transaction and prohibiting diversion of third country goods needs to be enforced. Gender sensitivity in border trade also needs attention to facilitate women to actively participate in the economic initiative.

(r) *Maritime Connectivity*: It is critical for the littoral states to sustain economic growth and deepen economic integration. This can be achieved through an efficient maritime connectivity ecosystem in the Bay of Bengal built around ships, ports and associated supply chains that connect the production hubs in the heartland to the sea. India's Sagarmala project could provide the stimulus to the region.

(s) *Digital Connectivity*: This will be a catalyst for augmenting maritime infrastructure, economic development and efficient commerce. The future maritime infrastructure would be characterized by cutting-edge science and disruptive technologies such as Big Data, Marine Cyber Physical Systems (MCPS), Artificial Intelligence (AI), Autonomous Systems, etc., which would necessitate BIMSTEC member countries to upend investments in digital maritime infrastructure.

(t) *Blue Economy*: A sustained dialogue to encourage public-private partnership enterprise that serves as a bridge that links all the relevant stakeholders.

(u) *Blue Bonds*: Blue Bonds for the Bay of Bengal that can help regional countries to pursue ocean-related projects.

(v) *Promote Short Sea Shipping (SSS):* This will be done through regional shipping networks is three maritime spaces, i.e. Bay, Strait and Sea. This is a significant aspect of SSS which can identify unique opportunities and challenges for maritime connectivity.

(w) *Marin leisure industry and cruise tourism:* These are highly promising areas for growth given that several destinations in ASEAN countries are already well known to Indian tourists.

(x) *Heritage tourism*: Given the civilizational connections, heritage tourism can be a potential trigger for a new set of cooperative agendas centred on marine archaeology.

(y) *Cyber Cooperation*: It could be the new dimension of the larger regional connectivity architecture including capacity-building initiatives which necessitates cooperation.

(z) *Establish Port Cities Cooperation Network Working Group*: This will help augment maritime commerce in the Bay of Bengal.

(aa) *Connectivity for landlocked including India's northeast*: This will add to regional maritime trading ecosystem.

(bb) *Cabotage Laws*: Harmonization will be a critical element in the promotion of India Bay of Bengal shipping networks.

(cc) *Digital connectivity*: This will help enhance "quality and efficiency" of the maritime connectivity ecosystem.

(dd) Removal of tariffs of non-sensitive items.

(ee) Time bound schedule for reduction of sensitive list.

(ff) Elimination of para-tariff.

(gg) Reduce logistic cost.

(hh) Increase people-to-people contact through border haats.

(jj) Awareness to be generated about accredited labs by NABL for testing.

(kk) Rules of customs across borders to be customised.

(ll) Electronic data exchange at border through single window.

(mm) Rules of origin negotiations to be expedited.

(nn) implementation of economic corridor will require accession to international conventions, improving intra-nodal transport, and strengthening regulations and standards.

(oo) Regional value chain would need to be customised to unique manufacturing and resource patterns of the region.

(pp) Imformed transaction at the borders to be curbed.

(qq) Border tarde facilitation should become gender sensitive to enable active participation of woman in border trade.